Charles A. Platt

The Architectural History Foundation is a publicly supported, not-for-profit foundation. Directors: William Butler, Colin Eisler, Edgar Kaufmann, jr., Elizabeth G. Miller, Victoria Newhouse, Annalee Newman, Adolf K. Placzek. Editorial Board: George R. Collins, Columbia University; Christoph L. Frommel, Bibliotheca Hertziana, Rome; Henry-Russell Hitchcock, New York University Institute of Fine Arts; Spiro Kostof, University of California, Berkeley; Vincent Scully, Yale University; John Summerson, Sir John Soane's Museum, London.

Special thanks go to Mr. and Mrs. Geoffrey Platt, and Lila Acheson Wallace, whose generous grants helped make possible the publication of this book.

AMERICAN MONOGRAPH SERIES

General Editor: David G. De Long

Bertram Grosvenor Goodhue, Richard Oliver. 1983

The Almighty Wall, The Architecture of Henry Vaughan, William Morgan. 1983

On the Edge of the World, Four Architects in San Francisco at the Turn of the Century, Richard W. Longstreth. 1983

Mizner's Florida, American Resort Architecture, Donald W. Curl. 1984

Charles A. Platt, The Artist as Architect, Keith N. Morgan. 1985

Portrait of Charles A. Platt, Thomas W. Dewing, 1893.

Charles A. Platt
The Artist as Architect

KEITH N. MORGAN

With a Memoir by GEOFFREY PLATT

THE ARCHITECTURAL HISTORY FOUNDATION,
NEW YORK
THE MIT PRESS, CAMBRIDGE, MASSACHUSETTS
and LONDON, ENGLAND

Keith N. Morgan is Assistant Professor of Art History, and Director of the American and New England Studies Program at Boston University.

Library of Congress Cataloging in Publication Data

Morgan, Keith N.
    Charles A. Platt, the artist as architect.

    (American monograph series)
    Includes bibliographical references.
    1. Platt, Charles A. (Charles Adams), 1861–1933.
I. Title.   II. Series: American monograph series
(Architectural History Foundation (New York, N.Y.))
NA737.P5M67 1985   720′.92′4   83-42518
ISBN 0-262-13188-9

Designed by Gilbert Etheredge

Contents

To my parents

Florence Payne Morgan and
Harry Edward Morgan, Jr.

With special appreciation to
Richard W. Cheek, principal
photographer for this book.

Acknowledgments

DURING THE years in which I have pursued the career of Charles A. Platt, I have been privileged to meet and to benefit from the knowledge of many people. Foremost among these were Mr. and Mrs. William Platt and Mr. Geoffrey Platt who patiently shared their memories and thoughts with me. Charles Platt was fortunate to have two sons who understood his importance and carefully maintained his office drawings, professional records, and personal papers. Without their continuing assistance, and that of other members of the Platt family, the project would have been impossible.

To the owners of Platt buildings, I express my appreciation for the opportunity to visit these properties; their names, unfortunately, are too numerous to mention. For help in locating Platt buildings and gardens, I wish to thank William E. Buckley, Chanler Chapman, David Ransom, Richard Longstreth, William L. Bauhan, Jack Quinan, Philip G. James, Alfred Branam, Jr., Donald Smith, Francis Jencks, Alexander James, Robert MacKay, and Hutcheson Page. Among the libraries and manuscript collections I visited, I am grateful for the kindness of: Adolf K. Placzek and the staff of the Avery Library; Andrew Zaremba, the Century Association; Juliet Kellogg, Phillips Academy, Andover; Susan Cosgrove, American Institute of Architects Library; Maynard Brichford, University of Illinois Archives; Anne Radice and Florian Thain, Office of the Architect of the Capitol; Michaelle L. Biddle, Deerfield Academy; Priscilla Smith, Freer Gallery of Art; Michael Richman, D. C. French Papers; Edgar deN. Mayhew, Lyman Allyn Museum; Sue Kohler, Commission of Fine Arts; Bartlett Hayes, Addison Gallery of American Art; Mark A. Nickerson, State Historical Society of Wisconsin; Christopher Monkhouse, Museum of Art, Rhode Island School of Design; Edward Nygren, Corcoran Gallery of Art; and Robert Lovett, Harvard Business School.

The initial research for this book was made possible by a fellowship from the Center for Studies in Landscape Architecture, Dumbarton Oaks, Trustees for Harvard University, Washington, D.C. For assistance and kindness during my two years at Dumbarton Oaks, I thank especially Elisabeth B. MacDougall, Director, and Laura Byers, Librarian. For a leave of absence to prepare part of the manuscript, I thank Brent Glass and the North Carolina Division of Archives and History. Completion of the manuscript was made possible by an Andrew W. Mellon Faculty Fellowship in the Humanities at Harvard University. I am grateful to Richard W. Cheek, Catherine Bishir, and William E. Buckley for faithfully reading and criticizing drafts. Robert A. M. Stern, an ardent admirer of Platt, brought my work to the attention of the Architectural History Foundation, and David G. De Long, general editor of the American Monograph Series, greatly assisted with detailed criticism. Doreen Bolger Burke and Patricia Hills generously shared their knowledge of American painting in the late nineteenth century. And the intellectual challenge and personal friendship of William H. Jordy were essential throughout the preparation of the dissertation on which this book is based.

Most importantly, my wife, Elizabeth, read and edited all chapters, typed drafts, and supplied patience and support whenever necessary. To her and our children, Julia, Ned, and Will, a special thanks for endurance.

Keith N. Morgan
Boston University

Foreword

This book arrives on the scene with near perfect timing. Like the *Charles A. Platt* monograph of 1913, which clarified that moment for American domestic architecture and became "the Bible" for a few designers, this one has chosen its entrance well. It will doubtless be read in different ways. Those interested, as some architects are today, in a fairly strict classical revival will find much to praise here: restraint, dignity, and the universal approach that comes from making one's proportions as canonic and balanced as possible. Those interested in a free-style classicism — considerably greater in number than the former group — will have their freedoms challenged by this book, their immodesty and perhaps excessive invention reproached by the quality that comes from limitation. For Platt, this limitation was to the Italian Renaissance, as he understood it directly and as it was modified by the classical periods of English and French architecture. Platt didn't copy as a revivalist might, nor did he transform his sources as a Post-Modernist would; rather, he adapted them to American conditions. The High Church of Classicism, with Sir Joshua Reynolds as its arbiter, always contrasted an "imaginative imitation" with a "servile copying," and Platt's "adaptation" clearly marks the same distinction.

A third group of readers will be excited by the story told in these pages, the success story of the etcher turned painter then landscape architect, architect, and finally urbanist. Here is the obvious twentieth-century Renaissance Man, a self-taught amateur who learned partly through the example of friends, fellow painters, and architects. If there are any doubts about the width of approach, they concern a relative lack of interest in engineering, science, and the new movements in art: in short, all those things summarized as Modernism. And those who might classify themselves in this last category will be the fourth kind of reader to find something of interest in this book, apart from the issue of style: the architect as a conscientious professional who takes responsibility for running a large office and delivering a well-made product, both in its details and overall conception. This professionalism acts as an implicit rebuke to the fast-food architecture that prevails today.

So this finely researched book will illuminate even as it causes debate. Based on wide reading and long discussions with two of the architect sons of Charles Platt (William and Geoffrey), it shares some of the virtues of its subject: sensible opinions and a good sense of proportion—here between description, comparison, social history, and formal analysis.

What does this last reveal? Three basic principles of classical design. First, the building will always be well connected with its site, and this invariably includes a geometrically designed garden. The route through the building is dramatically related to this landscape so that the final culmination—the grand view of Mt. Ascutney, for instance—is suggested, veiled, and then delivered, framed by a loggia. Photographs are absolutely hopeless at bringing out this drama.

Secondly, Platt always used sculpture, furniture, painting, and tapestry to underline and fill out the architecture. He sometimes went to Europe—as Frank Lloyd Wright went to Japan—to acquire furnishings and art for the houses. As the subtitle of this book—*The Artist as Architect*—makes clear, Platt, like Wright, knew the truth that has been overlooked in the last fifty years: no architecture is complete until it is complemented by art. The last classical principle evident in Platt's work is the geometrical basis of design. All the regular geometrical figures will be found, disciplined by the grid layout, but lessened in their severity by a few asymmetries and much informality. Perhaps Platt's popularity with clients stemmed in part from his mixture of regular, sober formality on the public side, with growing, changing, informal elements on the more private, garden side. In any case, his lesson of the ordered Italian garden became the major challenge to the prevailing picturesque mode of F. L. Olmsted, and all of his works stand out as clear geometrical propositions set in nature. Most dramatic is "Gwinn," his version of the White House and the Temple of Vesta in Rome, which heroically dominates its lakefront view.

Platt eschewed the heroic and expressive in favor of the understated and dignified. It is this last aspect of his work that might cause misunderstanding. We often tend to dismiss this quality, finding it dull, accommodating, or snobbish. Aristocratic taste, for that is what it is, does not flourish in a commercial or frenetically creative society. It is likely to be confused with its odious first cousin Good Taste, that moribund conformity that has spread over most of suburbia like sleeping sickness. Aristocratic taste can be defined as a series of paradoxes: as a taste for the monumental without ostentation, for the dignified without solemnity, for the understated without reticence, for the sensible and rational without dogmatic rigor. It takes more than a first glance to perceive and distinguish it from "ghastly Good Taste," and thus Platt's architecture definitely demands a second, even third look before its qualities fully reveal themselves. And again this can't altogether be perceived through photographs, which do not convey the relationships between garden, furnishings, space, and architecture.

It is this aristocratic taste that distinguishes Platt not only from his contemporaries and competitors — McKim, Hardenbergh, Carrère & Hastings, Goodhue, and almost everyone else but Stanford White — but also from Wright and the English architect with whom he was sometimes compared: Edwin Lutyens. Platt said the latter "had more influence towards bad architecture than anybody in England." Like Adolf Loos, another contemporary who was "preaching to the aristocrat" (as he said in *Ornament and Crime*), Platt liked that architecture best which showed no hand of a designer; the building that seemed just to "happen," like a Greek landscape.

This method of design, known in England as the silent-butler approach, could not be further from Frank Lloyd Wright's, who was Platt's nearly exact contemporary. One of the strange and sad encounters of their careers (although they never met, as far as I know) was over the Harold McCormick house. Platt ultimately got the job, a plum American commission, and most architectural historians have seen this as marking the death of the Prairie School. It remains for future critics and historians to get to the bottom of this and work out the complications that ensue from a contentious pluralism. For if one thing can be said with certainty, it is that both Wright and Platt were good architects operating at the height of their powers in good, but contending, traditions. The pluralism and conflicts haven't changed much today.

Although Charles Platt could censure the free-style classicism of Lutyens, he was also a tolerant man, particularly tolerant of artist architects. I say that partly from personal, if indirect evidence: he was my great-uncle, and my father always spoke of "Uncle Charlie's" wit and consideration, and of how he provided encouragement when each of the children followed a different career in the arts. Not only did I learn about landscape architecture by coming across some old Platt photographs of the Villa Lante (painted over, incidentally, in the most free-style manner), but I also received my first name and initial in honor of his memory. Everyone in our family was aware of his commitment to other artists, his involvement with the Cornish Colony as much as with his practice. This larger dimension to his personality, his friendships with those such as Judge Learned Hand, ultimately gave his work a broad, humanist depth. Geoffrey Platt in his contribution here, "A Memoir," rightly concentrates on Platt's open, generous, if reserved, character. Perhaps the most surprising thing about him is that, in spite of all his hard work as a successful architect and artist, he took considerable time and effort to be a thoroughly agreeable person.

Charles A. Jencks

Charles A. Platt

Introduction

. . . the Artist must out

To spend a long life in the creation of works of beauty, to care unswervingly for the things of the spirit and the mind, to wake the love of innumerable friends through the prompting of a generous heart — to do all this is surely to fulfill a high destiny. Such was the achievement of Charles A. Platt. He was an artist in the core of his being.[1]

Royal Cortissoz, *Pencil Points*

CHARLES A. PLATT (1861 – 1933) was a man of few words but high ideals. He shunned small talk. He seemed cool to casual acquaintances, retaining the proper reserve of his Late Victorian upbringing. Yet, behind this public reticence, Platt was an artist of all-consuming intensity. His friend, the sculptor Augustus Saint-Gaudens, once characterized Platt as a potbellied stove — he could appear cold on the outside but there was always a fire burning within.[2] This exterior aloofness and interior concentration were both part of Platt's continuing and total commitment to the life of an artist.

Platt achieved national prominence consecutively as an etcher, painter, landscape architect, and architect. With each new form of expression, he built upon his earlier experience, so that his work as an architect became the culmination and synthesis of his ideas on art. In all phases of his career, Platt thought of himself as an artist and saw his mission as the creation of beauty. An understanding of his perception of beauty and his method of achieving it is the purpose of this monograph.

Despite wide recognition throughout much of his lifetime, neither Charles Platt nor his work is well known today. In many ways, Platt epitomized the architectural and artistic philosophy that the modern movement sought to oppose. In the 1920s, due to his professional position, age, and ill health, Platt increasingly became a symbol of the old

1

order. In his final years, he was president of the Century Association, the Saint-Gaudens Memorial, and the American Academy at Rome. He was a Fellow of the American Institute of Architects, an Academician of the American Academy of Arts and Letters, and the recipient of several honorary degrees. Before his death on September 12, 1933, he was one of the few remaining leaders of the architectural establishment that had dominated the New York profession from the 1890s through the First World War. As such he became an institution, a representative of the values that were denied and rejected by the generation attracted to European modernism.

Even during his lifetime, the influence that Platt exerted upon his profession began to decline. After the 1910s, his new designs were rarely published or discussed by the architectural press. Commenting on the domestic work of the late twenties, Thomas E. Tallmadge in *The Story of Architecture in America* (1927) said, "[it] shows little or no improvement on the work that Charles Platt, Delano and Aldrich, Albro and Lindeberg and Howard Shaw did fifteen to twenty years ago."[3] And one year later G. H. Edgell in *The American Architecture of To-Day* pointed to only the formal garden design for Maxwell Court (1902–4) and the Freer Gallery (1913–23) as works by Platt meriting attention.[4]

Since his death, Platt has received infrequent recognition. Wayne Andrews in his 1947 *Architecture, Ambition and Americans* was one of the first historians to treat sympathetically the work of the early twentieth century in general and the designs of Charles Platt in particular.[5] More characteristic of midcentury scholarly appraisal was the brief notice of Platt by Henry-Russell Hitchcock in his 1958 *Architecture, Nineteenth and Twentieth Centuries* where Platt is grouped with Delano & Aldrich as designers who were "quite as competent" as McKim, Mead & White in exploiting a "formal Neo-Georgian" mode of domestic architecture.[6] But in the past decade, with the increasing skepticism toward the modernist philosophy and the reappraisal of history's potential contribution to contemporary design, Platt and his generation have received wider critical attention.

Although Platt was admired by his generation as an artist in four media, this book will discuss in depth only his career as an architect and landscape architect, leaving others to assess his work as a painter and etcher. The chronological progression of his landscape and architecture commissions, divided into four distinct phases of gardens, country houses, urban commissions, and public buildings, permits a convenient typological discussion of his designs. The 1890s were years of growth dominated more by landscape design than by architecture. From 1901 until the publication of a monograph on his work in 1913, Platt became one of the most accomplished and best-known country house architects in America. The uncertain years of the mid- and later 1910s saw Platt move from primarily domestic projects to predominantly urban commissions, with public buildings consuming an ever larger part of his work. And after the First World War, he was drawn to institutional projects and served as a consulting architect for museums, universities, and private schools. The evolution of his commissions, from private to public, was the standard route for financial and professional success. But Platt's more memorable and influential works remain the country houses he designed during the first fifteen years of this century.

Changing conditions in American patronage clearly affected the course of his career. He worked in an age when fashion demanded, and expanding fortunes permitted, the construction of large-scale country estates and cultural institutions. Like many beginners in a profession, Platt relied at first on family and personal friends for commissions, but the publication of laudatory articles in the professional press quickly brought him some of the most prestigious projects of his time. The enactment of the graduated income tax in 1913 signaled the decline of the country-house market, a trend further accelerated by the unsettling effects of the First World War. But even as Platt turned to more public commissions, his skillful way of dealing with wealthy and powerful clients remained a key to his success.

The intellectual and economic climate of his generation also determined Platt's philosophy of design. When he reached maturity around 1890, Platt joined a society in transition caused by the ascendancy of an urban, corporate-capitalist industrialism over the rural, individually dependent, agrarian economy that had been the basis of American life for nearly three centuries. Culturally, the Eastern establishment, of which Platt was a thorough product, was assuming an aggressive posture in response to the rapid economic and social changes. Artists of all persuasions now confronted the need to embrace or reject, to varying extents, corporate capitalism, political imperialism, and the attendant self-conscious longing for a high art culture reflective of America's evolving world status. That cultural ambition acquired cosmopolitan inclusiveness of all past forms, especially from western Europe, and a genteel idealism on which the dominant society relied for self-justification. His generation also believed in the improvement of American civilization through the application of large-scale planning and scientific organization to all problems of contemporary life. Especially in his work as an architect and landscape architect, Platt sought, through self-study and adaptation of the best examples of past cultures, to achieve an idealized beauty thoroughly appropriate to modern needs.

This book seeks to provide a context and a method for the evaluation of all Platt's work. Since he neither wrote about his ideas on art nor left a corpus of private papers, it is in the formal analysis of his commissions that one meets Platt on his own basis and best perceives the merit and influence of his works. Describing him, his friend Royal Cortissoz wrote:

He makes a work of art because he cannot help himself. The constructive nature of the artist must out. It is this fact which made him such a commanding figure in the field of architecture as a designer of houses. He was born to design them. He could not help but make them beautiful.[7]

1

New York and Paris

CHARLES A. PLATT emerged from a background characteristic of the professional and artistic position he was destined to achieve. His parents, John Henry and Mary Elizabeth Cheney Platt, held a secure position in the cultural and social life of New York City and provided a happy and prosperous home for their four sons and one daughter.[1] From a childhood enriched by contact with talented relatives and leading artists and intellectuals, Charles developed a self-confidence and independence of mind that encouraged the formation of a strong personal aesthetic. And he used that artistic vision to serve the economic and social class in which he was reared.

Charles's ancestors were typical of the determined and inventive race that first settled in New England. The Platts came from England to the New Haven Colony in 1638–39 and by the mid-eighteenth century had migrated to the Hudson River Valley.[2] There, William Barnes Platt, Charles's grandfather, became a merchant in Rhinebeck, New York, investing successfully in Hudson River transportation and retiring early to serve as the director of a railroad and two banks.[3] William's sister, Elizabeth, married Charles Henry Adams, a lawyer, politician, and congressman from Albany County. It was for this great-uncle that Charles Adams Platt was named.[4]

The Cheneys, Charles's mother's family, came to Connecticut in 1625 and eventually settled in the town of Manchester, where, in 1745, Timothy Cheney opened a clock shop.[5] In the 1830s, the eight sons of George Cheney focused the family's mechanical and manufacturing interests on the emerging field of silk production. They established a silk industry that prospered for a century as the basis of Manchester's economy.[6] The eight Cheney brothers, of whom Charles's grandfather,

George, was the eldest, presided over the growth of the silk mills and provided the social and cultural focus of Manchester. It was in the relaxed and healthy environment of a controlled rural-industrial countryside, supported by the success of Cheney Mills, that Charles spent many pleasant and instructive holidays.

Two of Charles's great-uncles, John and Seth Wells Cheney, while receiving income from their interests in the mills, pursued careers as professional artists.[7] During the 1840s, Seth carried on an active practice as a crayon portraitist in Boston, interrupted by two years of study in Italy. He also practiced painting and sculpture in the course of his short career. His brother, John Cheney, primarily an engraver, lived until 1885 and knew Charles well. John's biographer remarked that in old age the artist occupied himself "with frequent trips to . . . his niece in New York [Charles's mother]."[8] A peculiar mixture of vestigial Puritan theology and a Rousseau-inspired belief in Nature, John held "theories of severe economy, of rigid simplicity in dress, food, and manner of life, [that] were at variance with his tastes, which were delicate, and appreciative of beauty and refinement."[9] Young Charles seems to have inherited his great-uncles' restraint, love of beauty, multiple artistic talents, and rejection of formal training, but without the stiff moral constraints that had characterized these forebears.

Although extremely close to both his parents, Charles was more strongly influenced by his father. Born at Rhinebeck in 1829, John Henry Platt was graduated from Union College in 1849, then moved to New York City where he was admitted to the bar after one year of reading law.[10] Through his father's business connections, John entered the law firm of Schell & Slosson, which, within two decades, became the firm of Hutchins & Platt, pioneers in the practice of corporate law. Waldo Hutchins was an accomplished trial lawyer and a prominent New Yorker who declined a seat on the United States Supreme Court and served as a commissioner of Central Park for twelve years.[11] In contrast, John Platt gained his reputation as a lawyer in the library, not the courtroom, "being restrained by a singular timidity which rendered any public effort distasteful."[12] Charles definitely inherited his father's shyness, as well as many of his less inhibited qualities. A cousin described John Platt as a "gifted man — gifted with intelligence, personal beauty, a fine voice, a keen sense of humor, discerning appreciation of literature . . . [he] had the social gifts to a higher degree than any man [I] knew."[13] "He was fully informed upon subjects which interest men of taste and education," remembered his fellow Century Association members, "and as he also possessed an unfailing fund of humor, added

6

to unusual ability as a raconteur, his conversation was extremely brilliant and effective."[14] Charles succeeded to John Platt's reputation as a humorist, storyteller, and joiner of clubs. Later, as an architect and businessman, he also benefited from this early contact with the legal issues of the emerging corporate capitalist structure of the American economy.

Mary Cheney Platt's influence on her son's development is harder to judge. "She was a kind and sympathetic woman with the power of entering the things that . . . John and her children enjoyed."[15] Mrs. Platt had been reared by a family that instilled in its members self-respect, simplicity, and responsibility. Charles acquired these qualities as well as the Cheney artistic inclination. And at an early age, he began to dwell often in his imagination, becoming a "self-contained person . . . who had the ability to amuse himself," and selectively learning from his parents and their world.[16]

John Platt's social and professional associations attracted a fascinating group of visitors to the family residence at 90 Lexington Avenue. The friends fell into two general categories: publishers and artists. The former included William Cullen Bryant, poet of "Thanatopsis" and editor of the *Evening Post;* George Palmer Putnam, publisher of *Putnam's Magazine,* whose son, Herbert, was one of Charles's close friends; and Horace Greeley, would-be politician, editor of the *Tribune,* and voracious eater of pancakes at the Platt family Sunday breakfasts.[17] The artist group consisted of men whom John Platt met through the Century Club. He was a charter member of this organization founded in 1847 by "one hundred gentlemen engaged or interested in Letters and the Fine Arts."[18] Significant for Charles among his father's Century colleagues were Frederick Law Olmsted, designer of Central Park, and George Henry Hall, a landscape painter, who accompanied both John and Charles on two separate trips to Europe. Eastman Johnson, Sanford Gifford, Jervis McEntee, and John Bunyan Bristol were all fellow Centurion painters, for whose work Charles expressed an early admiration.[19] There were doubtless many other, perhaps closer associates, who made "Literature and the Fine Arts" part of growing up in the Platt house.

Following the pattern set by some of his father's New York friends and by his great-uncles in Manchester, Charles decided by the time he was eight years old that he would be an artist of some kind. Years later he recalled his initial efforts:

As I remember it, my first artistic interest was in trying to make in paper imitations of objects I had seen, chiefly houses, horses and carriages, and I composed complete country houses with the surroundings including inhabitants—all in paper.[20]

However, drawing and painting were his first loves. According to a Cheney cousin, "when he was 15 or 16 he was already absorbed in painting and his sketches seemed remarkable to us. He used to go off by himself with his painting things day after day when he was quite young."[21] But vacations in Manchester exposed Charles to artistic opportunities beyond just sketching in the countryside.

The Cheney brothers evinced an enlightened concern and vision for the physical environment of their mill village. Through both architecture and landscape planning, the family attempted to create a model industrial community. They emphasized light and ventilation in their mill buildings, as well as in boarding houses and cottages of extraordinarily high quality.[22] "The grounds about the mill are laid out like a park," commented *Harper's Magazine* in 1872, and ". . . the Cheney Brothers [have] purchased a wooded knoll, which has been left an unchanged natural forest, traversed by picturesque walks."[23] The importance of comprehensive order in community planning shown in South Manchester is relevant background for Platt's understanding of the symbiotic relationship of buildings and landscape, especially in his large campus-planning projects of the 1920s.

Visits to Manchester may also have provided Charles with first-hand knowledge of contemporary movements in American architecture. In 1875–76, Henry Hobson Richardson designed the polychromatic Cheney Block in nearby Hartford and later proposed an addition to the family store.[24] One of Charles's earliest etchings was a view of Hartford from across the Connecticut River with the Cheney Block dominating the skyline. Also in the 1870s, Stanford White, while still working in the Richardson office, designed South Manchester houses for James and Rush Cheney, Charles's great-uncles.[25] Although neither of these shingled, Shavian manorial houses was built, Charles may well have met White, who was not so much older and whose friendship he would later enjoy. If Charles's earliest artistic memory was the composition of country houses on paper, he would certainly have been interested in these architects' work for his relatives. In the second half of the 1870s, Richardson and White were both seeking to discipline American architecture through rational planning and a selective dependence on historical forms. As their work matured in the early 1880s, it established the philosophical basis that would inform Platt's own career as an architect.

In comparison with the artistic associations that his family provided, formal education was far less important for Platt. He had evidently finished a private secondary education of unexceptional achievement by the age of seventeen.[26] Then, in the fall of 1878, he enrolled in the Antique School of the National Academy of Design and registered for life drawing classes the following March.[27] The Ruskinian Gothic building stood on the northwest corner of Fourth Avenue and 23rd Street, not far from the Platt house on Lexington Avenue. "The goal of the school was . . . to provide not only visual and technical training but also a thorough analytical knowledge of anatomy and perspective."[28] It required ten weeks of drawing from casts of antique sculpture before the student advanced to the art drawing class. Platt's instructors included Lemuel Wilmarth, director of the school, who had trained in Munich and Paris; James Wells Champney, lecturer in anatomy, who had studied in France and Holland; and John George Brown, an English immigrant, who had trained in Newcastle-on-Tyne and Edinburgh.[29] All three were genre painters whose work and teachings Platt would soon reject although he benefited from their instruction in technique. "In the late seventies, Wilmarth introduced in the life class the rapid sketching of models in briefly sustained poses, imposing on the students a new way of seeing the model."[30] The technique demanded charcoal and chalk and emphasized a quick rendering of light and shadow, rather than studied draftsmanship. Wilmarth's approach responded not only to new directions in painting but also to the increasing interest in etching as fine art and as illustration, an interest that Platt would soon share.

Missing from the academy curriculum was training in painting, for which Charles joined the Art Students League. Founded in 1875 by dissatisfied students and teachers from the academy, the league provided self-governing, cooperative classes at the nominal fee of five dollars a month. "Classes at the League were held daily and were in session for periods of three hours. Afternoons were reserved for the ladies. The gentlemen studied at night."[31] Thus, Platt was able to improve his drawing during the day at the academy, while attending painting classes in the evening at the league. His painting instructors, Walter Shirlaw and William Merritt Chase, were younger than the academy professors and more familiar with current European ideas and practices, both having been trained in Munich. Chase, Shirlaw, and "other artists who studied in Munich sought *brio* in their paintings of exotic subjects and felt a kinship to Franz Hals," which may partially account for Platt's later attraction to the Old Masters and to the contemporary landscapists of the Dutch School.[32] Even after taking full advantage for three years of all that the academy and the league had to offer, Platt was later forced to admit, "My training in the New York schools, you know, was neither long nor thorough."[33]

Charles supplemented his winter studio work with summer sketching trips in the country. Like most people of their time and economic class, the Platt family visited various resorts, including Newport, Lenox, and Lake George; they also spent considerable time with the Cheneys in Manchester. On one such vacation at Bolton's Landing, New York, in 1879, Charles met Stephen Parrish, a Philadelphia artist, the father of Maxfield Parrish, and an experimenter with the newly revived art of etching.[34] Platt became his informal pupil and joined the Parrishes the following summer at Gloucester, Massachusetts. There Charles made sketches for his own first etching, "Gloucester Harbor," which he produced in the winter of 1880. He chose a horizontal format, marked by great voids of water and sky, and opposed by the vertical lines of ship masts and their reflections. More mature etchings, such as "Buttermilk Channel" of 1887, show similar subject matter and technique (Fig. 1). He worked his etchings with extreme economy of line, showing the light, quick quality of Wilmarth's academy training. This reduction and simplification of compositional elements would remain a basic characteristic of his work in all aspects of his artistic career. And for several years he concentrated on the amorphous effects of light, air, and water in seascapes and harbor views as the primary subjects for his etchings and paintings.

Platt was soon caught up in the enthusiasm for etching as an art form, a revival that had begun in France in the 1850s and had spread to England in the following decade. In 1866, a Parisian publisher named Cadart held an exhibition of French etching in New York City which inspired various American artists to begin experimenting with the plate and needle. The Centennial at Philadelphia gave further impetus to the movement, and in the winter of 1877 a group of about twenty artists gathered to form the New York Etching Club.[35] The founders emphasized the personal, noncommercial quality of the art etching, which they considered as "suggestive rather than elaborated" when compared to the engraver's etching used for contemporary commercial illustrations.[36] This distinction of "suggestive rather than elaborated" is also reminiscent of the quick sketch techniques that Wilmarth had introduced at this time in the academy curriculum. And Platt acquired a condescending attitude toward commercial engravers, emphasizing the more genteel and elevated purpose of the artist etcher.[37]

Platt joined the New York Etching Club and quickly established a reputation in this new medium. In 1881, one year after completing his first print, Charles was the subject of one in a series of articles on major American etchers written by Sylvester Rosa Koehler for the *American Art Review:*

Charles A. Platt is, if not the youngest, one of the youngest, of the school of American etchers which has developed with such surprising rapidity within a few years. . . . His first plate was etched in December of last year and the art had such fascination for him that he devoted much more time to it than he had originally intended, to the neglect of his studies in drawing and painting.[38]

Charles was nineteen when he began etching, and John Platt was soon referred to by his fellow Century Club members as "the father of the boy-etcher."[39] By the time of the 1881 article, Charles had already etched seventeen plates, eleven of which he had destroyed because he was dissatisfied with the results. Koehler rightly saw Platt as working in the manner of Stephen Parrish and allowed that the young man's drawing held room for improvement. Nevertheless, Charles had become a recognized American etcher within a year of his first attempt and before

1.   "Buttermilk Channel," 1887.

11

he was twenty.[40] His ease in mastering the techniques of etching forecast his later shifts to landscape design and architecture, again without any academic training. But Platt was not a facile dilettante. Regardless of medium, he approached his work with total seriousness, taught himself the necessary skills, and evolved a personal style.

Both Platt and Parrish were soon characterized as American disciples of the etching style of Seymour Haden. Haden, a British surgeon, etcher, and print collector, was a meticulous and exacting technician of the etching process. Platt would visit Haden in 1882 and be impressed by the Englishman's elaborate equipment and printing press. In 1880 Haden founded the Society (now Royal) of Painter-Etchers which began holding exhibitions in 1881. Parrish was one of the American contributors to the first show, and Platt sent a frame of etchings the following year.[41] Other Platt contemporaries, such as Frank Duveneck and Joseph Pennell, were more heavily influenced by the work of the expatriate American, James McNeill Whistler. In the 1860s, Whistler had begun to execute etchings that had a profound influence on several other American artists working abroad. His work was characterized by attention to light and tone. Platt adopted some of Whistler's effect of understatement in presentation, but he followed Haden more closely in his concern for careful craftsmanship to create more exacting effects of light, water, and atmosphere.

Even though Platt received national recognition and financial reward, etching was not a career that he considered fully satisfying or expressive of his talents. He continued to etch and to hold periodic exhibitions throughout most of his life, but this art form now became a secondary interest. To achieve maturity as a painter, he felt that he needed more sophisticated training and a greater exposure to the masterpieces of the past and present than New York could offer. Like many contemporaries, he believed that the best opportunities for study and criticism were in Paris, which was quickly becoming the unchallenged international center for the arts. So, with the moral and financial support of his parents and new confidence from his rapid success as an etcher, Charles sailed for Europe in May 1882.

Platt spent nearly all of the years between 1882 and 1887 studying in Paris and traveling throughout Europe.[42] During these five years, he was exposed to the dominant influences of his career and formulated a personal artistic philosophy that he applied to his work as a painter, architect, and landscape architect. He perpetuated an annual cycle of summer sketching tours with winter studio work in Paris. The friendships and acquaintances that he made abroad greatly fostered his personal and professional growth. Throughout his sojourn, he shared his changing assumptions on the nature and purpose of art with family friends and former classmates from the National Academy of Design and the Art Students League, as well as with new colleagues from America and Europe. Typical of his natural self-confidence, he attached himself to no school or master but evolved his ideas in reaction to a broad range of influences. By the end of this period of study, Charles had synthesized the issues of design that he would continue to explore and refine throughout his life.

Although it was not a financial burden for the Platts to support Charles's studies, he helped through the sale of his etchings and paintings.[43] In fact, while on his way to Paris he stopped in London to meet Seymour Haden and to view the second exhibition of the Society of Painter-Etchers. He gleefully reported: "I have found that all the etchings I had in the exhibition here were sold except the one selected by the Society of Painters and Etchers, so I have reason to be much pleased."[44] This financial success continued throughout his time abroad, from works he sold directly in his Paris studio and paintings and etchings he sent to dealers in New York.

During the first two years in Paris, Charles worked completely on his own, attending exhibitions, visiting museums, and preparing the standard submissions to the spring Salon, where he had only modest success, despite his strong performance in the salesrooms. Initially, the artists he met during summer sketching trips were more influential than the institutionalized art world of Paris. He spent his first summer wandering through Normandy and Brittany until he settled in August 1882 at Grand Camp in Normandy, where he met an American expatriate painter named Frank Myers Boggs. Platt's original reaction to this new colleague in no way forecast his later affection for the man and admiration for his work:

I find there is an American artist named Boggs. I remember seeing some of his pictures in Philadelphia and there were two at the Salon this year bought by the government. They were weird sort of things, almost totally lacking in color and to me uninteresting.[45]

Boggs was a pupil of Léon Gérôme and had been in France since 1877, having started as a scenic designer in New York. A contemporary American reviewer characterized him as "an impressionist who is particularly sensible to the delicacies and subtleties of the grays and blues and greens of the seacoast and of the sea that is rather sulky and menacing."[46] Already fascinated by the nuances of seascapes, Platt was gradually

13

attracted to Boggs and his work.

More important than the influence of Boggs's own work was the introduction he provided for Platt to the modern Dutch School of landscape painters. In the summer of 1883, both men decided to paint in Dordrecht. There and on excursions to Antwerp they met artists who emphasized tone and color and who took inspiration from the Barbizon group, the Englishmen John Constable and J.M.W. Turner, and seventeenth-century Dutch painters such as Franz Hals and Anthony Van Dyke.[47] Platt's affinity for the Dutch artists was reinforced by three factors: his pleasure in the landscape of Holland; his appreciation for earlier works in museums; and his friendship with important contemporary painters, especially Jacob Maris, a leader of the Dutch School.[48] Platt never accepted Maris's use of thick, unmixed pigment, but he experimented with the potential of using landscape to express emotion and warmly embraced the principle of learning from earlier works of art.

In addition to Boggs, Platt met other American artists who eventually drew him into more academic training in Paris. His close friends and frequent traveling companions were Dennis Miller Bunker and Kenneth Cranford, whom Charles described in a letter to his family:

I think you know who Bunker is. A New Yorker, nephew of Mr. Gifford. I used to know him in New York and have seen a good deal of him this winter. He is a small and rather handsome fellow and is, I believe, one of the strongest draughtsmen in Gerome's "atelier." Cranford is another N. Yorker. He is also an excellent draughtsman from the Beaux Arts, but of his work I know nothing.[49]

But even with two friends in Gérôme's studio and another at the Ecole des Beaux-Arts, Platt's native self-confidence made him reluctant to pursue formal academic training.

It was only his lack of success in Salon entries that convinced Platt of the need for greater structure in his studies. The two etchings and the painting of a harbor scene that he submitted to the Salon in 1883 were rejected.[50] The following spring he reported to his parents: "I sent two pictures and they are hung! I said last year that I would make them do it this year and you see I have."[51] Even though he later wrote that he was "charmed to find one of mine hung on the line in one of the best rooms," there is no listing for Platt in the 1884 Salon catalogue or in the coverage of the exhibition in the American art periodicals.[52] A Salon failure in the first year and no public recognition in the second, as well as a desire to include figures in his landscapes, probably persuaded him finally to seek instruction during his third winter in Paris.

2. "The Etcher," 1885.

Given Platt's passion for personal and artistic independence, it is not surprising that he enrolled at the Académie Julian, the most informal of his possible choices. He described his new training in a November 1884 letter to his parents:

The atelier is managed by Julian, who makes a living out of it. . . . There are four ateliers, two of them criticized by Bougereau and Robert Fleury and two by Boulanger and Lefèvre. It is under the last two that I am. The professors come twice a week & give each man 1 or 2 minutes criticism. They are not paid for their time but give it for the sake of having someone to swear at as he always gives it to the fellows in the strongest possible language.[53]

Platt was one of approximately eighty students who worked under the guidance of Jules Lefèvre. Julian's was popular among Americans, Platt's fellow students including Will Low, Kenyon Cox, and Willard Metcalf, among others. Admitting that he needed "to just go to work and plough away at the nude," Platt concluded that "if I could get 2 years of hard study in the schools here it would be of the greatest use to me."[54]

The fruit of Platt's labors was his success in the Salon of 1885, to which he submitted a figure study called "The Etcher" (Fig. 2). Although he initially denied an intention to enter, he confessed to his family in March:

I have just heard that it was very well received . . . and will be hung on the

15

line!!! It is a small picture & my first attempt at the figure. I took the corner of the studio & placed my own working clothes on the model, all the materials of the aquafortist are in the background and I painted them as I did the figure "my level best." I feel considerably encouraged. Hard work in the school is doing me lots of good & I think if I stick to it long enough I will be able to do something some day.[55]

The *Art Amateur* acknowledged Platt's entry in the 1885 Salon, but the reviewer preferred "Low Tide at Larmor," a marine landscape Platt had exhibited at the American Art Association that year.[56] French critics applauded Platt's figure study, a painting that was the culmination of his Paris training, while the American reviewer favored his landscapes, subjects that he had begun to treat seriously at home and had refined under the influence of the Dutch School. When he decided not to submit in 1886, Platt ended his surprisingly brief Salon career. The process of public competition and criticism did not fit his temperament. And he used these years in Paris more to satisfy his consuming curiosity about current activities in the arts.

One important indication of his widening interests was his unsuccessful attempt to gain entrance to the architectural section of the Ecole des Beaux-Arts. Strangely, Platt's correspondence with his family contains no mention of his taking this examination, but three decades later he recalled the event in a letter to the art critic, Royal Cortissoz:

Regarding my architectural education — it began by beaux arts examination in Paris '83. They require you to know the Orders, perspective etc., the elements in fact. This got me started on a few fundamentals so that I was studying architecture all the six years I was abroad from the point of view of the artist, for fun. Of course, I knew architectural students in Paris and criticized their projects and discussed their performances from my point of view.[57]

Characteristic of Platt's love of understatement, he presents this occurrence as if it had been simply a student lark. It would have been uncharacteristic of him not to have prepared for this examination as he constantly sought to expand his artistic parameters. An interest in buildings is certainly evident in the frequency with which he chose architectural subjects for his etchings and paintings. For example, the "Quai des Orfèvres," etched in 1886, shows the reflection of water and forced perspective that characterized his views of city architecture (Fig. 3). But there is no further archival documentation for his experimentation with architecture while in Paris.

Among Platt's architectural student friends at the Ecole was James Archibald Campbell, a tall, handsome, reserved Scotsman, pupil of Pascal, and later partner of Sir John J. Burnet.[58] They met during

3. "Quai des Orfèvres," 1886.

Platt's first year in Paris and maintained contact after Campbell returned to Scotland the following year. Although Platt generally disliked philosophical discussions on the meaning of art, he and Campbell engaged in frequent "studio talk." And the Scotsman's penchant for mannered classicism is one of the strains that eventually emerged in Platt's work as an architect, especially in his designs for the Freer Gallery of Art (1913–23) and the competition entry for the Theodore Roosevelt Memorial (1925), both in Washington, D.C.

Out of these conversations and his own reflections on painting and architecture, Platt formulated a personal "sense of the beautiful" during these student years abroad. From his training in New York, he arrived in Paris intent upon the pursuit of the Picturesque—the rough, the irregular, and the ruined—as an appropriate subject for art. "What I want," he wrote his family in the summer of 1882, "is some God-forsaken place where the people are content to let their houses tumble about their ears, without taking the trouble to restore them (their houses, not their ears)."[59] While the earliest Parisian influences on Platt's work were technical, such as his adoption of the current habit of painting outdoors, directly from nature, by 1884 his ideas on the choice and treatment of subjects also had begun to shift.[60] In criticizing the highly narrative paintings of the contemporary German and English schools, he observed:

This is all wrong. An artist should interest one's sense of the beautiful and make that his great object. He must have a subject, of course, but he should *use* the subject to make his picture and not use the picture to render his subject.[61]

He had now divorced himself completely from the training he had received in New York, especially at the National Academy of Design.

Platt not only rejected history and genre painting as appropriate subjects, he also turned away from the quaint scenes of cluttered harbors and dilapidated houses that had previously been his major interest. In another letter to his family, he continued to clarify his evolving philosophy:

I think it is often difficult to separate the beautiful from what is curious and extraordinary and in my case it is usually a rather long operation. I find that I carry with me longer & with constantly recurring charm the impression of something beautiful, while the effect of the wonderful & curious & seemingly picturesque may be remembered just as long but never with the same pleasure.[62]

In this statement, Platt identifies the contrast between the Picturesque and the Beautiful in art, much as it had been understood since the second half of the eighteenth century. He clearly characterizes the picturesque qualities of his former work as a painter — the effect of the curious, the wonderful, the extraordinary. But he was only beginning to understand what he meant by "the sense of the beautiful."

He now began to conceive of the beautiful as an abstract ideal of smooth, even, balanced, complete forms. The rejection of picturesque values in both painting and architecture was a predominant lesson of all academic training in Paris. But to Platt, beauty in painting meant something different than it did to those American contemporaries who emerged from a similar background. Unlike Will Low and Kenyon Cox, after leaving the Académie Julian, Platt did not retain an interest in figure painting, a frequent vehicle for those who shared his admiration for classic beauty. Nor did Platt even use figures in his landscapes to create an allegorical reference or a specific mood, as did Thomas Dewing, who had previously studied at Julian's and would later become a friend and neighbor of Platt. In his devotion to pure landscape, Platt might seem to have sympathized most closely with fellow Julian student Willard Metcalf. Although both men shared a thin, dry palette, Platt did not succumb to the influence of Impressionism, so central to Metcalf's work. Rather, Platt reduced his search for beauty to the depiction of landscape devoid of people and emotion, where only color, texture, and composition remained the tools of the artist.

For Platt, the "sense of the beautiful" had a life of its own, separate from the moral and literary overlays he had rejected with the picturesque subjects. As Royal Cortissoz later stated, Platt "played more or less into the hands of those of us who were talking ardently . . . about the now slightly old-fashioned gospel of 'art for art's sake.'"[63] This philosophy, derived from both academic training in Paris and his own response to varied personal experiences, became the foundation for all his later work. When Platt turned to architecture, Herbert Croly, critic and editor of the *Architectural Record,* saw no remnant of the romantic viewpoint in Platt's work:

But as he was too well-informed a painter to seek for picturesque landscapes, so he is too well-informed an architect not to discern the artificiality of merely picturesque houses. The picturesque ideal is not pictorial; it is not architectural; it is literary.[64]

This contrast between classic and romantic, beautiful and picturesque, which Platt defined as a student in Paris, became the touchstone for all his work as an artist.

Toward the end of his stay in Paris, Platt yielded to parental

19

pressure and went "into society" more. In 1885, Stephen Parrish moved his family and students to Paris, providing a new circle of friends for Platt. A photograph of a dinner party organized by Charles for this group shows the interior of his studio with sketches and etchings covering the walls (Fig. 4). In addition, he attended the "Salons" and "days" held by residents of the American quarter in Paris but found these occasions boring and avoided them whenever possible. Also at the urging of his parents, he returned to the United States for the summer of 1885. His father had not been well, and Charles had postponed several previous requests for a visit. But Platt still felt he had much to learn abroad and in September he boarded the boat for France again.

Although he little expected it, the coming year in Europe would be momentous for Charles and would lead to a period of compounded tragedies. The major changes were personal, not professional. For several years he had been writing home half-serious predictions of engagements to pretty, young French girls or daughters of American friends. Upon his return from America, his tone became more sincere: "I've got

4. Photograph of party for Stephen Parrish family and friends, Platt's Paris studio, 1885.

a good deal of affection in me, although I have always shown so little that you might easily doubt it."[65] By November 1885, he had definite objectives and hinted as much in a February letter to his parents:

Some very charming people that I have seen a good deal of this winter, Mr. & Mrs. Hoe and their daughter have urged me very much to join them in their travels to the sunny south. I like them very much, especially the *daughter*! so I have about as much as promised to run across them somewhere on the "Riviera" & proceed to Rome in their company.[66]

Since Charles had intended to go to Rome the previous year, before an outbreak of cholera there changed his plans, he needed little persuasion to join the Hoe party.

The daughter, Annie Corbin Hoe, was born in New York in 1852 to Colonel Richard March Hoe and Mary Corbin Hoe.[67] Her father headed R. Hoe & Co., manufacturers of printing presses. The family residence was "Brightside," a large estate located in the Bronx when the area was still farmland. The Hoes traveled extensively and lived in Paris throughout the Civil War. They were friends of Kenneth Cranford, who introduced them to Platt. Charles reported to his parents: "She is not exactly pretty although she has a most charming face, extremely interesting and a smile that is quite impossible to resist." Annie was nine years older than Charles, but he found her "considerably younger in many ways."[68]

On his way to meet the Hoes, Platt stopped at St. Raphael on February 16, 1886, to see the Parrishes. Commenting on Platt's taciturn yet intensely critical nature, Mrs. Stephen Parrish recorded in her diary:

Platt came this afternoon, he will only stay a week en route for Italy to join some friends. . . . Steve is quite discouraged with his Salon picture and Platt's coming does not help him as he criticizes faults but does not see or at least does not speak of virtues; his coming is always depressing as he seems to give so little, he is a queer fellow and we always have to get used to him over again, after an absence, the first impression is always chilling.[69]

As Platt grew older, the "chilling" effect of his personal relationships certainly decreased, but he always remained an exacting critic and never faltered in his artistic convictions. His son, Geoffrey, recalled, "In looking at a work of art, or a design that he had made, or a drawing that someone else had made . . . he was only interested in what was wrong and what could be done to make it right. He was incapable of flattery."[70]

At the end of February, Charles joined the Hoes at San Remo, and they proceeded by carriage for a leisurely tour through Genoa, Pisa, and Siena to Rome. Charles found time to sketch and to "rummage with

21

mademoiselle." With Miss Hoe rather than the masterpieces of the Renaissance uppermost in his mind, Platt's letters contain little information on his intial reactions to the country that so strongly influenced his later career. Before reaching Rome, Platt announced to his family his engagement to Annie:

I may as well tell you that it has been going on for a long time and that my journey to Italy was not altogether with a view to seeing old masters. . . . You can imagine what the ride along the Riviera was for me. It was very soon after arriving in Genoa that I found a good opportunity to have an explanation with Miss Hoe. I have never understood exactly how it happened that I persuaded her to "enter into my views."[71]

Annie's parents consented to the match, and the couple decided to return to New York in June. They continued to Naples and then back to Rome, but in early April, Charles caught "Roman fever" (typhoid) while crossing the Campania. He and Annie thought to marry at once so that she could be with him day and night, but he slowly began to recover, and they decided to marry in Italy when he regained his health.

Charles and Annie were married on April 10, 1886, in Florence, although Platt was still bedridden. Then, on June 7, Colonel Hoe died, and his widow and the Platts returned immediately to New York with the body. Charles's father also died that summer on August 21. The young Platts stayed on in New York through the summer to comfort their families and sailed for Paris in October. Then, incredibly, death struck a third time. Annie died in childbirth, losing twin girls on March 18, 1887. The disasters were unexpected and difficult to accept. Platt returned to New York but found little comfort. Charles C. Burlingham, a relative of the Hoes, remembered:

[Charles] was devoted to his mother & sister, and they to him; but they had never known Annie and he could not talk with them about her. . . . Every night, for months, Charles came up to our house & climbed the stairs to the top storey and listened at the door to learn if we had any visitors; and if there were none, we sat there talking of Annie.[72]

Not for several years did Platt recover from this stunning series of deaths, culminating in the loss of a marriage that had hardly begun.

Following the tragedies, Platt only slowly regained his strength and momentum. He became heavily involved in the expanding art scene in New York, joining the mildly revolutionary Society of American Artists, while continuing to exhibit at the annual shows of the National Academy of Design and New York Etching Club.[73] In 1887 friends nominated him for membership at the Century Association and in 1889 at The Players, a club for professionals in the theater, literature, and the arts.[74] He spent the summers along the seacoast, at Gloucester, Massachusetts, in 1887 with Dennis Bunker and another Paris friend, Henry Oliver Walker, and alone in Holland in 1888.[75] The following summer, Walker invited Platt to join him for several weeks of sketching in Cornish, New Hampshire. The colony of artists that had gathered in the Cornish hills provided the close fellowship and communality of interests necessary for Platt's recovery. While the uncertainty of his potential success as a painter lingered, it was at Cornish in the 1890s that Platt found the opportunity to explore and expand his talents in the design of houses and gardens. These changes in form of expression, however, did not alter Platt's principles or goals as an artist.

Platt's family background, his development of a personal aesthetic as a painter, and his reaction to the tragedies of 1886–87 were significant influences on his work as an architect and landscape designer. Within his own family can be traced the basic economic change from an agrarian society to corporate capitalism that would underlie the financial conditions of his architectural and landscape commissions. The Cheneys symbolized the evolution from artisans within an essentially rural, agricultural environment to a family-controlled industrial complex. John Platt, as a corporate lawyer, carried the economic evolution one step farther as a servant of the centralizing corporate-capitalist system that New York came to dominate in these years.

Just as the national evolution of the capitalist structure represented a clear ordering of society, Platt's own understanding of the purpose and process of art shows a desire for organization and for universal cultural ideals. His rejection of the curious, decayed, and irregular in landscapes and of the sentimental moralizing of contemporary history and genre painting demonstrates the emergence of a refined and abstract sense of beauty. This reduction to a visual ideal would become even more pronounced in his work as an architect than it was in his canvases and etchings.

Finally, the personal tragedies of losing his father, father-in-law, wife, and daughters in such numbingly rapid succession reinforced character traits that naturally would affect his art. The taciturn, self-reliant youth turned in upon himself even more as he attempted to resolve the confusion he felt during this period of grief. As he searched for a new framework of stability, he became a man of firm convictions derived from a belief in his own abilities and ideas. He moved into a period of personal and artistic maturity that allowed him to create his idealized visual forms.

23

2

Gardens and Early Houses

DURING THE 1890s, Platt established a new life for himself, personally and professionally. He married for a second time in 1893 and celebrated the birth of three of his five children before the turn of the century. He continued to etch and paint and applied his artistic philosophy to the design of small houses and gardens for himself and friends in the summer colony at Cornish, New Hampshire. He based these experiments on his Paris training and his familiarity with Renaissance villas acquired during tours of Italy in 1886 and 1892. The Italian villa especially had impressed upon him the value of integrating buildings and landscape. He published and illustrated his observations on Renaissance gardens in 1893 and 1894, and during the second half of the decade he designed a series of large gardens based on Italian villa principles adapted to American conditions. By 1902, he had been instrumental in creating a formal landscape revival in America and was embarked on a successful career as the architect of large country houses.

Platt's personal and professional relationship to the Cornish summer colony was immediate and far-reaching. He first visited Cornish in 1889 at the invitation of his artist friend H. O. Walker. At the time Platt was a painter in search of landscape subjects for his canvas. The summer colony at Cornish was an informal gathering of artists, writers, and other professionals, primarily from New York City. Seeking refuge from the heat of the city, they found the New Hampshire hills an ideal place in which to work.[1] The central figure in the Cornish colony was the sculptor Augustus Saint-Gaudens, who first summered there in 1885 and urged friends to join him. In 1890, the year after his initial summer visit, Platt purchased property for the house he was to build and in which he would spend nearly every summer thereafter.

In choosing Cornish as his summer residence, Platt developed associations with a community of kindred spirits who deeply influenced his work. Most of his Cornish friends were artists. In addition to Walker and Saint-Gaudens, Thomas Dewing, portrait and landscape painter, and his wife, Maria Oakey Dewing, were already established when Platt first came to Cornish. Stephen Parrish, who had been Platt's friend and teacher for more than a decade, arrived with his family in 1893, followed by his son Maxfield three years later. Also in 1896, Kenyon Cox, muralist, art teacher, and critic, bought land in Plainfield, just north of Cornish, and built a house. Among the resident sculptors, Platt developed friendships with Saint-Gaudens, Daniel Chester French, and Herbert Adams. He later collaborated with each, supplying the landscape or architectural setting for their public monuments.[2] Platt also became friends with writers at Cornish, including Herbert Croly, editor of the *Architectural Record* and later founder of the *New Republic;* the American novelist, Winston Churchill; and the playwright, Louis E. Shipman, and his wife, Ellen.

These artists and writers shared many common attitudes toward their work and life, especially a love of the classical tradition in literature and the arts. The extent to which this enchantment penetrated the colony was epitomized by the masque staged in 1905 as a Greek festival in honor of the Saint-Gaudens' twentieth summer in Cornish. A portrait plaque presented to Platt by Saint-Gaudens the previous summer equally symbolized the classical-Renaissance fascination in its jargonized Latin-Italian inscription and the representation of Platt as a garden herm (Fig. 5). This devotion to the classical past as inspiration for the modern world was evident in the work of many Cornish colonists, from the bas-reliefs of Saint-Gaudens to the allegorical figures in landscapes by Dewing, to the history murals by Cox. While this attitude was not as obvious in Platt's landscape paintings, his houses and gardens, in Cornish and elsewhere, owed as clear a debt to the classical heritage as did the work of any other colonist.

Gardening was a passion of the Cornishites, and the colony served as a training ground for several important landscape architects, including Ellen Shipman and Rose Standish Nichols.[3] The Dewings were credited with the introduction of flower gardening to Cornish.[4] Dewing conducted horticultural experiments to determine which plants could survive the area's harsh winters. His recommended plantings emphasized hardy, herbaceous material. In contrast to the gaudy exotics in common use at the time, Cornish gardeners favored what a contemporary writer described as "simpler, not nurserymanic" plants and "old-fashioned flowers."[5] While never a horticultural innovator, Platt developed a plant vocabulary from the gardening enthusiasm in Cornish and used this material to reinforce the architectonic nature of his landscape plans.

Platt's schemes for Cornish and later gardens evolved from the character of the topography and the vegetation. He worked broadly with existing stands of mature trees, favoring groves of birches and pines and adding Lombardy poplars for architectural accents. For hedges, he selected barberry, especially for Cornish, and privet in less severe climates. Within a strict geometry of rectilinear beds, he planted generous clumps of daffodils, poet's narcissus, scilla, columbines, phlox, iris, hardy chrysanthemums, poppies, Michaelmas daisies, larkspurs, or hollyhocks, all varied for height, color, texture, and scent. At the intersections of paths or flanking architectural elements, he commonly placed pots of hydrangeas, orange trees, or other dwarf fruit trees. And to soften the sharp angles and straight lines, he introduced climbers, especially grape vines for loggias. All these plants served to fulfill his spatial conception for the landscape.

The Cornish house and garden that Platt designed for himself provided the first opportunity to formulate his ideas on the interrelationship of architecture and landscape. His simple, clapboarded studio house was built on land along the Plainfield Stage Road, now known as

5. Augustus Saint-Gaudens, medal presented to Charles A. Platt, 1904.

26

6. Charles A. Platt house, Cornish, New Hampshire, 1890–1912.

Platt Road. The house site overlooked sheep pastures and had a clear southern view directly down the Connecticut River Valley. On the sloping site was an abandoned apple orchard, and the house was made to nestle cozily behind one of the gnarled old trees. To make a level site for the house, he cut into the hill rising to the rear and built a terrace across the south front. Below the terrace, he gently graded the foreground to make it ready for a garden he was to develop in detail after his second trip to Italy in 1892. In positioning his house on the site and orienting it to the distant landscape, Platt revealed at once the instinctive command that would guide his future double-sided career. The original plan of the house consisted of a studio-living area, a dining room, and a kitchen on the first floor, with bedrooms above.[6] As expanded over the next two decades, the house acquired a drawing room, a loggia, and an increased service area, as well as additional bedrooms (Figs. 6–8).

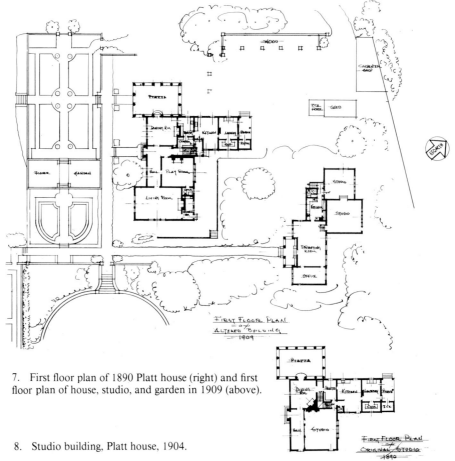

7. First floor plan of 1890 Platt house (right) and first floor plan of house, studio, and garden in 1909 (above).

8. Studio building, Platt house, 1904.

28

Even more suggestive of his sensitivity to the integration of a building and its surroundings was the 1889–91 scheme he developed for the house and garden of his neighbor, Miss Annie Lazarus. She was the daughter of a New York banker and sister to the poet Emma Lazarus, and unlike her fellow Cornishites, she was a patron of the arts rather than an artist.[7] Her property, opposite Platt's on the Plainfield Stage Road, was set on the exposed crest of a barren hill, with a commanding view of the surrounding country. High Court, her choice of name for the house, immediately became a landmark of the area and a harbinger of Platt's later work.

Whereas his own residence initially resembled a clapboard farm-house of the New Hampshire hills, High Court's hilltop site at once reminded Platt of similar scenes and situations in Italy, remembered so vividly from his 1886 tour. There was certainly no mistaking the origins of the two-story, stuccoed, hipped-roof dwelling with a U-shaped plan and interior colonnaded courtyard. In August 1890, in the course of planning, he wrote to his friend, the architect Stanford White: "What I want to build is an Italian villa 3 sides of a court with a collonade [sic] in the middle. The wings to be one story & the main part two."[8] The sketch he sent White showed the simplicity of his conception (Fig. 9). Although

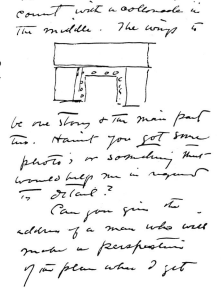

9. Letter, Charles A. Platt to Stanford White, August 29, 1890.

29

10. Annie Lazarus house, High Court, Cornish, New Hampshire, 1891.

11. First floor plan, High Court, 1890.

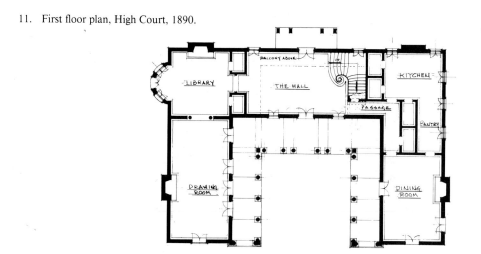

the original High Court was destroyed by fire in 1895, the nearly identical brick replacement constructed the following year maintained the
basic plan, with drawing and dining rooms occupying the wings on
either side of a central, monumental entrance hall defined by a sweeping
staircase and arcaded balcony and positioned to provide an immediate
view of the courtyard and vista (Figs. 10, 11). The location and treatment of the entrance hall alone forecast Platt's mastery as an architect.

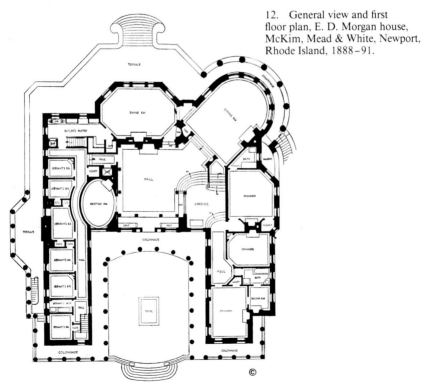

12. General view and first floor plan, E. D. Morgan house, McKim, Mead & White, Newport, Rhode Island, 1888–91.

31

13. Entrance hall, High Court.

High Court has a superficial similarity to a commission on which
McKim, Mead & White was working at the time of Platt's letter. The
Edward D. Morgan house, called Beacon Rock, at Newport, Rhode
Island, was designed in 1888 and constructed in 1889–91 (Fig. 12).[9] It
also incorporated a three-sided courtyard with a two-story body and
one-story wings fronted by a colonnade. The similarities stop there,
however. Since the McKim, Mead & White design had been established
two years before Platt wrote to White, his letter did not provide the idea
for Beacon Rock. Conversely, since Platt's conception for High Court
was already fixed at the time of writing, he was not influenced by the
Morgan project. Also, the organization of the two houses was entirely
different. McKim, Mead & White used the loggia courtyard as the entrance, while Platt made it the rear or vista elevation. Of course, the
Cornish house was also much simpler and smaller than the Newport
example, in which semicircular, oval, and hexagonal rooms encircled an
asymmetrical living hall.

Nevertheless, both the Morgan and Lazarus houses were early
nonurban examples of the classical-Renaissance formula that came to
dominate American architecture in the 1890s. As early as 1883,

McKim, Mead & White had signaled a return to classical formalism in the design of the Villard Houses in New York City.[10] Inspired by the Palazzo Cancelleria in Rome, this group of town houses was organized around a U-shaped courtyard with an inset, arcaded walkway across the first story of the central section. High Court's similarity in aesthetic and image to both the Villard and Morgan commissions indicates how closely the still amateur Platt was paralleling and anticipating the general trends in American architecture often referred to as "the academic reaction" or "revival" (Fig. 13). The next chapter will include a fuller description of this movement and of Platt's role in it.

Platt approached the siting and landscape plan of the Lazarus project from the perspective of a landscape painter. In fact, he later painted a view of the house as seen from his own garden farther down the hill (Fig. 14). Platt designed the Lazarus house, guest house, and gardens to represent the kind of simple, well-sited villa eagerly sought by a painter for his canvas. But his innate architectural insight was also immediately evident in his plans for High Court (Fig. 15).

14. "High Court." View of Lazarus property from Platt's own garden, n.d.

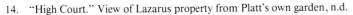

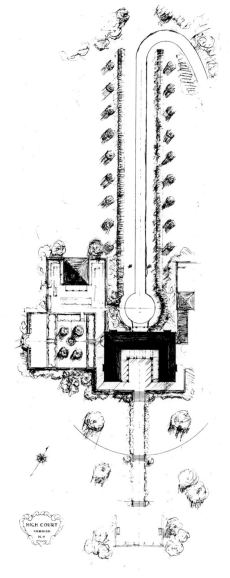

15. Plot plan, High Court.

His training as a landscape painter had instilled in Platt a constant concern for the importance of views into the landscape when siting
a building. The Lazarus house, like almost all those built at this time in
the Cornish area, was laid out to capitalize on the view of Mt. Ascutney
in Vermont and the Connecticut River Valley. High Court's position
permitted excellent views of both, but Platt carefully controlled these
advantages. He designed the entrance drive to circle around the hill and

approach the house on the side away from the main vista. Rows of hemlocks, backed by poplars, channeled the visitor to the door and prevented an early view of the landscape. A central axis through the house brought one into the rear courtyard which framed a panorama of the valley. Mt. Ascutney only became visible as one walked to the edge of the terrace. To conceal these views until the precise moment was one of Platt's major objectives in the design of High Court.

Another technique of the landscape painter that Platt carried over to villa planning was attention to depth recession. Generally, he relied on a formal and architectural treatment of the foreground with a naturalized handling of the middle distance leading to the natural landscape beyond. The setting of High Court, however, required a different approach. In one of the rare public statements on his work, Platt commented:

To a house set high upon a hill, the ground falling away from it with some abruptness, the whole site chosen for the view, the landscape gardener will give surroundings of the utmost simplicity that they may not compete with or disturb the larger without. This was recognized in the Frascati villas of Italy, which were terraced to give a view of the distant Campagna, and in America there was an example in High Court.[11]

The land sloping away to the south of High Court was treated as a series of earth terraces intended as viewing platforms. A wide set of steps on axis with the house connected these terraces, which were adorned only by wood and stucco balustrades.

On the west side, totally separated from the sweeping vistas, Platt placed a walled flower garden of intimate scale. Its proportions reflected the size of the house, and it was carefully isolated from competition with the distant landscape. Again following Italian precedents, the flower garden was divided into four rectangular beds with a circular fountain at its center. Along the west wall of the garden, that farthest from the house, Platt pushed out a semicircular loggia as a place to sit and view Mt. Ascutney. The loggia repeated the bowed window of the library, both aligned on the cross axis through the base of the house's U-shaped plan.

Both his own house and High Court were designs of direct simplicity and great charm, as his fellow artists in Cornish readily recognized. Few first projects by trained architects could match the unselfconscious dignity and quiet repose achieved by this landscape painter. High Court, in particular, revealed Platt's ability to rival the finest country house commissions then being executed by leading architectural firms. It is astonishing that this obvious success did not lead him at that time to consider becoming an architect. Instead, he continued his painting.

Platt's admiration for and understanding of the Italian villa model was obvious in his 1890 plans for High Court. But his first-hand knowledge of Renaissance architecture and garden art was greatly increased during an important systematic tour of Italian villas that he made in the spring of 1892. Charles's younger brother William was then an apprentice in the office of Frederick Law Olmsted, the great park maker and landscape architect. Charles felt, however, that his brother's training was deficient in the formal aspects of landscape design, such as he had shown in his own plans for High Court. So Charles proposed that William join him in an expedition to Italy to sketch, photograph, and measure the gardens of the Renaissance. The excursion was conceived as having value for both a landscape painter and an aspiring landscape architect.

Olmsted reacted to the proposed expedition with only mild enthusiasm and recommended that William first discuss the tour with Charles Eliot Norton, influential professor of fine arts at Harvard College and recognized authority on the art and culture of Italy.[12] Norton's opinions, first seen in his 1860 *Notes of Travel and Study in Italy,* were fully consistent with the ethical criticism of art professed by the Englishman John Ruskin.[13] Olmsted, who shared with Ruskin and Norton a belief that art must project moral values, practiced a picturesque, naturalized style of landscape design that he believed could inspire the mind and refresh the spirit of the observer. Assuming that Norton could best prepare young Platt to discern the relative value of what he would see, Olmsted sent William with a letter of introduction summarizing his understanding of the trip's purpose:

His brother, who is a painter and etcher, is going to Italy with the intention of obtaining material by sketching and photography for a volume of which an appropriate title might be *Al Fresco*: its contents being . . . illustrations of gardens and garden furniture, seats, fountains, terraces, staircases, pergolas, rustic paths and other amorettes of Italian out of door life. That at least is my understanding of his project which I think is still lacking definition a little partly because of hazy information as to what is practicable.[14]

Olmsted hoped that Norton would think of something to say to William from "the abundance of your knowledge in Italian petty scenery that would be of invaluable service to him and his brother."[15]

If it is impossible to know exactly what Norton told William Platt, at least it is easy to see Frederick Law Olmsted's opinions in the tone of the note he wrote to William on February 1:

I am afraid that I do not think much of the fine and costly gardening of Italy, and yet I am enthusiastic in my enjoyment of much roadside foreground scenery there in which nature contends with and is gaining upon the art of man. I urge you again to hunt for beauty in commonplace and pleasant conditions; . . . and all of such things as are made lovely by growths that seem to be natural and spontaneous to the place, especially vines.[16]

Olmsted's concern about the seductiveness of the formal Italian garden is well expressed in this letter to his pupil. Elsewhere in the note, the repetition of the words "rustic" and "picturesque" clearly indicates Olmsted's focus on the natural value of common landscape settings.

Olmsted had good reasons for offering this persistent advice, since brother Charles was exerting a strong and opposite influence on William's landscape training. As an etcher and painter, Charles had originally embraced the cult of the Picturesque, but he had evolved a personal sense of the Beautiful during his student years in Paris. He now sought to reveal to his brother his understanding of beauty in landscape. Charles later recalled:

The way I got interested in landscape gardening was through the fact that my youngest brother had adopted landscape gardening as a profession . . . I was very much interested in his studies and felt that they [Olmsted] were not teaching him on the side of landscape architecture which interested me most — that is, the purely architectural side of it. So I decided to take him abroad and go through the great gardens of Europe with a camera, etc., prepared to study them and make drawings.[17]

In essence, Charles was intending to subvert the teachings of William's mentor. Instead of the naturalized landscape of Olmsted, which was ultimately based on the concept of the Picturesque, Charles was attracted to the geometric, axial gardens of the Renaissance, a style of landscape architecture that came to be known as the formal garden and which corresponded to Platt's general understanding of the Beautiful.

The exact dates of the Platt brothers' tour of Italy are not recorded, but they left sometime after February 1 and returned before the middle of July 1892. The list of gardens visited, approximately twenty-five, can be determined from the labeled photographs that Charles mounted in an album after their return.[18] The brothers concentrated on the villas and gardens surrounding Rome and Florence, but they also traveled to Genoa, Naples, Palermo, and "Isola Bella" in the Lake District. Although none of the plot plans they drew has survived, the measured drawing of the Villa Costanzi, which Charles made on a later trip, is probably representative of their investigations (Fig. 16). Correspondence reporting the success and progress of their venture also has

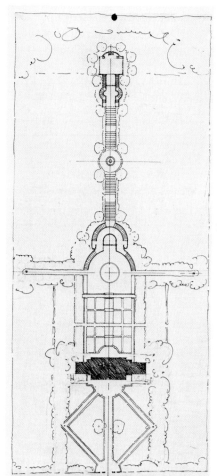

16. Plot plan, Villa Costanzi, near Rome, 1915.

17. Garden wall, Villa Medici, Caprarola, 1892, Platt photograph.

38

18. "Hedge Walk, Quirinal Garden," ca. 1893.

been lost. Extant, however, are many beautiful photographs that Charles took and developed which show the painter's eye applied to a new medium, and watercolor drawings which capture well the spirit of these villas (Figs. 17, 18).

On their return trip, they stopped briefly in Paris, where Charles remained to squire around the widow of Dennis Bunker, his close friend in Paris and New York. Bunker had married Eleanor Hardy of Boston in 1889, then died of pneumonia three months later. A tragedy so like his own brought Platt's sympathies immediately to the fore. Following the period of mourning, Charles had begun to court Eleanor in New York

19. Plot plan, Platt house, 1892–1912.

20.   View across the flower garden of Platt house toward
pine grove concealing Mt. Ascutney.

and he resumed his suit during his return visit to Paris. William returned
to America alone, and on July 16 he was drowned in a swimming
accident while vacationing in Portland, Maine. Charles had been devoted to his brother and was deeply grieved by yet another death.[19] The
experiences they had shared so recently brought some consolation, however. He was still inspired by them and strove to apply his new knowledge of Italian gardens here in America.

In the remaining months of that summer, undeterred by
Olmsted's advice, Platt greatly enlarged and refined the plan of his
Cornish property to reflect concepts he had observed in Italy (Fig. 19).

41

He divided his garden into distinct geometric units carefully defined by walls, fences, and hedges. Using as the dominant axis his promenade across the south side of the house, he connected all these elements by a grid of paths that visually tied the house to the flower and vegetable gardens, tennis court, and distant landscape. Unlike almost all his neighbors, he did not choose to make Mt. Ascutney the central focus from his house. Instead he centered the vista on the Connecticut River Valley (Fig. 20). He retained a stand of tall white pines to create a composition of shaded verticals in the right middle distance which teasingly revealed Mt. Ascutney beyond. The transition from the tight control of gardens adjacent to the house to a carefully chosen natural landscape again demonstrated his ability to translate the principles he had learned as a painter to his practice of landscape gardening.

Although the villa tour had certainly reinforced Platt's growing interest in landscape design, the characteristics of his 1892 garden were not changed significantly from those shown in his 1890 scheme for High Court. In both cases and in all his later work, Platt relied upon two fundamental tools of landscape design: clear definition of spatial units, and axial alignment of all elements along sightlines, including the relationship of the garden to the house. If anything, the landscape development of his own place at Cornish shows as casual and sympathetic a response to the natural conditions as any garden Platt ever designed. The geometric formality of the flower and cutting gardens is merged gently with the topography. The organization of paths and vistas provides a framework for a balance, not a symmetry, of garden parts. Platt's personal knowledge of and association with the site allowed him to devise a scheme in which he distilled the essence of the Italian landscape principles he had studied without relying upon specific Italian models.

The summer of 1893 was highlighted for Platt by a number of events significant for his life and work. The World's Columbian Exposition on Chicago's waterfront drew thousands of Americans to the gleaming "White City." Platt exhibited both paintings and etchings at the fair and won awards for his work, but it was the architectural and landscape plan developed by many of his older friends that left a lasting impression on him.[20]

After returning from Chicago, Platt married Eleanor Hardy Bunker on July 13, 1893, in a small ceremony at the Boston home of the bride's parents. According to the Platts' mutual friend, Barry Faulkner, Eleanor "was one of the most beautiful women of her time and was much admired and painted by artists."[21] The portrait of her by Dennis Bunker shows a woman with golden hair, strong features, and a confident posture (Fig. 21). Especially fond of gardening, she brought her talents to bear on the flower garden at Cornish, making it "bloom and spread like a fabulous Persian carpet."[22] She was attracted to artists, and throughout her married life she sought to provide for Charles the stable and stimulating home life that would encourage creativity. Her devotion and support allowed him to reestablish the sense of direction and purpose so badly eroded by the death of his first wife.

In July 1893, the month of the Platts' wedding, *Harper's Magazine* carried the first of two articles written and illustrated by Charles on "Formal Gardening in Italy." These essays and the book that followed were the most influential result of the 1892 tour. *Garden and Forest,* the principal organ of the landscape profession, had alerted its readers as early as November 2, 1892, to the forthcoming article on "the old gardens of Italy by Mr. Charles A. Platt, the well-known landscape painter and etcher."[23] The magazine's reaction to the essays, however, was one of mild disappointment. Allowing that "much of the interest which invests these pictures . . . is derived from the fact that they [the gardens] are, in a measure, ruined," the review proceeded to state that only

21. Dennis Bunker, "Eleanor Hardy Bunker" (later Mrs. Charles A. Platt), 1889.

43

in the American South would such gardens be climatically appropriate.[24] It continued:

But after all, works of this kind only appeal to the aesthetic sense; they delight the eye and satisfy the cultivated taste as a beautiful piece of tapestry or pottery does. It is beauty for its own sake. It expresses no sentiment and carries no inner meaning; it does not address itself to the nobler part of our nature as simple natural scenery does.[25]

The reviewer hit on the key conflict for landscape architecture in the 1890s. Following the philosophy of Ruskin, Norton, and Olmsted, *Garden and Forest* criticized Italian gardens for a lack of "sentiment and . . . inner meaning." It was precisely the "beauty for its own sake," which the magazine denigrated, that Platt sought to create. And unlike *Garden and Forest,* he saw the Italian villa as a useful model for American gardens in general.

On April 17, 1893, even before the articles appeared, Harper & Brothers signed a contract with Platt for a book that would be a composite of these articles. Platt was to supply, "free of charge, a water color drawing to be reproduced as a frontispiece . . . and matter to the amount of one thousand words in addition to that which is to appear in *Harper's Magazine.*"[26] Harper also agreed to reproduce between fifteen and twenty full-page illustrations beyond those to be used in the magazine. The book, called *Italian Gardens,* was published early in 1894.

In the articles and book, Platt discussed nineteen sites, including examples from the fifteenth through the eighteenth centuries. Frankly admitting that he was "leaving out the matter of research all together," he attempted "to illustrate . . . the existing state of the more important gardens of Italy."[27] He drew conclusions, however, about the fundamental principles of the Italian villa:

The evident harmony of arrangement between the house and the surrounding landscape is what first strikes one in Italian landscape architecture — the design as a whole, including gardens, terraces, groves, and their necessary surroundings and embellishments, it being clear that no one of these component parts was ever considered independently, the architect of the house being the architect of the garden and the rest of the villa.[28]

The comprehensive unity of design that Platt observed in the Italian villa was the logical extension of the total control of a medium which he had evolved as an etcher and a painter. In concluding his essay, he expressed the hope that "as there is a great similarity in the character of the landscape in many areas of our country with that of Italy, [the book] might lead to a revival of the same method" of gardening here.[29] Although

Platt's original purpose for the expedition to Italy had been simply to record the character and mood of Renaissance gardens, his enthusiasm for these villas made him a strong proponent for the revival of the formal garden.

Despite the previously unpublished material contained in *Italian Gardens,* some landscape architects and periodicals criticized both the topic of the book and its form of presentation. For example, Charles Eliot, a partner in the Olmsted office and the creator of the Boston Metropolitan Park System, called the book "unsatisfactory" for its brief notes, lack of plans, and ignorance of foreign scholarship on the Italian garden.[30] Platt's writings may have met with skepticism and criticism in part because the book potentially represented the beginning of an American parallel to the professional schism then raging in England. There the landscape designers had taken sides in support of the theories of either William Robinson or Reginald Blomfield.[31] Robinson, primarily a plantsman, espoused reliance on naturalized garden layout and use of hardy natives or hardy and half-hardy exotics as a formula for overcoming the artificiality of late-Victorian landscape design. He advanced his ideas in *The Wild Garden* (1881) and in his more influential *English Flower Garden and Home Grounds* (1883). The chief opponent was the architect, Reginald Blomfield, who, in *The Formal Garden in England* (1892), described landscape *gardening* as the fuzzy work of amateurs. Instead, he proposed a landscape *architecture* of formally organized compositions which he considered a true art form.

Although Americans never reached the abusive extreme of their English contemporaries, landscape architects in America in the 1890s certainly were divided between the formal- and natural-landscape schools. It was the entrance of architects, sculptors, and painters, like Platt, into the field of landscape design that replaced the irregular, naturalized plans espoused by Olmsted and Charles Eliot Norton with an emphasis on Renaissance-derived designs and an art-for-art's-sake mentality. The publication of Platt's *Italian Gardens* was the keystone of this evolution.

Platt's articles and book fit into a pattern of increasing American interest in Italy throughout the second half of the nineteenth century. Yet *Italian Gardens* represented the first illustrated study in English on the Italian Renaissance garden. The publication of Platt's book anticipated an avalanche of writing on Italian landscape design that continued through the 1920s, gradually becoming more scholarly and less romantic.[32] The best-known early work in this series was Edith Wharton's *Italian Villas and Their Gardens,* significant for the author's research

45

22. "Clouds," 1894.

and descriptive facility, as well as for the charming illustrations by Maxfield Parrish.[33] Wharton held a purist's devotion to the original configu-
ration of Italian gardens and was critical of recent attempts to emulate
those models in America.[34] Platt, however, saw the villa as the appropriate precedent for the American country house and increasingly pursued
the translation of Renaissance forms to modern needs.

The middle years of the 1890s were important as a period of
transition for Platt. With his bride, he was in Rome in 1893–94 for a
successful winter of painting. Later in 1894 the Society of American
Artists awarded Platt the Webb Prize for landscape painting at its annual
exhibition. Platt's entry, entitled "Clouds," shows a view of the Cornish
hills — smooth, regular, rolling forms that well represent the concept of
abstract beauty he had formulated in Paris (Fig. 22). Despite this honor,
however, Charles was becoming more frustrated and discouraged about
his future as a painter.[35] The arrival of the Platts' first child, Sylvia, on
September 30, 1895, only increased his concern about his limited financial achievements. Fortunately, Eleanor Platt's social connections
helped ease this awkward period by providing his first design commission for a location outside of Cornish. According to one member of the

Platt family, "Dr. and Mrs. John Elliot, friends of the Hardy family in Boston, had read Platt's Italian Gardens and had been impressed by his knowledge and flair for the subject."[36] The house and garden that Platt designed for the Elliots at Needham, Massachusetts, in 1895, and two others for Cornish neighbors in successive years, showed his initial struggle to create an American villa model and marked his transition from landscape painter to professional architect and landscape designer.

Platt exhibited his Italian sympathies in the stuccoed walls, low hipped roof, deep overhanging eaves, and attached loggia of the Elliot house. He also revealed here his novice rank as a planner. He chose an L-shaped plan and placed the entrance, flower garden, and service court on separate sides of the L. This scheme meant that the drawing room abutted the service court and that meals had to be carried from the kitchen to the dining room across the entrance hall. The Cornish projects that followed deserve closer attention. In these he moved further away from his Italian sources and overcame the early awkwardness in planning shown in the Elliot commission.

The first of these New Hampshire houses was a project in 1896 for Miss Grace Lawrence, a concert pianist, and her sister (Fig. 23). The Lawrence design shows a comfortable integration of the vernacular nineteenth-century New England farmhouse and the Italian villa. Platt

23. Entrance elevation, Misses Lawrence house,
Cornish, New Hampshire, 1896.

retained the hipped roof, overhanging eaves, and loggia of the earlier Italian-derived projects but replaced the stucco-on-wood construction with a grooved horizontal boarding. He had these boards rough-cut and left unplaned so that the surface was enlivened by the texture and by the interplay of light and shadow from the deep offsets of the boards. And the plan is more traditionally American—a central stairhall, three-bay scheme, the drawing room being on the left and the dining room with a kitchen and pantry behind it on the right.

In 1897, Platt designed a Cornish house for his close friend, Herbert Croly, the architectural critic.[37] The Croly house (Fig. 24) resembled the Lawrence project in its hipped roof, rough clapboarding, and projecting loggia, but it followed an L-shaped plan that improved on the Elliot design. Here the drawing room and loggia formed one wing of the L with the dining room at the corner and the service area extending at a right angle. Platt later repeated this plan in various modifications because the drawing room and loggia provided views of the flower garden on one side and of the distant landscape on the other. All three houses represented Platt's adaptation of the Italian villa to the requirements of a small, inexpensive, American summer house.

If Platt had felt some dissatisfaction with his design for the Elliots at Needham, his clients were delighted. "Dr. Elliot was so enthusiastic over my plans for him," Platt recalled, "that he suggested me to a rich

24. Garden facades, Herbert Croly house,
Cornish, New Hampshire, 1897.

client of his named Sprague, and I got my first chance at a really important piece of landscape work in the Sprague Gardens, Faulkner Farm,
Brookline."[38] How Platt won this commission is a story that his sons
vividly remember hearing from their father:

Platt went to see the Spragues, and after examining the site, told them that he
could not design the garden unless the entrance road was relocated. He returned
home convinced that the Spragues would never agree to such an expense and
that his imposition of this condition would lose him the job.[39]

Platt was astounded when the clients agreed to his recommendations on
the road. What Platt may not have known was that Charles Eliot, who
had been working previously on this project, had failed repeatedly to
persuade the headstrong Sprague to follow his plans and recommendations for the road and other features of the property.[40] This commission
is the first example of Platt's innate ability to convince and control even
the most willful patrons.

Charles F. Sprague had won a Congressional seat in 1896 and
then had built a new house on his Allandale Road estate in Brookline,
Massachusetts. He commissioned Platt to design the gardens the following year.[41] Himself a man of independent means, Sprague had married
Miss Anna Pratt, heiress to a $20-million fortune, making him the
richest member of Congress and a patron eager to display his political
and social importance. He was also aware of current landscape theories,
having been a member of the Boston Park Commission since 1893 and
in 1897 serving as its chairman.

At Faulkner Farm, the Spragues asked Platt to design a garden
and landscape setting for an existing three-story white frame house,
designed recently by Little & Browne and sited near the crest of a hill.
The plot plan Platt devised included a long, straight approach drive into
a walled entrance court on the uphill side of the house and ending in a
monumental statue on axis, where the service drive turned off to the left
(Fig. 25). A terraced promenade and woodland garden capped the top of
the hill, with a view of the house and grounds on one side and of the
Boston skyline on the other. He placed the formal flower garden adjacent to the house, to the left of the approach drive but concealed from
view by a wall and plantings. A broad grass terrace across the rear of the
house served as the transition from architecture into the surrounding
farmland. To create this terrace required the construction of a very high
retaining wall, a bold but essential move.

A comparison of the plan of Faulkner Farm with that of the
sixteenth-century Villa Gamberaia near Settignano shows how fully

25. Plot plan, Charles F. Sprague estate, Faulkner Farm,
Brookline, Massachusetts, 1897–98.

Platt had absorbed the principles of the Italian garden (Fig. 26). Both
houses were sited below the crest of a hill with nearly identical disposi-
tion of a woodland garden on the hilltop, an allee across the front of the
house ending in a monumental statue, a grassed terrace behind the
house, and an adjacent formal garden with semicircular end.[42] Given an
identical problem and similar site, Platt produced a design at Faulkner
Farm that showed his mastery of the Renaissance villa concept.

Other elements within the Faulkner Farm scheme also display
Platt's knowledge of specific Italian villas and gardens. For example, the
stuccoed pavilion at the far end of the flower garden was inspired by the
pair of lodges at the top of the Villa Lante at Bagnaia, one of which Platt
had photographed for *Italian Gardens* (Figs. 27, 28). But he greatly
modified this form to suit his needs. Instead of a small, isolated stone
structure, Platt designed an ample stuccoed pavilion which he extended

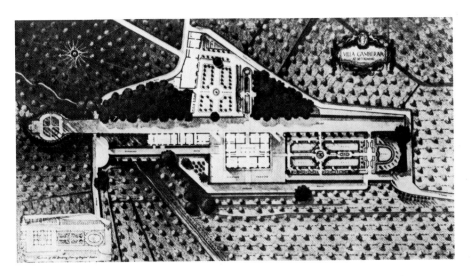

26. Plot plan, Villa Gamberaia, Settignano, 1610.

27. Pergola and pool in flower garden, Faulkner Farm.

28. Pavilion, Villa Lante, Bagnaia, Platt photograph, 1892.

through inward-curving pergola arms. He decorated the interior with Pompeiian-like wall paintings and furnished it with tables and chairs modeled on antique forms or made from sculptural or architectural fragments. Like many of his New York colleagues, Platt carefully studied appropriate historical models. But in the design process, he altered his sources so completely that they were almost imperceptible.

While Faulkner Farm is significant, it is not the first example of the formal garden revival in America. The Boston area especially had notable precedents. As early as the mid-1860s, H. H. Hunnewell had begun to lay out his lakeside estate in Wellesley with a series of terraces with clipped topiary that he called "the Italian garden." And beginning in 1885, Isabella Stewart Gardner developed Green Hill, her forty-acre estate in Brookline. Typical of contemporary eclecticism, the grounds included an open lawn, a Japanese garden with dwarf trees, and an Italian garden with pergolas, box-edged flower beds, pools, fountains, and statues.[43]

Among Platt's contemporaries, the architectural firms of McKim, Mead & White and Carrère & Hastings had designed country estates with formal gardens that predate Faulkner Farm. Indian Harbor, the Greenwich, Connecticut, estate of E. C. Benedict, which Thomas Hastings designed in 1895, was the most conspicuous predecessor (Fig. 29).[44] But Hastings handled the landscape as a totally architectonic setting for the house, extending his Ecole des Beaux-Arts training to the design of gardens. Platt's schemes always revealed the painter's sensitivity to the landscape and his allegiance to Italian models. Hastings's designs were more generalized and could be adapted with ease to several landscape styles, most frequently the seventeenth-century French garden. Platt's Faulkner Farm, designed two years after Hastings's Indian Harbor, was a more complete transformation of the villa principles and a more influential model for American landscape architecture.

29.   Plan, E. C. Benedict estate, Carrère & Hastings, Greenwich, Connecticut, 1895.

Well before Faulkner Farm, Platt's enthusiasm for Italian gardens had also attracted the attention of Charles L. Freer, the Detroit industrialist and collector of Oriental art, who subsequently was to become an important Platt client. Freer had come to Cornish as early as 1890 to visit Thomas W. Dewing, whose paintings he was collecting, and through Dewing he met Platt. Freer was already a friend of Augustus Saint-Gaudens, Stanford White, and many of what Freer called "the New York gang."[45] In a letter of introduction that Freer later wrote for Platt to a friend on the isle of Capri, he stated: "He [Platt] is a charming man in every way, and I am indebted to him for the itinerary of Italian gardens and sights at the time of my first trip to Italy."[46] Freer's trip, in the fall of 1894, included gardens at Verona, Florence, Rome, Tivoli, Caprarola, Bagnaia, and Naples.[47] The knowledge of Italian architecture and gardens that Freer acquired during the 1890s led directly to a number of important commissions for Platt up until the industrialist's death in 1919.

The first of these Freer-instigated projects came in the summer of 1897 when Colonel Frank J. Hecker, Freer's business partner, commissioned Platt to draw up a master plan for the development of some farmland as a residential neighborhood near Detroit. On July 21, 1897, Dewing wrote to Freer from Cornish:

He [Platt] has showed me the sketch he is sending to Mr. Hecker and it seems to me a very good scheme — it is not worked out in detail and the lots are merely drawn freehand without being in scale — in this plan he gets over 300 very fine lots . . . the great thing about Platt's [plan] is the Central Park like Gramercy opposite the Players Club with gates and everybody who lives there to have keys, this gives an absolutely safe place for children to play.[48]

Hecker liked the plan and slowly began its execution. By June 1898, Freer could write to William G. Mather, Cleveland iron ore magnate and soon a Platt client too, that Hecker had begun to develop a hundred acres of land and that if he followed Platt's plan, "he will establish one of the best resident tracts thus far started in this country."[49] Unfortunately, no plan for the laying out of the subdivision survives, but a plan of the communal park shows a fenced square with a central colonnaded casino from which axes of "malls" and "basins" project, dividing the space into four "campuses" for children's play (Fig. 30).

The economic recession of 1898–99 dealt a heavy blow to Colonel Hecker's financial capabilities and ended Platt's scheme.[50] Although residential land development would soon experience a boom, Platt did not receive another commission to lay out a subdivision. Given the generally flat character of the lake-plain farmland south of Detroit where

54

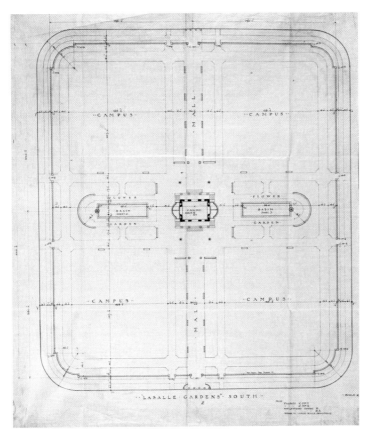

30. Plan of central square, LaSalle Gardens South, Detroit, Michigan, 1897.

the subdivision was to be built and the strict formality of this central park, a geometric grid would have been the logical organization for the three hundred lots in this 300-acre parcel. When compared to contemporary developments, such as the curvilinear schemes by Olmsted, Olmsted & Eliot for Log Cabin Lands (1895), also in Detroit, or for the better-known Roland Park District (1891–1924) in Baltimore, Maryland, LaSalle Gardens South would have been a rare early example of formal landscape principles applied to suburban residential planning.[51] If the Detroit project had come to successful fruition, Platt's developing career might have focused more on landscape planning alone.

While LaSalle Gardens South came to a dead end, the Sprague commission held more promise for Platt. Although Faulkner Farm did not immediately bring Platt to national attention (the architectural magazines showed little interest in landscape and *Garden and Forest* had ceased publication in 1897), this project generated several related commissions over the next few years and eventually became Platt's most

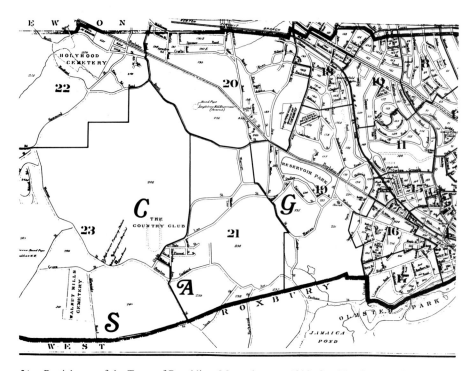

31. Partial map of the Town of Brookline, Massachusetts, 1890. C = The Country Club; G = Isabella Stewart Gardner estate; A = Larz Anderson estate; S = Charles F. Sprague estate.

often published garden. A contemporary map of the Town of Brookline graphically demonstrates the geography of developing country house life (Fig. 31). Grouped near The Country Club (C), founded in 1882 as the first such suburban recreational and social club in the nation, were Isabella Stewart Gardner's Green Hill (G), Faulkner Farm (S), and Platt's next project, Weld (A), for the Larz Andersons.[52]

Located two hills closer to Boston than Faulkner Farm, Weld was another Italian garden that Platt designed, this time for Mrs. Sprague's cousin, Mrs. Larz Anderson, and her diplomat husband. Here the garden extended from one end of an earlier house basically on a level along the top of the hill. For the Andersons Platt designed a much simpler plan than the Sprague garden: a bowling green, then a grove or wooded section, and finally a formal flower garden—all of which comprised a long rectangle (Fig. 32). He completely enclosed the flower garden with earth banks on the sides and walls or pergolas at the ends (Fig. 33). Here Platt eliminated the busyness of the planting scheme at Faulkner Farm by designing a central narrow greensward, flanked by beds of flowers, that united the overall composition. Platt imported more antique sculp-

32. Plot plan, Larz Anderson garden, Weld, Brookline, Massachusetts, 1901.

33. General view of garden, Weld.

ture for use in this garden, and, following an Italian practice, set inscriptions in walks and walls alluding to the ancestral home of the Welds (from whom the clients' wealth had come), which supposedly had stood on this site.

Platt began work on the plans for Weld in late 1899 or early 1900. In a letter to Eleanor Platt postmarked Boston, February 19, 1900, Charles reported:

Everything is going well. . . . Mrs. Anderson is very nice, but Larz seems to be the boss and he thinks he knows a great deal. They were both very cordial and [I] spent a pleasant day and night at their place. There has been a blizzard and the wind and snow were not exactly propitious for examining garden sites but I managed to do it.[53]

To explain his proposal to the Andersons, Platt built a cardboard and plaster model of the hilltop site and carried it back to Brookline. By October 14 he could tell his wife that "the Anderson Garden now seems to be an assured thing. They seem to have fallen in love with the model and want to realize it as soon as possible."[54]

His client being so eager to "realize it," Platt sailed for Italy in early December 1900 to purchase sculpture and architectural fragments for the garden. After stopping to inspect the villa partially owned by Charles Freer on Capri, he proceeded to Rome and reported to Eleanor:

I haven't done much since my arrival here but going the rounds of the antiquarians as I want to get that done before I can feel free. I have found some beautiful things here and have unloaded a considerable stack of *mun.* belonging to les autres.[55]

It was not unusual for wealthy clients to commission their architects not only to design the house and gardens but also to acquire the furnishings and art objects. "My evenings I find are pretty well occupied in making lists of purchases," wrote Platt, "and dividing them up among owners to be."[56] In addition to sculpture for the Anderson garden, he purchased a "corker" tapestry for the Maxwells, commissioned a sculptor named Rudolfo Apolloni to make copies of a couple of antique statues for Mrs. Clark, and "bought a lot of wonderful copies of Pompeiian paintings."[57] After passing through Bologna, Modena, Mantua, and Venice to look at architecture, Platt sailed home with his purchases in January 1901.

The Mrs. Clark for whom Platt had Apolloni copy classical statues was Mrs. Randolph M. Clark, another Boston socialite. She too had commissioned Platt to design a large garden for her estate in Pomfret, Connecticut.[58] Called Glen Elsinore, the Clark property was fully developed when Platt was called in to design a walled flower garden,

34.   General view of garden, Randolph M. Clark estate, Glen Elsinore,
Pomfret, Connecticut, before 1902.

completely separate and at some distance from the house (Fig. 34).
Larger than the flower gardens at Faulkner Farm or Weld, Platt envisioned this complex as a pleasure haunt in the woods. Walled on three
sides and with a bowed terrace overlooking a ravine on the fourth, the
center section was completely devoted to geometric flower beds with a
central circular pool and the usual examples of classical ornament
placed at the intersections of paths. Along one end, an elevated promenade provided an overview of the scheme. In the center of the long side
nearer the house, Platt designed two tile-roofed pavilions connected to
an extended pergola. Opposite, a similar facade masked a casino where
the Clarks held balls, suppers, and musical galas. Immediately adjacent
to this walled flower garden, Platt placed a kitchen garden and cutting
garden with three large greenhouses. No plans or interior photographs of
the casino are known to exist.

At Glen Elsinore the Clarks presented Platt with a situation entirely different from his earlier commissions. The garden was unique
because it was totally isolated from the main house and contained the
casino, making it an independent entertainment facility. Platt designed
a landscape setting that more closely resembled a villa of the Ancients
than one of the Renaissance. Pliny the Younger's letter containing a
description of his Tuscan villa, written in the first century A.D., bears a

59

resemblance to the plan of Platt's Pomfret garden.[59] Although it appears that Platt intended to evoke the image of a villa of antiquity, by no means did he attempt an archaeological reconstruction of the Tuscan villa of Pliny. Platt already had shown his interest in classical villas in the murals he painted for the pavilion at Faulkner Farm and the photographs and copies of Pompeiian wall paintings that he had purchased in Italy. Thus, both the Renaissance villa and its Ancient source formed the theoretical and design models for Platt's gardens of the late 1890s.

Platt discussed the gardens of the Ancients and of the Renaissance in the definition of the term *villa* that he wrote for Russell Sturgis's *A Dictionary of Architecture and Building* (1901). Following the ideas that he presented in his earlier articles and book, he defined *villa* as "a country residence designed particularly with a view of affording all the enjoyments of country life, consisting of a house and surroundings, such as gardens, terraces, groves and all appurtenances which may be brought into direct connection with the design."[60] While tracing the development of villa design from antiquity to the present, he admitted that "the villa is usually, though not necessarily designed for occupancy during the summer."[61] As for the United States, Platt feared that the term "has come to imply merely a suburban dwelling with small grounds."[62] But he predicted a change in attitude:

The habit of life of the people in the United States is distinctly congenial to the villa idea. The winters are spent in the city and the summers in the country. Men go to the country for recreation, health and pleasure, while in the city they leave their real interests, business, etc. Climate leads them to be as much as possible out of doors in the summer. The country houses should be extended and the scheme of gardens, terraces, etc., which does this in the Italian villa can be applied here. It seems not improbable that within the next generation or so this country may be the centre of development in villa design.[63]

Platt's prediction was based on the success of his own initial efforts and was destined to be proved correct.

The influence of work by Platt and his contemporaries upon the emerging profession of American landscape architecture was rapid and extensive. Within a decade after Platt's initial gardens and publications appeared, the formal-landscape school had achieved supremacy over the natural-landscape theories of Frederick Law Olmsted, Sr. Guy Lowell, a prominent architect from Boston, documented the rise of the architectural landscape group in his 1902 book, *American Gardens.* While warning that changes in climate and plant material had to be considered judiciously in transposing Italian forms to the United States,

Lowell concluded that "it is the appropriate adaptation of the established European principles of gardening to American surroundings that will perfect an American style."[64] The landscape design philosophy that Lowell stated here clearly parallels the architectural theories that were the background for Platt's work, from his earliest designs in Cornish onward, and for the designs of many of his architectural contemporaries throughout the 1890s. The formal garden is essentially the landscape corollary to the architecture of the academic reaction. The illustrations in Lowell's book show the extent to which the Italian garden formula had been embraced by American designers. According to Lowell, the leaders of the movement included established architects, such as Carrère & Hastings and McKim, Mead & White, as well as landscape architects. The most frequently illustrated works were gardens by Philadelphia architect Wilson Eyre and by Charles A. Platt. But, as both an architect and landscape architect, Platt would continue to explore this design formula with greater consistency and wider influence.

By the time Guy Lowell's book appeared, Platt had completed his evolution from painter and etcher to landscape designer and architect. In 1898–99, Platt changed his occupation listing in the New York City Directory from artist to architect.[65] With the turn of the century, Platt also ceased to think of himself as a landscape designer alone. When he moved his office in 1901, he no longer stamped the books in his library "C. A. Platt landscape architect."[66] In the same year, Platt received four substantial country house commissions — not summer places for artists in Cornish or gardens to embellish other architects' houses. These new projects required the total integration of Platt's multiple talents. Thus, as the century turned, he declared himself to be a professional architect, again without academic training other than as an artist. He assumed the role of architect even more confidently than he had that of landscape architect a few years before, and his confidence was quickly rewarded.

In the years between his arrival at Cornish and the start of the new century, Platt evolved from a landscape painter of moderate reputation to a nationally recognized designer of residential gardens. His marriage to Eleanor Hardy Bunker and the growth of their family had provided new stability and purpose for his work as an artist. His writings on the Italian villa generated popular interest in the subject and significantly influenced the work of other designers. If he was not the sole originator of the American return to formal landscape design, Platt certainly was the leader of that movement.

His experimentation in houses and gardens for Cornish neighbors and in estate plans for Boston gentry established a new American landscape formula. He provided a firm break from the curved lines and naturalized planting of the English landscape school that had dominated American gardening throughout the nineteenth century. Instead, he emphasized a landscape of clearly defined geometric spatial units tied together by a system of axes. Even more so in succeeding projects as an architect, he carefully interrelated the house and its landscape environment. He established a gradual transition from the architectonic spaces nearest the house to the natural landscape beyond. That formula recalls the works and writings of the English landscape gardener Humphrey Repton, from the turn of the nineteenth century. But Platt and his colleagues derived their ideas from direct observation of Renaissance models and adapted these sources to contemporary American needs. His garden plan for High Court was one of the earliest American landscapes to demonstrate this revived formality, and Faulkner Farm represented the decade's most extensive and visually successful reinterpretation of the Italian garden. His seminal publications and exactingly integrated projects made his villa concept the timely model for the rapidly expanding field of country house architecture which he soon came to dominate, thus fulfilling his prediction that "in the next generation," America would be "the centre of development in villa design."[67]

3

Philosophy and Practice

BEFORE TURNING to the mature work of Charles A. Platt as an architect and landscape architect, it is necessary to discuss his philosophy of architecture and method of design. Because he wrote so little about his own work or its supporting concepts, this task is a difficult one, requiring recourse to other writers' opinions of Platt and a comparison of his work with that of contemporaries who aspired to similar ideals or who worked within a comparable environment. The fact that Platt was not trained as an architect, either through formal education or apprenticeship, may make his ability to practice architecture in the early twentieth century surprising to the modern reader, so an analysis of his office organization—his assistants and their design relationship to Platt— must precede any investigation of his work.

Platt was not a man who enjoyed speculative discussion. If the philosophy of architecture became a topic of conversation during lunch at the architects' table of the Century Club, Platt had not initiated the topic and probably held little interest in expressing an opinion.[1] The book and articles he wrote and illustrated on the Italian garden were primarily descriptive and only tentatively advanced a belief that these villas were appropriate models for contemporary American architecture and landscape design. The other occasion on which Platt published his ideas on architecture was a one-paragraph foreword to a 1927 book on interior architecture.[2] In 1914, he agreed reluctantly to give three lectures to architecture students at Harvard University on the history of the country house in Italy, France, and England, and on his own work as a country house architect.[3] His notes for those lectures survive. But little of his personal or professional correspondence still exists, and what does contains scant information on his work or thoughts.[4] From these meager gleanings, only a partial statement of Platt's architectural philosophy can be assembled. More worthwhile are the statements on Platt's work by his contemporaries, a comparison of his designs with the work and words of select colleagues, and a description of the architectural community of which he was a member. There is, of course, a danger here of imposing upon Platt ideas or opinions he would not have espoused, but the larger problem is one of not confronting the ideas behind his designs.

By birth, Platt was the close contemporary of John Merven Carrère, Thomas Hastings, Wilson Eyre, Cass Gilbert, and Ralph Adams Cram. These men were representative of the northeastern architectural establishment that existed from Boston to Philadelphia but was centered in New York City. As such, they provide a test group for comparison with Platt. Because of his progression from etching to painting to landscape to architecture, Platt emerged as an architect a decade later than his contemporaries, who were all established in their own practices by at least 1890. Among these colleagues only Platt and Cram had not received academic training in architecture, while the others had studied at the Ecole des Beaux-Arts or the Massachusetts Institute of Technology or both. Platt had served no apprenticeship, unlike all five of the others, three of whom apprenticed in the office of McKim, Mead & White, the dominant eastern firm of the late nineteenth century. It is surprising that an architect who emerged from a background as unconventional as Platt's became a designer so thoroughly devoted to the adaptation of traditional forms.

Even though Platt had not apprenticed in the office of McKim, Mead & White, he inherited and supported basic trends in architecture that this firm had largely initiated. In the early 1880s, as Platt himself stated, McKim, Mead & White began a reform of American architecture through reliance on an eclectic historical vocabulary, especially the classical, and on symmetrical and axial planning learned by Charles F. McKim at the Ecole. Richard Morris Hunt and Henry Hobson Richardson had been the first Americans to attend the Ecole des Beaux-Arts, and both men, in separate ways, set the stage for the reforms that McKim, Mead & White instituted.[5] Hunt sought to improve American architectural taste through designs inspired by a wide spectrum of historical models, especially the early French Renaissance, which he treated with a new archaeological sophistication.[6] Richardson used medieval-derived forms, particularly a weighty stone vocabulary, as a vehicle to achieve a new sense of discipline and large-scale order in plan and elevation.[7] Charles McKim and Stanford White had served as successive chief draftsmen in the Richardson office, and they synthesized a design

64

formula that merged Hunt's stylistic variety and Richardson's clear planning. While experimenting with designs inspired by Greek temples, Renaissance palaces, Romanesque cathedrals, Roman baths, or French chateaux, McKim, Mead & White, from the mid-1880s onward, evolved a recognizable, corporate architectural manner distinguished by clear planning and a powerful handling of scale and ornament.[8] While Platt saw McKim, Mead & White's work as the most positive force in American architecture at the start of his career, he was one member of a group of younger men seeking to refine the process inaugurated by this predominant firm.

Continuing to emphasize balanced, axial planning as the generating spirit of good design, Platt and others sought a more sophisticated and appropriate use of past forms through a limited choice and comprehensive study of historical models. A.D.F. Hamlin, professor of architecture at Columbia University and former member of the McKim, Mead & White office, was one of the first to distill the aims of Platt's generation in an article he wrote in 1892 entitled "The Battle of Styles."[9] Complaining that "we behold in modern work a bewildering variety of styles whose employment in most cases seems to have been determined by no more serious consideration than the architect's personal predilection,"[10] Hamlin still concluded that "there is no alternative but to use the forms of a historic style in modern architecture."[11] He rejected the possibility of pure invention as a desirable route to a modern, national style, his ultimate goal, but encouraged the intensive study of selected past forms to "penetrate the spirit and find out the animating principles of the style."[12] Selectivity, according to the prejudices of the individual designer and the needs of the society, was the goal, as "a man cannot well succeed in mastering more than two [historic styles] in a lifetime."[13] As Hamlin pointed out, the rapid increase in publications on historic architecture both permitted in-depth study and demanded limits on which models were appropriate to contemporary conditions. For Platt, the choice was limited to two phases of essentially one historic style — the classical revival as it flourished in the Italian High Renaissance and as it influenced the architecture of eighteenth-century England, America, and — to a lesser extent — France. Although Platt never stated that refinement of forms through close study of limited models was his objective, his designs and even the books in his office library clearly illustrate this personal selectivity.

By 1904, when the first major article on Platt's work as an architect was published in the *Architectural Record,* Herbert Croly reiterated the belief that "the trouble with the first generation of well-trained architects [Hunt, Richardson, and McKim, Mead & White] was not that they were too imitative, but that they were perhaps too indiscriminate in their imitation. They tried experiments in too many styles."[14] And he agreed that "the next step in the regular improvement of American architectural practice must consist in the more careful selection by the individual designer of his favorite architectural forms and the persistent endeavor to give to those forms a more individual and local rendering."[15] Croly saw Platt as one of the leaders of this reform effort among younger architects, one "whose designs show plainly the influence of this selective ideal."[16] Croly further pointed out that Platt, up to that date, had essentially explored one type of project — the country house and its gardens — giving him increased opportunities for study of related historical models from which to formulate a personal design mode.

But how did Platt's work and ideas differ from other young architects who pursued "the selective ideal" at the turn of the century? The newly dominant force in American architecture at this time was the ascendancy of the influence of the Ecole des Beaux-Arts. Carrère and Hastings at the Ecole and Gilbert and Eyre at MIT had received, to differing extents, architectural educations that molded the character of their work and distinguished it from Platt's.[17] In contrast, Ralph Adams Cram vehemently opposed the philosophy that the Ecole dictated and wrote about the limitations and dangers of these ideals for contemporary American architecture.[18] Having studied painting in Paris and having discussed the Ecole method with architecture students there, Platt was aware of Ecole theory but, as always, he steered an independent course that resulted in a personal philosophy and method of design. Thus, the relationship to Ecole principles and to the concept of stylistic selectivity become central issues in comparing Platt to his contemporaries.

John Merven Carrère and Thomas Hastings were among the architects of this generation most committed to adapting the Ecole teachings to contemporary American needs.[19] Hastings was the design partner and spokesman for the firm. In a lecture in 1915, he touched on the Ecole question and explained the benefits he saw for America in the Parisian ideals:

We American architects are ofttimes confronted with the question why we have not an architecture of our own — one which is essentially American; and why it is that so many of us who have studied in Paris seem inclined to inculcate the principles of the Ecole des Beaux-Arts into our American architecture. The majority of people do not seem to realize that in solving the problems of modern life the essential is not to be national, or American, as it is to be modern and of our own period.[20]

66

35. Henry Clay Frick residence, Carrère & Hastings, New York, New York, 1914.

For Hastings, to be modern was to follow the international leadership of Paris and the Ecole. Thus, Carrère & Hastings's designs predominantly displayed an ornate French classicism in style, derived from models as early as the Renaissance or as recent as current fashion, and a rigid monumentality in planning, demonstrated by sculpted and intricate spatial schemes (Fig. 35). Platt would have agreed with Hastings's dismissal of the need for a national style, but instead of following the French lead, he sought a more personal architectural expression, more direct and simple in plan, more minimal and severe in elevation.

Another aspect of Ecole training that reveals differences between Platt and his colleagues was the importance placed on monumental civic architecture. The initial mission of the Ecole to provide architects for the French state, and the elaborate *projets,* often designs for vast public buildings, required of students at the Ecole, inspired a taste for grandeur in many of the school's graduates. Hastings's hope that "our monuments [will] adequately record the splendid achivements of our contemporary life . . . the elevated character of our institutions"[21] illustrated his enthusiasm for noble civic art and architecture. Cass Gilbert, trained in the school of architecture at MIT modeled on the Ecole, was equally committed to celebrating the increasing power and sophistication of American urban culture through the design of monumental public buildings. As the architect of several state capitols in the early twentieth century, he lavished soaring domes, heroic sculpture, and vast murals on the new symbols of public magnificence (Fig. 36). In his more limited number of public commissions, Platt would share Gilbert's belief that "the greatest element of monumental architecture is good proportion,"[22] but Platt did not aspire to the grandiose and gave his public buildings a more modest scale and restrained character that achieved dignity without bombast. Design competitions were also an integral element of the Ecole system and a frequent method for choosing the architects of public buildings in early twentieth-century America. Unlike Gilbert, however, Platt almost never entered competitions, but he was able to develop a reputation for certain types of public commissions, especially the design of art museums and academic buildings.[23]

36. Minnesota State Capitol, Cass Gilbert, Minneapolis, Minnesota, 1896.

Platt would have shared both Hastings's and Gilbert's basic assumptions about good design and contemporary architecture which Hastings expressed emphatically:

. . . surely modern architecture should not be the deplorable creation of the would-be style inventors, the socialists who have penetrated the world of art further than they have the world of politics. . . . No more should modern architecture be the work of the illogical architect, living in one age and choosing a style from another without rhyme or reason, to suit his own fancy or that of his client.[24]

The "style inventors," into whose camp Hastings and Platt would have placed men like Louis Sullivan or Frank Lloyd Wright, broke the canon of reliance on traditional forms as the basis of good design. Wright is reported to have once observed that Platt "was a very dangerous man — he did the wrong thing so well."[25] Platt would probably not have been so generous in his opinions of Wright's work. Another group among the "style inventors" would have been the followers of the Arts and Crafts Movement and its commitment to handicraft and the creation of forms derived from or related to local historical traditions or conditions. Although Platt, like most of his contemporaries, appreciated the importance of fine craftsmanship, he remained almost totally unaffected by the arts-and-crafts ideal. The character of the site was of primary importance to his design philosophy, but he only rarely used local building materials or suggested a regional historical pattern in his buildings or landscapes. The perfection of an abstract visual ideal remained his constant aim.

Hastings's "illogical architect living in one age and choosing a style from another without rhyme or reason" was a slightly veiled attack on the modern Gothicists, whom both he and Platt abhorred. For Platt, the Gothic, in any form, was inappropriate for modern needs. If clients requested a Norman-cottage-style country house, Platt would ask whether "they wanted a house for this year or for twenty years."[26] And when he was invited to design a chapel for Trinity College, Hartford, he declined the commission when he learned that the design would have to be in the Gothic style.[27] In particular, Platt disliked the work and methods of Gothic revivalists Charles Klauder and Bertram Grosvenor Goodhue. And when Goodhue deserted the Gothic to design the stripped classical Nebraska State Capitol in the 1920s, Platt complained to Royal Cortissoz: "It won't do. Tradition can't be chucked so abruptly and the design is fundamentally bad."[28] To Platt's eyes, the Goodhue capitol flaunted a disregard for the appropriate classical models and

69

attempted to create a new form out of thin — Platt would say very thin — air. But it was Goodhue's early partner, Ralph Adams Cram, the leading spokesman and architect of the modern Gothic movement, who was the target of Hastings's salvos against the "illogical architect." Platt also totally disagreed with Cram's belief in a living Gothic tradition, but there are several instructive similarities in the two architects' philosophies.[29]

Platt resembled Cram most in being a specialist who restricted his design choices to the models he felt best served modern American civilization. This was seen equally in the two men's concentration on specific building types and historical styles: for Platt, the country house in Anglo-Italian variants of the Classical Revival; for Cram, the church in the English Perpendicular Gothic style. Platt would have ardently shared Cram's belief that "art is the measure of civilization"[30] and that "art is the result of beautiful ideas, of beautiful modes of life, of beautiful environment."[31] As Platt counseled architecture students, "your minds must be so filled with beauty that you can think of nothing else."[32] For both men, art and beauty were the mediating factors that gave direction to modern life, "not," as Cram stated, "commercial enterprise, not industrial activity, not the amassing of fabulous wealth, not increase of population; these may accompany civilization, but they do not prove it."[33] These men saw the artist as a central, motivating figure for contemporary society.

But the beauty that drove Platt and inspired Cram was not the same muse. Cram turned to the Late Gothic Revival church as the greatest opportunity to achieve beauty and mold civilization. As an institution that should be changeless, the church, to Cram's mind, inherited a rich tradition directly from the Middle Ages:

There is one style, and only one, that we have a right to; and that is the Gothic as it was when all art was destroyed at the time of the Reformation. But this is only the basis; from this starting-point we must advance, in order to prevent a dead archaism. . . . But the base of it all, the primary architectural impulse, must be that of the last days of Gothic architecture in England, namely the end of the fifteenth century.[34]

Cram viewed the Gothic as a living tradition, halted by the Reformation, that could now continue its natural development. Like a preacher from his pulpit, Cram spread the gospel of a new Gothic in scores of books and articles and in highly publicized designs produced alone or in partnership with Goodhue from 1891 to 1913 (Fig. 37).[35] In practice, however, Cram often deserted his crusade for revival of English Perpendicular, turning to a number of other historical styles including classical modes, especially for secular commissions.

In 1914, Platt observed that the American country house is "the best opportunity at the present time to produce a work of art in architecture."[36] Unlike Cram and the church, Platt saw the country house as the heir to the finest traditions of the classical revival, not as a style that should evolve from the last pure statements in the early nineteenth century before the romantic viewpoint and the picturesque aesthetic released a flood of competing stylistic choices. Cram preached devotion to a perfect historical model; Platt practiced it. But Platt should not be seen as simply a secular Cram. Despite protestations to the contrary, Cram dreamed of a modern Anglo-Catholic church that would once again achieve the spiritual dynamism that he attributed to the pre-Reformation period. Platt, however, saw in the Renaissance villa and the Georgian country house forms and functions ideally suited to modern needs. Certainly, he was far from unique in his basic historical prejudices. McKim, Mead & White, Carrère & Hastings, Cass Gilbert, and

37. All Saints' Church, Ashmont, Ralph Adams Cram, Dorchester, Massachusetts, 1891.

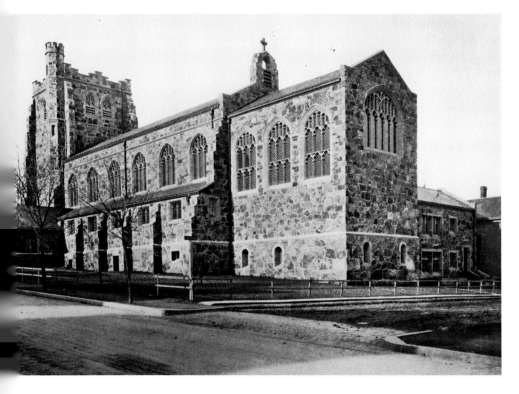

38. John W. Pepper house and garden, Wilson Eyre, Jenkintown, Pennsylvania, 1886.

many others could all be characterized from the 1890s onward by a devotion to the classical heritage. But Platt, just as Hamlin and Croly had advised, restricted his stylistic options and approached design from a domestic viewpoint. Throughout his four-decade career, more than half of Platt's commissions were residences, and even his nonresidential work maintained a uniform, restrained scale and character.[37]

A similar reputation for residential design is a major link to the last of Platt's close contemporaries to be considered, Wilson Eyre.[38] As we have seen, both men were also leaders of the formal garden revival. Eyre spent the first eleven years of his life near Florence, so he early acquired a prejudice for the Italian garden. But unlike Platt, Eyre never shed a love for the Picturesque that remained evident in his plans, elevations, and details. Platt designed his plans in concert with the elevations so that all elements stressed the axial growth, balance, and order he desired. Eyre worked from a plan that accommodated the spatial needs and then expressed those functions in elevations of variety and movement (Fig. 38). As Julian Millard commented in his *Architectural*

Record review of Eyre's work, "a strong individuality is always interesting."[39] Although Platt developed a distinctive, personal design formula, he resisted any temptation to show such individuality, seeking rather to have his commissions appear so resolved that the hand of the architect seemed less evident. "The most successful work an architect of a villa can accomplish," Platt believed, "is to make it appear as if no architect had ever been about the place. You must make it look as if the owner had done it."[40] Strangely, the very casual nature of Eyre's designs sometimes gave his project a similar sense of no architect having been involved.

Beyond a few close contemporaries, Platt rarely spoke of or thought about the work of his fellow architects. Instead, he always advised draftsmen and young architects to "go to the original sources."[41] But the opinions he did hold about the work of his generation were strong ones. The American architects Platt admired most were John Russell Pope and Henry Bacon, men whose architectural philosophy and concern for quality closely paralleled his own. Both men returned this respect, but Platt and Bacon were especially close; Platt completed his friend's current projects after Bacon's death in 1924. And Pope, until his death in 1939, remained true to the basic architectural assumptions that he and Platt shared.

On the other hand, Platt considered Sir Edwin Lutyens, the English country house architect, to have "had more influence towards bad architecture than anybody in England," because of Lutyens's playfulness and contempt for the traditional standards that Platt thought were so important.[42] When major monographs were published on Platt and Lutyens in 1913, the two men were compared as the leading country house architects in America and England.[43] Throughout his career, Platt remained loyal to the design philosophy he had evolved by the late 1890s, but Lutyens continued to experiment with a nervous intensity that seemed to forget all he had previously produced. Unlike Lutyens's work, Platt's architectural designs did not evolve. He did not pursue change. Throughout his career he sought universal approaches to each specific design problem, whether it was a country house, a museum, or an apartment building.

To achieve this consistency of expression and to handle those technical problems with which he was at first unfamiliar, Platt had to organize carefully and supervise constantly his design team. While the early projects in Cornish and the major gardens of the late 1890s were solitary efforts, by the turn of the century he had begun to assemble a professional office staff comparable to that of other large offices of the period. Platt's conviction that successful design required the control of all elements—from site development, to landscape planning, to architecture and interior decoration—meant that he needed a diverse range of talents. He showed a marked executive ability in selecting his assistants and determining their activities. He established definite lines of authority and assigned specific responsibilities to each office member, under his ultimate control. While he developed a personal knowledge of practical aspects of architecture, he willingly admitted that there were parts of his architectural practice for which he had little training and gladly hired qualified assistants. In a 1913 letter to Royal Cortissoz, he explained how he had learned the technical aspects of construction:

I never, however, had any formal training in architecture. In the early years, I picked something off every one I could talk to on the practical side—architects, contractors, draftsmen, etc.—I learned to do a lot of things that I am not particularly fitted to do & it was a great relief to me to employ 1st class men to leave me to do what I can't have any one [else] to do.[44]

He was fortunate in his choice of loyal lieutenants, who relieved him of technical problems and left him free for design conception, client relations, and final supervision.

The key designers in the office were Platt, George T. Goulstone, the head draftsman, and Schell Lewis, the office renderer.[45] The design began with Platt, who established the basic scheme. He sketched a plan of a building and its site, indicating critical dimensions, arrangement of rooms, and even placement of furniture. He often made a rough sketch of the exterior, or he showed Goulstone books from the office library with illustrations of the type and character of elevation he wanted. Goulstone, who "bubbled with ideas," would then make a series of elevation studies, and Platt would prod him until the right scheme emerged, always restraining Goulstone's tendency to design overly elaborate elevations.[46] Goulstone's studies were made with pen and ink and wash on tracing paper and were remarkably accurate in representing the color and texture of the design. While these elevations were being studied, Platt and Alfred C. Cass refined the plans.

When the scheme had assumed its final form in plan and elevation, Schell Lewis began an exhaustive study of the details.[47] After consulting the library, Lewis began to draw. Platt taught him a rapid rendering technique using charcoal and the flat edge of a pencil on tracing paper placed over a measured drawing.[48] His responsibility was to show Platt what a molding or doorway would look like. "We'd try out moldings in the form of full size drawings," Lewis recalled, and study them to gauge the effect of light and shadow.[49] Throughout this process, Platt laconically criticized Lewis and the draftsmen, giving a small shake of the head if displeased, or saying "that's the cheese" when satisfied. Next "they made a clay model in plasticene [with] a cardboard template."[50] Platt regularly turned to the modeling studio of Angelo Andriole for plaster casts of proposed details. And when concerned about the overall effect of a design, he had a full-scale model built, such as the steps for the Maxwell Library (1902), which he erected in his backyard, or the trial exhibition room for the Freer Gallery (1916), which he had built on the roof above the drafting room of his office.[51] When the scheme and details had finally been established, Lewis rendered a perspective drawing for presentation to clients or for publication. Although he remained involved with every phase of design, Platt willingly admitted, "Goulstone is my right arm and Lewis is my left."[52]

Following these studies came production of working drawings and supervision of construction. Robins L. Conn oversaw completion of working drawings and coordination of architectural, structural, and mechanical work. Francis L. Henderson, a civil engineer, made topographic surveys of sites and engineering drawings of roads and drainage and sewerage systems. For landscape schemes, Platt frequently collaborated with Ellen Shipman for planting plans and with the Olmsted Brothers for large-scale work. A central figure in the office was the business manager. The first was Charles Dunbar, followed by Charles Cullen. Cullen also managed all the very profitable projects from the Vincent Astor Estate Office, for which he had worked before joining Platt. In addition, depending upon the amount of work, the office employed as many as twenty draftsmen.

Another key member of the Platt team was Edwin Wheeler, who wrote specifications and supervised construction of buildings. Wheeler and the designers were often in conflict as he attempted to meet their exacting standards. Practical necessity sometimes called for a solution that made the designers unhappy. There were many shouted arguments in the drafting room. In the design of the Manor House (1909) for John T. Pratt, Goulstone called for joints in the brickwork of 3/16" which was unusually thin. Goulstone visited the job and found the joints were slightly more than 3/16". He returned to the office and threw a brick at Wheeler's desk.[53] Not all office disputes were as volatile, but the office members were all equally serious about the quality of their work.

Despite Platt's skill in office organization, he discovered that his methods required modification with every project. In 1914, he wrote:

. . . I have never been able to establish for my own work or for those who work under me, any system of rules and principles to govern their plans and designs. At times I have thought that I had discovered some principles that might be the

75

basis upon which to work, but experience has shown me in many cases that in order to accomplish results that I particularly wanted, it was necessary to violate those rules.[54]

While Platt's personal supervision of every design ensured work of uniform character and quality, the other members of the design team helped to provide constant variety for office commissions.

The Platt office library was of central importance to his work and reflected the respect for history that he and his contemporaries shared.[55] The collection of approximately two hundred volumes had been continuously enlarged through purchases on European tours and through regular acquisitions from B. T. Batsford in London and William Helburn in New York. While small in comparison with the architectural libraries of some contemporaries, the Platt collection was highly selective, focusing primarily on the architectural styles that inspired his designs. In addition, the library contained fifty-one photograph albums assembled between 1901 and 1906 that paralleled the subjects of the printed sources. Platt knew the volumes well, and Goulstone and Cass, both bachelors who had not traveled abroad, spent their evenings poring through these books. Under Goulstone's direction, draftsmen also consulted the library as drawings were studied to determine the appropriateness of every detail.

The degree of study, the concentration on certain historical models and specific modern building types, the clear hierarchy and organization of office personnel under the continuous supervision of the master architect are characteristic of the search for order that Platt and his contemporaries pursued in American architecture and modern life. Emphasis on professionalism and specialization also typified the rising middle-class urban society of Platt's generation.[56] In 1909, Herbert Croly wrote *The Promise of American Life,* presenting a vision of a new American civilization founded on a powerful state administered by enlightened managers pursuing national goals. As early as 1903, Croly had praised a "nationalizing" process in contemporary architecture in which the "selective ideals" of historical models were producing national solutions for specific building types, such as Platt's country houses and gardens.[57] In *The Promise of American Life,* Croly argued that a new elite class of leaders, "constructive individuals," was needed to achieve the unity of national purpose. While the importance of Croly's book as a rallying point for reformers and politicians, from Theodore Roosevelt to Woodrow Wilson, is fully appreciated, architectural historians have failed to recognize that the modern American architect was the model for the "constructive individual." Many elements of Croly's hypothetical model manager fit Platt's adoption of his new career and the reasons for his easy success:

> . . . the work of the [architect] who does his very best is much more likely to possess some quality of individual merit, which more or less sharply distinguishes it from that of other architects. He has a monopoly of his own peculiar qualities. Such merit may not be noticed by many people, but it will probably be noticed by a few. The few who are attracted will receive a more than usually vivid impression. They will talk and begin to create a little current of public opinion favorable to the designer. . . . The designer will in this way have gradually created his own special public. Without in any way compromising his own standards, he will have brought himself into a constructive relation with a part at least of the public and will soon extend beyond the sphere of his own personal clientele. In so far as he has succeeded in popularizing a better quality of architectural work, he would be by way of strengthening the hands of all his associates who were standing for similar ideals and methods.[58]

Whether Croly had his friend Platt in mind while writing this model of the spreading influence of the progressive professional specialist, he was describing, in this quotation and elsewhere, qualities that Platt possessed and the manner in which Platt affected his "special public" of patrons and associates.

Perhaps as much as any member of his generation, Platt synthesized a personal artistic ideal and did not waver in his commitment to that standard. Entering the profession without academic training or apprenticeship, he inspired a small community of admirers and built his reputation on the consistent quality of his work, not on public visibility or polemics. The "moral courage" and "intellectual efficiency" that Croly described for his architect model correspond to "the certainty of mental movement — a mark of genius" that Croly saw in Platt and his work.[59] Platt possessed a directness of vision and action, a clear logic for the organization of spaces or individuals, an ability to eliminate the unnecessary or superfluous, and the quiet strength of personality that brought enthusiastic recognition for his designs. These qualities, along with his commitment to the reform of American architecture through close study and adaptation of select historical form, must be understood as integral elements of his philosophy of architecture and as the essential background for an examination of his work.

4

Country Houses

HAVING "ENTERED architecture through the garden gate" as one critic suggested, Platt achieved his greatest success as a country-house architect.[1] These projects that involved architecture, interior decoration, and landscape design allowed him to exercise the full range of his artistic talents. He developed a distinctive manner that, despite the limitless variety of his designs, was recognizable to the trained eye. Building on his past experiences, he formulated a design philosophy combining traditional architectural forms, comprehensive interrelationship of building and landscape, reduction of all unnecessary elements, and creation of beauty as he perceived it. And he inspired in his clients complete confidence in his total control of each commission. From the simple beginnings at Cornish in the 1890s, he rose quickly to national prominence in the opening years of the twentieth century and was preeminent in this field of architectural practice until the country-house market declined after the First World War. Platt set standards emulated by his contemporaries and helped establish the image of the American country house.

Although wealthy Americans had maintained houses in the country since colonial days, the purpose, use, and popularity of these residences, as we have already seen, began to change at the end of the nineteenth century. Prosperous Victorians had been primarily urban dwellers, with railroad and streetcar suburbs an increasingly popular and possible option. Enjoying rural pleasures often meant escaping to a resort area, such as Newport or Bar Harbor, for the summer or a shorter holiday. Near the end of the century, the summer house at the shore or in the mountains was generally replaced by a permanent residence in the environs of a major city that could be lived in year-round, often in conjunction with an apartment or house in town. This pattern was especially true of older, eastern cities, but it was adopted in urban areas across the country in the first decade of this century.

The reasons for this new interest in the country were as numerous as the architects who provided designs for houses. The pastoral revival was primarily a reflection of the fluid economy in which, unfettered by income taxes, great fortunes were amassed quickly.[2] European society was still dominated by a land-based aristocracy. With increasing awareness of European customs, the well-traveled and newly rich American sought to emulate the aristocrat of England and the Continent by spending at least part of the year at his country estate. The American fashion for building country houses, however, arose just as the habit was beginning to fade in England. Landed families there ceased to hold a majority of seats in Parliament in 1885, and in 1908 H. H. Asquith became the first prime minister not to own a country estate.[3] Yet, by 1927, the *Architectural Record* could report that the Prince of Wales on an American tour "learned at first hand . . . that a characteristic and well-developed country house life, not inferior in charm to that of England itself, existed in the United States."[4] Unlike their models, the American gentry almost never farmed or derived their income from the land.

At the same time, the rapid rise in urban density produced a nostalgia for the healthier and more tranquil world of the countryside.[5] This spirit was manifested by a renewed interest in nature, gardening, and outdoor recreation. "Bird books were published by the score," noted the *Architectural Record* in 1901, and "within the last six months two periodicals devoted to different aspects of country life have started and will, we hope, have a most prosperous existence."[6] The move to the country was facilitated by improvements in public transportation, and, more importantly, by the popularization of the automobile. "During the first decade of the century, automobility became an integral part of American life . . . [and] by 1907 the automobile was commonly referred to as a necessity."[7] Finally, large-scale immigration provided an inexpensive labor force to build and staff large rural estates.

Platt emerged as an architect just as, and at least partly because, the demand for country houses began to escalate. Between 1901 and 1917, he designed an average of five domestic projects each year, ranging from suburban houses on small lots to mansions surrounded by several hundred acres. Many of his earliest professional commissions came from relatives and friends of his Cornish neighbors or from the Cheneys and their friends in nearby Connecticut. Around 1904 Platt's projects, now executed by an office of up to seventeen men, increased in scale and cost, and he received greater attention from the professional press, especially the *Architectural Record* which published most of his new designs. After 1907 his practice became truly national with projects in the suburbs of metropolises like Philadelphia, Washington, D.C., Chicago, and Seattle, or in the periphery of smaller cities like Elmira, Youngstown, Louisville, or Saginaw.[8] And by 1913, the year in which a monograph was published on his work, Platt had climbed to the top of his field. But as the 1910s progressed the climate for country-house work became less favorable, and these projects consumed a decreasing percentage of Platt's work.[9] Platt continued to design a small number of country estates until the end of his life, but through the 1920s he devoted his major energies to public commissions.

By reviewing forty major commissions that Platt executed between 1901 and his death, it is possible to sketch a profile of the characteristic "Platt house."[10] In his domestic commissions, as in all his work, Platt did not strive for inventive solutions but varied his designs according to established themes. His devotion to traditional architectural forms and belief in the careful study of appropriate models meant that all of his houses had a certain historical stylistic character. In all cases, however, he designed houses that were eminently suited to their time — contemporary — and many then called them modern.

The major characteristic of all Platt's domestic projects was certainly the importance placed on the interrelationship of the house and its surroundings. Whenever possible, he sited a house facing south and placed the main entrance on the north. The service court and formal gardens also were segregated so that extending from the house in four directions were the entrance, service area, view, and garden. Platt often withheld the view for which the site was chosen until the visitor entered the house, at which point an axial vista opened from the entrance to the distant landscape. Although Platt's procedure in siting a house conformed to basic patterns typical of nineteenth-century English country houses and to the work of many of his contemporaries, he handled each site in a clear, exact, and confident manner.

Platt believed that symmetry or its effect was essential to a beautiful building, and thus he soon rejected the asymmetrical plans of some of his early houses in favor of bilaterally balanced schemes. The central sections of his principal elevations were almost always symmetrical and any lateral wings were balanced if not identical. When the plan required wings of different sizes or only one wing, Platt used his landscape plan to conceal this imbalance. Although hardly unique for his generation in this preference for symmetry, Platt was unswerving in his drive for clear order in elevation and plan.

80

Within the house, Platt located the major rooms in relation to the site and views. The rooms' shapes were almost always rectangular, not the varied geometry that McKim, Mead & White explored or the intricate spaces that Beaux-Arts-trained firms like Carrère & Hastings preferred. The entrance or stairhall was always centered in the main elevation and received careful attention as the focus of circulation in the house. He handled the stairs with great variety, sometimes looping them over the entrance, sometimes tucking them away to the side. Reached directly from the entrance hall, the principal rooms usually were arranged along the south side of the house and generally included the dining room, library, and drawing room. Depending on the client's needs, other rooms could include a study, office, reception room, breakfast room, morning room, music room, and on very rare occasions, a billiard room or conservatory. The most characteristic space of all was the loggia, a columned porch which served as a place for outdoor living. A Platt house almost always included a loggia and often two or three. The loggias were placed adjacent to principal rooms so that they served as transitional spaces from architecture to landscape.

The number of bedrooms a client required directly determined the scale of the house. With one exception, Platt located all principal bedrooms on the second floor. To provide maximum light to these rooms, he relegated the hall to the center of the upper floors and provided natural illumination through skylights when possible. The number of bathrooms in relation to bedrooms increased throughout Platt's career, and sleeping porches were a popular extension of major bedrooms, echoing the loggias below. The service area of a house invariably included a servants' hall, butler's pantry, kitchen, and laundry. The servants' bedrooms, ranging from four to ten or more, were normally above the service wings or on the third floor of the main house. All houses included a service stairway.

While the size of rooms varied greatly, the height of ceilings on the first floor was generally between 10 and 12 feet and on the upper floors at least 9 feet. The walls in the principal rooms, including the stairhall, were usually fully or partially paneled. The woodwork was stained or painted a light color. When not fully paneled, walls generally were papered or hung with brocades or tapestries. Platt devoted great attention to the design of ceilings, favoring intricate molded plaster in the Adam manner or painted beams of Italian Renaissance inspiration. All interior detail was designed by the Platt office specifically for the house. Platt's interiors were both distinctively expressive of his design philosophy and representative of the best work of his generation.

In the majority of commissions, Platt also selected and arranged the furnishings, from the paintings to the light fixtures. Following his general philosophy of domestic architecture, Platt formulated basic principles for interior decoration:

. . . first, that structure is the basis from which form arises; second, that decoration is an element of architectural design and that its purpose is to accentuate architectural lines and proportions; and third, that a completely furnished room may be likened to a composition in which the various components — architectural motives, decorative features and furnishings — bear a definite relationship to each other and to the whole. There should be continuity between interior architecture and interior decorations just as in the painted picture the work is entirely that of one artist.[11]

For his interiors, Platt chose the objects and arranged the furniture with the same spatial clarity and balance evident in his house and garden plans.

As has been pointed out, Platt was able to carry out these comprehensive schemes of gardens, houses, and decorations because of the total trust most of his clients had in him. He felt the need for a close

39. River facade, Anna Osgood house, Hadlyme, Connecticut, 1902.

40. Pergola and loggia,
Osgood house.

relationship with a client, which is one reason why he almost never entered public competitions. Barry Faulkner described Platt's influence:

The effect of his character upon his clients was almost hypnotic. They held him in awe and respect, and turned themselves and their pocket-books inside out to meet his every demand. Not that he was unreasonable or over-extravagant, but his clear vision and untroubled certainty of intention made unthinkable any solution other than his own. The secret of his power with clients lay in the remark that he made to his son William, that an architect had failed in his duty by his client if he had not educated him to desire better and finer things than he had been conscious of before.[12]

Platt alone handled all client relations for the office, which meant that he could undertake only a limited number of commissions. And his clients sought Platt's advice about every aspect of their building, including, occasionally, how to live in it.

The year 1901 was a propitious moment for the American economy and, consequently, for Platt's emerging architectural career. Following the financial uncertainty of the mid-1890s, economic recovery was obvious by 1901.[13] During the previous decade, Platt had developed in the Croly and Lawrence houses at Cornish a variable model that he considered appropriate for the informal summer life of sophisticated, but not ostentatious, urbanites. He now reworked the low-massing, deep overhanging eaves, textured facades, essential loggia, and balanced plans for later clients in Cornish and in Dublin, New Hampshire; Northeast Harbor, Maine; Hadlyme, Connecticut (Figs. 39, 40); and Woodstock,

83

41.   Rear facade, Frank Cheney, Jr., house, Manchester, Connecticut, 1901.

42.   Clifford D. Cheney house (right), 1904, and Philip Cheney
house (left), 1927–29, Cheney family complex, Manchester, Connecticut.

Vermont, as late as 1906. Invariably painted white and carefully set in
their sites, these houses spoke with proper proportions and great charm
of New England and the Renaissance, fresh air and recreation. Here is
the first of a series of design solutions for specific conditions that he
varied but rarely deserted.

A new initiative — for more substantial residences than the sum-
mer-house models he first evolved in Cornish — began to appear in the
opening years of the century, especially among the commissions he
received from seven members of the Cheney family in Manchester.[14]
The house for his cousin, Frank Cheney, Jr., begun in 1901, was among
the finest of the group (Fig. 41).[15] He designed a five-bay, two-story
elevation flanked by one-bay wings from which corner loggias projected
on the rear elevation. He built the house of red brick trimmed in limestone and painted wood. This residence was the largest of the group of
Platt houses that dotted the rolling land of the Cheney family compound
(Fig. 42). The simplicity and restraint of these commissions was a further
statement of the Cheney family character that Platt had inherited.

43. First floor plan, Winston Churchill house, Harlackenden Hall,
Cornish, New Hampshire, 1901–4.

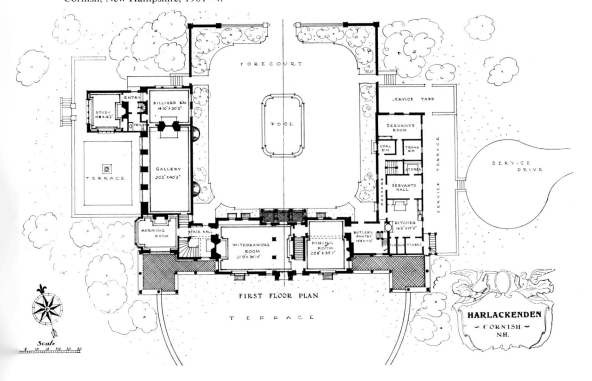

The spare and proper character of Frank Cheney's Manchester house was seen also in a more conspicuously colonial revival design constructed in Cornish at the same time. For the American novelist, Winston Churchill, Platt designed Harlackenden Hall to suggest the eighteenth-century Maryland setting of his client's most recent and successful novel, *Richard Carvel* (Fig. 43). The house was again built of red brick trimmed with white-painted wood and limestone and arranged in a U-shaped plan that initially recalled the High Court design. But the large music room, drawing room, and substantial service areas of the plan show that this house was conceived of as a country seat, not just a summer retreat. As such, it marks the transition in Platt's work at the turn of the century even more than any other of the contemporary Cheney projects.

The Cheneys' other major contribution to Platt's career was the introduction they provided to the Maxwell family of nearby Rockville, Connecticut. Like the Cheneys, the Maxwells were the mill owners of this small town, but unlike their friends, they were more willing, and perhaps more able, to construct buildings that embodied their gentry status. The earliest of three family commissions was for the George R. Maxwell Memorial Library, given to the town by his widow and children and designed by Platt in 1902 (Fig. 44). The library was T-shaped, with a

44. Maxwell Memorial Library, Rockville, Connecticut, 1902.

45. Rear facade, Francis T. Maxwell house,
Maxwell Court, Rockville, Connecticut, 1901–3.

monumental public reading room forming the top of the T closest to the street and a 30,000-volume stack room with a ninety-seat lecture hall above composing the shaft of the T.[16] Built of fine Vermont and Italian marbles, the building demonstrated a reverence for knowledge as well as the prominence of the donors. From 1897 onward, the generosity of industrialist Andrew Carnegie was helping to make public libraries a ubiquitous symbol of small-town America. But the Maxwell Library, proclaiming local philanthropy and family responsibility, more closely approached the austere propriety with which Charles McKim would soon endow J. P. Morgan's private library in New York City. Platt's design was his first public building commission and clearly showed, from the entrance stairs to the proportions of the reading room, his ability to create ceremonial grandeur even on a diminutive scale.

Much more important to Platt's developing reputation and philosophy of interrelating architecture and landscape was the first of two large houses that he built for George Maxwell's sons. Maxwell Court, the residence of Francis T. Maxwell, designed in 1901 but not completed until 1904, was the first comprehensive statement of Platt's villa theory (Figs. 45, 46). Set on the side of a hill, the two-story, red brick, limestone-trimmed house had a projecting pedimented entrance and a colonnaded rear entrance. Francis Maxwell gave Platt free reign, believing that "a true artist should not be held back."[17] And, realizing the limitations of life in a mill town, the patron wanted to surround his wife and daughters with beauty and elegance. Platt was uniquely suited to realize his client's ambitions, and Maxwell was willing to execute whatever his architect suggested. Maxwell Court is, in many ways, the fulfillment of the promise Platt showed at Faulkner Farm, no longer inhibited by another architect's house.

46. Entrance facade, Maxwell Court.

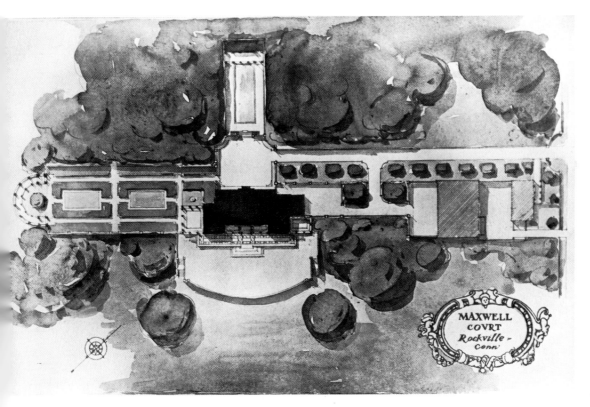

47.   Plot plan, Maxwell Court.

Indeed, the ground plan of the Rockville estate is very similar to its Brookline predecessor, while more unified and less ambitious (Fig. 47). Once again, Platt set the house into the side of a hill just below its crest, and organized the property on two major axes intersecting at the house. As Sprague had before him, Maxwell paid for the construction of a high retaining wall to support a large grass terrace across the rear of the residence, providing views of the valley and mill town below. Opposite, on the entrance side of the house, Platt located the enclosed forecourt, with a proposed swimming pool and pergola on the top of the hill.[18] The longer axis ran from the incurving gates at the eastern edge of the property, past the gate lodge and stables, into the entrance courtyard, and then on to the formal flower garden on the western side of the house. Thus, Platt intimately tied the house to its surroundings, a sector for circulation and service, an area for recreation, the flower garden, and the view, each extended in a cardinal direction and each visually segregated from the others with great care.

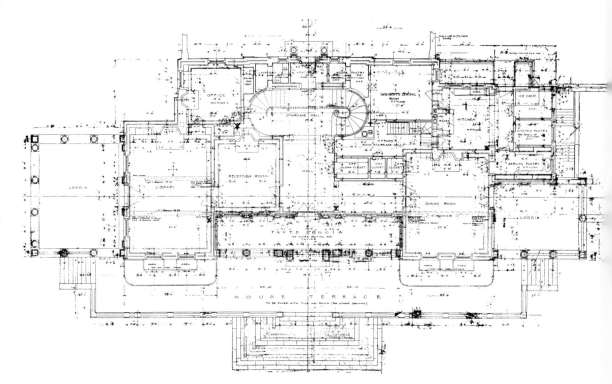

48. First floor plan, Maxwell Court.

The interior plan of Maxwell Court is the most imaginative of all his houses (Fig. 48). One enters from a small vestibule into a cross-axis stairhall with semicircular ends, one of the few nonrectangular spaces in his domestic production. The stairs climb over the vestibule, giving access at the landing to a loggia above the front door and continuing to a colonnaded second story corridor (Fig. 49). A short hall proceeds from the stairhall to the rear terrace, intersected first by a cross hall along the south elevation. Here he placed the major rooms—the library and reception room to the west, adjacent to the flower garden, and the dining room and kitchen to the east. And he connected these spaces by a vista from the dining room loggia at the southeast corner through to the library loggia at the southwest end and then to the path of the flower garden beyond. He reinforced the importance of this axis with both the inset loggia and the paved promenade of the rear elevation. He thus achieved internal coordination and internal-external relation in plan.

In elevation and massing as well, Platt experimented with the interpenetration of interior and exterior space. On the entrance facade, the central pedimented section projected to welcome and direct the visitor. The open loggia above the entrance was an enticing transitional area that could only be reached from within the house. On the rear elevation, the end pavilions, corresponding to the library and dining room, were pulled forward to mark the importance of their interior uses. And Platt gradually modulated from architecture to nature through the succession of inset loggia, paved promenade, and grassed terrace to frame the distant landscape.

Maxwell Court is also an excellent demonstration of Platt's neo-classical manner. He thoughtfully blended Italian, English, and American images to create a conspicuously personal mode. Here the red brick and limestone materials suggest English Georgian or American colonial models, but the balconies, loggias, and terraces provide a Mediterranean warmth and softness. Even the antique held sway in the staircase hall's

49. Stairhall, Maxwell Court.

91

50.   Entrance hall, Dr. Arthur C. Cabot house, Cherry Hill,
Canton, Massachusetts, 1902.

51.   First floor plan, Cherry Hill.

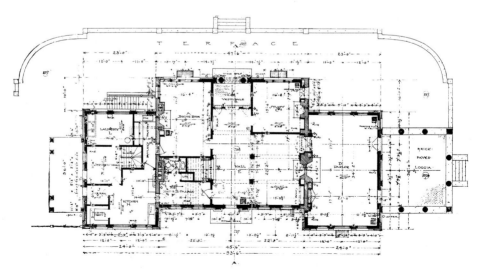

Pompeiian red walls ornamented by medallions of Roman figures. The way he selected and modified his sources was personal and distinctive, although his ideas were quickly adopted and imitated by many of his colleagues.

Throughout his career, Platt often experimented with a particular model, varying the plan, massing, and orientation. For example, the red brick with white trim classicism of Maxwell Court was reduced and modified for three contemporary projects. In the C. L. Ring house (1903), for a lumber baron in Saginaw, Michigan, and in North Farm, the Howard L. Clark residence (1902–3), for a successful banker in Bristol, Rhode Island, Platt retained the balanced, pedimented facade of the Maxwell Court entrance elevation, but he radically reorganized the interior space around large central stairhalls. At Cherry Hill (1902), the Dr. Arthur T. Cabot house, in Canton, Massachusetts, he employed an open, central hallway with enclosed stair and column-screened reception area but divided the building into a series of major blocks which he projected and recessed along the axis through the house (Figs. 50, 51). As the progeny of Maxwell Court, these three houses show Platt as a composer developing variations on a dominant theme.

52.   Rear facade, William H. Rand house, Rye, New York, 1903–4.

For projects of more moderate size, Platt frequently turned to stucco as an exterior wall treatment from 1903 to 1905. Following the model of High Court, he continued to design hipped-roof, stucco houses that emphasized horizontal lines, such as the William H. Rand house (1904) in Rye, New York (Fig. 52). But he simultaneously developed a more vertical, cross-gabled prototype. Two Manchester projects, houses for Clifford D. Cheney (1904) and for J. Davenport Cheney (1905), are typical expressions of this Platt idiom. These and other stuccoed, cross-gabled houses are somewhat suggestive of the contemporary work of English arts-and-crafts architects, such as C.F.A. Voysey or M. H. Baillie Scott, without the self-conscious expression of battered walls, rough-cast finish, or quaint detailing.[19] Platt may have been partially influenced by these English designs, which were then being published in American journals, but he combined the appeal of vertical massing with classically proportioned doors and windows, projecting loggias, and his other characteristic elements.

A more complex example of this Platt variant is the Henry Howard house (1905) in Brookline, Massachusetts (Fig. 53). A compact design on a narrow suburban lot overlooking a park, the Howard house is two-and-a-half stories high and three bays wide. The house's 6,000-square feet are dominated by a gable, parallel to the street, from which two narrow gables project for the side bays of the entrance facade and a central loggia extends into the garden at the rear. Platt used an axial hall to divide reception and smoking rooms at the front corners and the library and dining room with service area on the garden side. In the basement he located the kitchen and servants' hall on the right, and on the left a garage reached by a curving ramp from the street. In 1905, a basement garage alone would have made this house noteworthy. Because of fear of the combustion engine, Platt designed the garage with fireproof walls and ceiling.

The Howard house, in general, reflected the contemporary interest in fireproof construction. The process and material Platt used for the Howard commission were described in an article for the *American Architect:*

In the construction of this house, the outside boarding had been omitted, and the metal lathing is put directly on the studs. On the inside between the studs another coat of cement is applied, making a two-inch reinforced wall. The outside wall has a white finish coat.[20]

The nature of the material and construction technique encouraged Platt to simplify the design of this building when compared to his earlier brick

53.   Entrance facade, Henry Howard house, Brookline, Massachusetts, 1905.

houses. An unmolded bandcourse provided the only exterior decoration
aside from the wooden door surround. The crisp meeting of wall and
roof in the gables expressed the pure volumes of the house. Wanting both
to provide the most fire-resistant buildings and to achieve greater plastic-
ity in these designs, Platt continued to explore alternatives in cement
and stucco construction.

At the request of his client, Platt stressed fireproof construction in
a 1906 country house for George L. Nichols at Katonah, New York (Fig.
54).[21] With the boxy shape of the house reflecting the construction
process of poured concrete, Alderbrook, as it was named, was one of the
stiffest and least unified of his country-house designs. Platt created boxes
for a three-story central section of five bays, flanked by two-story, one-
bay wings. The house has flat roofs concealed behind parapets, balustraded in the middle portions. Although the building was encased in
brick, poured concrete was used for decorative work, such as the bandcourses, cornices, balustrades, and loggia columns on the exterior and,
to a lesser extent, on the interior. The library, a room where fire preven-
tion was a major consideration, was built totally of poured concrete
ornamented with inset marble trim. Even the elliptical staircase was

54.   Rear facade, George L. Nichols house, Alderbrook, Katonah, New York, 1906.

constructed of poured concrete. These methods forced Platt to modify his schemes, especially the massing as seen at Alderbrook, but he still relied upon conventional designs of wood and masonry rather than create new ornament uniquely expressive of the material.[22] For clients not as fanatically concerned about fireproof materials, Platt preferred to use hollow tile block covered with stucco on the exterior and ornamented with stone or wood. This technique was more compatible with his philosophy as a designer since it did not conflict with the traditional nature of his sources.

Two of the earliest projects to be built in this manner were similar houses for the Reverend Joseph Hutcheson (1903–6) at Warren, Rhode Island, and for John Jay Chapman (1904–9) at Barrytown, New York. Villasera, the Hutcheson house, was the finer but has been demolished. Sylvania, the Chapman place, remains unaltered, including its original furnishings (Fig. 55). Both were two-and-a-half-story gable units with projecting monumental porticoes on the long elevations. They were designed for similar sites, the edge of plateaus overlooking land that gently sloped to a river. Their giant porticoes and simple massing related to the scale of their settings.[23] They were the initial step that Platt took toward large-scale geometric forms of minimal ornamentation.

The culmination of this thrust for monumentality and formal abstraction came with Woodston, the residence of Marshall Slade at Mount Kisco, New York, designed in 1904 and constructed in 1905–6.[24] In overall appearance, the house was a two-and-a-half-story, simple rectangle with gabled ends (Fig. 56). Only a small, one-story service wing, screened by plantings and the fenced forecourt, extended beyond the basic rectangle. The 8,000-square-foot building stood in a thick group of oaks on a prominent hilltop, visible for some distance from the surrounding countryside. Platt placed the house so that the public rooms faced south and west for maximum light. A single entrance drive served both the forecourt and the service yard. From the front door one looked back up an allee of trees to the swimming pool and pedimented bathhouse, both on a higher elevation than the house (Fig. 57). A tennis court abutted the pool area but was concealed by dense foliage. On the rear side of the house, flower gardens flanked a central greensward that descended to a second grassed terrace ornamented by a large, cross-axial, exedra-ended pool. The west elevation provided the best view, while the service area occupied the least desirable northeast corner.

The site suggested this simple formula. The conspicuous hilltop required a house of large proportions that would express its character

55. River facade, John Jay Chapman house, Sylvania, Barrytown, New York, 1904–9.

56. Garden facade, Marshall Slade house, Woodston, Mount Kisco, New York, 1904–8.

and look appropriate from a distance. Both the simple massing of the south elevation and the extension of the gable into the monumental end portico of the west facade beautifully achieved this result. Since his days as an etcher, Platt had been recognized as an artist of reduction, capable of eliminating components and keeping details to the barest mininum.[25] Although he had pursued these ideals in earlier projects, Platt realized at Woodston the culmination of his experiments in simplified massing.

Platt showed the same move toward fewer and larger spaces in the plan of Woodston (Fig. 58). A square entrance hall, centered on the north side of the house, served as the focus of a radiating circulation system, with direct access to all the major rooms and the enclosed staircase. Straight ahead was the drawing room, comprising the central

57. Plot plan, Woodston.

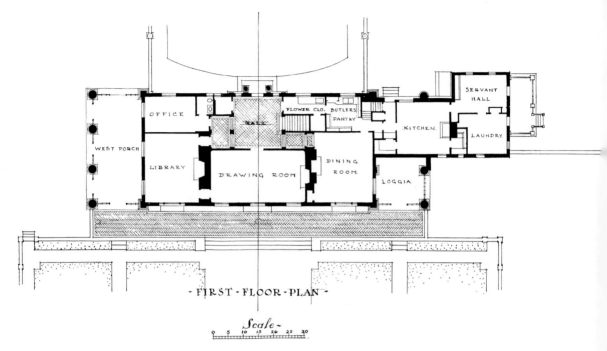

58. First floor plan, Woodston.

three bays of the rear facade. This space was flanked by a dining room and library of equal size. All three rooms opened directly through glass doors onto a brick terrace across the south side of the house, and the library and dining room provided access to the inset end loggias. The northern half of the house contained an office to the west of the hall and service areas to the east. The purity and logic of Platt's plan equaled the simplicity and grandeur of his elevations. In all elements of the Woodston design, Platt achieved a sense of breadth and quiet country dignity that was much admired by his contemporaries. The reduction of ornament and firm control of proportions makes the Slade house one of his most pleasing designs to late-twentieth-century eyes.

Despite the austerity of the scheme, Woodston was not without precedents, and Platt's use of those sources reveals clearly his methods as an architect. One of the photograph albums in Platt's office library contains views of Wyck, a house begun in 1690 at Germantown, Pennsylvania, that provided part of the inspiration for Woodston (Fig. 59). A stuccoed brick box with end chimneys and large glazed doors in the center of the side elevation, Wyck, like Woodston, was encased in a screen of lattice on which vines were trained.[26] For the Slade house, Platt lowered the pitch of the roof, continued the glass doors all along the garden elevation, and inserted giant porticoes on the ends. He adopted the simple lattice bracket above the entrance door at Wyck and repeated it above the ground-floor openings at Woodston to cast shadows, much as a molding would.

The image of Wyck also inspired the designs for The Mallows, a house Platt designed for C. Temple Emmet at Saint James, Long Island, in 1905 (Fig. 60). Mrs. Emmet was the sister of Mrs. John Jay Chapman, for whom Platt was currently building Sylvania. Mr. Emmet was a cousin of the architect Stanford White, whose own country place was

59.　Entrance facade, Wyck, Germantown, Pennsylvania, ca. 1690.

60. Garden facade, C. Temple Emmet house, The Mallows,
Saint James, Long Island, New York, 1905.

also in Saint James. Nearby White had designed Sherrewogue, a house
for Temple's brother, Devereux Emmet.[27] White had incorporated a
two-story loggia in the garden end of Sherrewogue, much as Platt did at
both Woodston and The Mallows. Also, White used a broken scroll
pediment on the center dormer of the main section of his Emmet house,
which Platt would repeat for the Slade project. Platt's handling in both
cases was much tighter than White's sprawling, shingled design. White
was using a Long Island vernacular vocabulary. Platt, although he was
working from a colonial model, showed no interest in re-creating
Wyck's picturesque character.

In an article on Woodston, a contemporary reviewer observed:

The architect has dared to be simple to the point of bareness; but the simplicity
never becomes either attenuated or empty because of the strength with which
the essential elements of design have been handled. There can be no doubt that
the great majority even of the better American architects do not dare to be
sufficiently simple. . . . Perhaps Mr. Platt's highest merit as a designer is the

increasing simplicity of his buildings; and that is one reason his large influence upon contemporary American practice is so wholesome.[28]

So, in the Slade house, Platt brought to bear aesthetic principles that had directed his work from his earliest days as an etcher (Fig. 61). Striving to minimize, to use nothing more than was really required, became the Platt image. And, as the reviewer noted, that simplicity exerted a positive influence on his fellow architects and attracted an ever wider circle of clients.

The architectural press was primarily responsible for the rapid spread of Platt's influence. His country houses were published so regu-

61. Garden terrace, Woodston.

larly in the middle of the first decade of this century that his clients (and imitators) were no longer drawn from the Boston-to-New York enclave alone, but from the country at large. His reputation moved west quickly. In 1907, he designed his first house near Philadelphia, and within two years he was working in Seattle, having built near Buffalo, Cleveland, Detroit, and Chicago en route. His clients now were generally wealthier and envisioned substantial houses set in expansive grounds. Platt devised two general models that he varied widely for these estates: red brick structures that suggested English and American prototypes, and stuccoed villas that evoked the Italian Renaissance. Which historical style he chose depended heavily upon the site and the intentions of the patron. Perhaps due to a sense of regional appropriateness, the brick Georgian projects were generally restricted to the East Coast. Similarly, the Renaissance villa formula was chosen most frequently for waterfront sites.

Two Connecticut projects show Platt's varying treatment of American colonial models. The first, called Eastover, was built in 1906 in New London, Connecticut, for George T. Palmer, a leading collector of American decorative arts who wanted a sympathetic setting for his

62. Garden facade, George T. Palmer house, Eastover, New London, Connecticut, 1906.

63. Rear facade, Robert H. Schutz house, Hartford, Connecticut, 1907–8.

collection (Fig. 62).[29] The model was Westover (1730-35), William Byrd's plantation on the James River in Virginia. Platt accepted Westover's basic exterior appearance, elements of the first floor plan, and some decorative details. However, he stretched the model horizontally, allowing for larger spaces than at Westover, yet retaining the vertical thrust of the original design in the high, hipped roof and four tall chimneys, now moved to the interior of the house. Despite these modifications, Eastover never escaped the specter of its obvious source, making it one of the less satisfying of Platt's large houses.

Less derivative and more representative was the house he designed in 1907 for Robert H. Schutz, a Hartford businessman.[30] Like Palmer, Schutz wanted a house with American character and took Platt to see buildings he admired. Unlike Palmer, however, Schutz did not compel his architect to copy a colonial model.[31] Platt created a two-and-a-half-story, five-bay brick block surmounted by a gambrel roof with four tall end chimneys and a delicate roof-top balustrade (Fig. 63). Within, a central hall with enclosed staircase divided the traditional double-pile plan with library, drawing room, dining room, and kitchen at the four corners. However, the inset loggia at the center of the rear elevation and the projecting loggia of the garden side provided elements of classical sophistication that liberated the design from close reliance on eighteenth-century America.

The more English inflection of Platt's brick country houses can best be seen in a slightly later project (1909–11) for John T. Pratt at Glen Cove, Long Island. Called The Manor House, the Pratt commission was far grander than either the Palmer or Schutz design, costing well over $300,000 and including the residence, gardens and pavilion, stables, a playhouse, a garage, a laundry building, a farmhouse and a camp.[32] Part of a large complex of Pratt family houses that eventually included other projects by Platt, The Manor House was designed to emulate the qualities of English country life. Platt planned the house along a single axis with the entrance in the center of the long south facade. A formal garden to the west, a view of Long Island Sound to the north, and the service

64. Entrance facade, John T. Pratt house, The Manor House, Glen Cove, Long Island, New York, 1909–11.

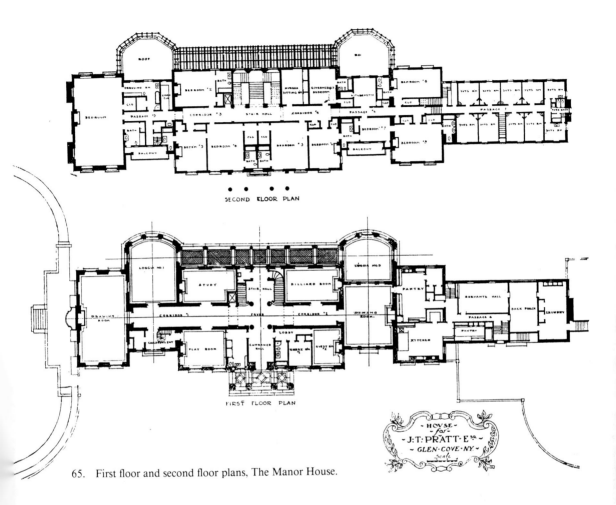

65.   First floor and second floor plans, The Manor House.

wing to the east completed the orientation of the residence. He broke up
the potential monotony of the principal elevations by projection and
recession of porticoes, pavilions, and hyphens along the major axis (Fig.
64). The monumental entrance portico suggested the grandeur of English country houses of the late Georgian period, while the intricate
wrought-iron balconies of the recessed hyphens were modeled on specific photographs of English ironwork in Platt's office library. The plan
of the first floor was anchored by the ample drawing and dining room at
either end of the central corridor with loggias, study, billiard room,
playroom, and guest bedrooms balanced along this axis (Fig. 65). Platt
planted a stand of mature elms around the residence, giving The Manor
House the immediate appearance of venerable age and providing a
domestic character to this imposing structure.

66. Garden facade, W. Hinckle Smith house, Timberline,
Bryn Mawr, Pennsylvania, 1907.

67. First floor plan, Timberline.

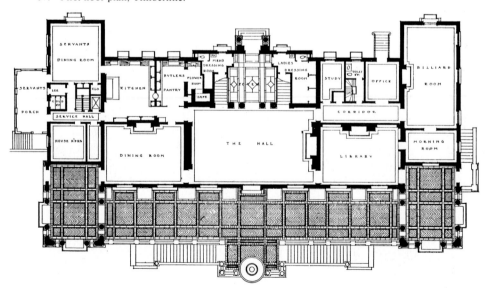

Equal in scale and quality to the Pratt house were a series of stuccoed villas that Platt began from 1907 through the end of the decade. The first of the group was designed for W. Hinckle Smith (1907) at Bryn Mawr, Pennsylvania (Fig. 66).[33] Called Timberline, the Smith house was set on a ridge overlooking parkland to the south, a formal garden and tennis court to the east, and a cutting garden and stable to the west. The interior plan demonstrated Platt's love of uncluttered, large spaces, with the dining room and library flanking an immense central hall with a 17-foot-high ceiling (Fig. 67). Stuccoed and trimmed in limestone, the house had projecting end pavilions on the entrance side and projecting end loggias on the back. From the tile roof to the stone door surrounds to the double-level fountain and ramped staircases of the terrace to the loggias overlooking the landscape, Platt pursued here a new archaeological attention to his Renaissance models that would continue in subsequent projects (Fig. 68).

Referring to his most famous villa projects, Platt once jokingly told architecture students, "I've been asked to develop the Great Lakes,

68.   View from rear loggia, Timberline.

you know."[34] In fact, his principal commissions in the closing years of the decade were major houses on lakes Erie, Superior, and Michigan. All were sited at or near water's edge and showed Platt's ability to incorporate and manipulate the water frontage as part of his design.

Gwinn was the most concise of the three designs. Built near Cleveland, Ohio, for William G. Mather, an iron ore magnate, Gwinn was developed on a five-acre site bounded on the north by a 28-foot drop to Lake Erie.[35] Platt placed the house at the edge of the cliff and created an artificial harbor by constructing incurving retaining walls with circular pergolas at their ends (Fig. 69). He arranged the lot compactly, with entrance and service drives along the west and east boundaries, respectively, providing access to the short ends of the house (Fig. 70). All the

69. Waterfront, William G. Mather house, Gwinn, Cleveland, Ohio, 1907–8.

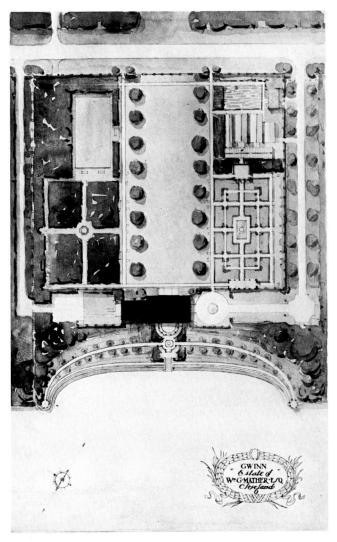

70. Plot plan, Gwinn.

area to the south of the house was devoted to gardens, recreation, and service. A tree-lined central lawn stretched from the house to Lake Shore Boulevard and continued as an allee of trees across the road. Platt flanked the greensward with a flower garden and greenhouse on the west and a woodland garden and tennis court on the east. He withheld the view of the lake until one entered the house and then revealed it through the monumental semicircular portico that projected toward the water. Platt showed his varied genius in merging a house and its environment through the different treatments of the two main elevations. The majes-

111

71. Library, Gwinn.

tic, theatrical presence of the waterfront portico contrasted with the domestic, quiet character of the garden facade and the warm rooms that overlooked the greensward (Fig. 71). Gwinn also showed Platt's adaptation of diverse design sources. While the stuccoed construction and lakefront terraces immediately evoked Italian images, the north portico of the Mather house resembles both the south front of the White House, an American building Platt greatly admired, and the circular temple of Vesta at Tivoli.[36]

Similar to Gwinn in site but larger in scale was The Moorings (1908–10) which Platt designed for Russell A. Alger, Jr., at Grosse Pointe, near Detroit (Fig. 72).[37] As at Cleveland, Platt placed the house on the highest land near the lake, here with a rectangular bowling green set between the house and the water. Unlike Gwinn, The Moorings's entrance drive, lined by elms, was centered in the property with gardens and service areas to either side. The interior plan resembled that of Timberline, having a large central hall flanked by dining room and library, all overlooking the water. Despite similarities in planning to earlier Platt projects, the elevations of the Alger house were a studied response to the site: the vertical thrust of the pedimented and heavily ornamented entrance elevation contrasted with the horizontal spread of the lake facade, pulled out by loggias, a pergola, and the architectural treatment of the shoreline.

The last and grandest of Platt's lakefront villas was a large and complex commission for Harold and Edith Rockefeller McCormick, heirs to two of the country's greatest fortunes.[38] The property consisted of three hundred acres on Lake Michigan in Lake Forest, Illinois, thirty miles north of Chicago. The estate, the largest one Platt ever designed, was constructed in two stages, with a third phase never executed, between 1908 and 1918.

The story of the search for an architect enhances the significance of the commission. As early as August 1906, Harold McCormick con-

72. Entrance facade, Russell A. Alger, Jr., house, The Moorings, Grosse Pointe Farms, Michigan, 1908–10.

73. Plot plan, Harold and Edith Rockefeller McCormick estate,
Villa Turicum, Lake Forest, Illinois, 1908–18.

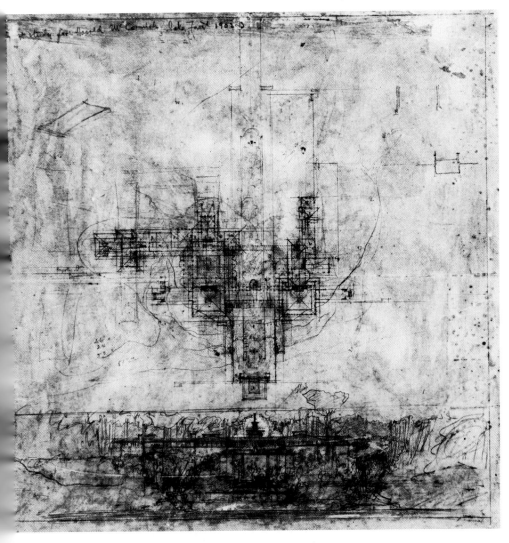

74. Frank Lloyd Wright, plan and waterfront elevation,
Harold F. McCormick project, Lake Forest, Illinois, 1907.

tacted James Gamble Rogers of New York and Chicago to prepare plans
for the house.[39] The clients were specific in their demands, requesting
"pure Italian lines," a "stucco exterior and very flat hipped roof," and a
house that was powerful yet peaceful. Mr. McCormick further explained
that his wife did not like overhanging eaves and gables because they
made a house dark and dreary.[40] For unknown reasons, the couple did
not accept Rogers's proposals but took no action until May 1908, when

115

they informed him that they were investigating another architect, Charles A. Platt. Given the McCormicks' prejudice for a stuccoed villa, it is surprising that they first approched Rogers, better known for public and commercial buildings at that time, rather than Platt, now nationally recognized for Renaissance-inspired country houses.

What is even more surprising is that the name of a third architect, Frank Lloyd Wright — whose involvement with the project occurred between Rogers and Platt — is totally missing from the McCormick correspondence. In 1907, Wright prepared a scheme for the McCormick place, using low pavilions grouped around gardens and terraces, a design which Henry-Russell Hitchcock observed "might suggest a group of exhibition buildings as much as an ordinary house."[41] Although Mr. McCormick had expressed an interest in Wright's work, Mrs. McCormick was evidently dissatisfied with the proposal and sought out Platt for alternative designs.[42] This change in architects by a nationally prominent family has been seen by some architectural historians as "a severe blow to Wright's early career and, indeed, the lowering of the curtain on the whole Chicago school."[43]

Should it have been a surprise? Platt once stated: "I believe it is the architect's business to express the ideals of the client, mixed with the architectural ideals of his own time."[44] The problem with Wright's scheme was that it imposed not only a physical setting but also a way of life upon his clients. The Prairie School house, of which Wright's McCormick project could be considered a palatial example, was not what the McCormicks, especially Mrs. McCormick, wanted. Coming from a comparable background, Platt respected the family, educational, and economic conditions of his patrons and understood how to provide them with a setting appropriate to their interests and social position.

In spite of Platt's and Wright's divergent approaches, it is interesting to see how similarly they responded to the site.[45] Both architects positioned the house at the edge of a bluff overlooking the lake and immediately south of a ravine (Figs. 73, 74). Both designed a system of artificial terraces down the face of the cliff and planned the house around a series of open and closed courtyards. Wright's scheme was more horizontal with sprawling wings of predominantly one story, emphasized by broadly cantilevered roofs. Platt's proposal was more vertical — two-and-a-half stories — and self-contained. Wright's design had a vaguely Eastern character, while Platt's was clearly inspired by Italian Renaissance villas. Both men conceived a full integration of the house with its surroundings, but for Wright, nature predominated, while for Platt, man established control.

116

75. Entrance facade, Villa Turicum.

In a telegram confirming Platt's initial visit to Lake Forest, Harold McCormick wrote: "Tract of land consists of 100 acres on shore. Proposed site consists of bluff 70 feet above water. Mrs. McC inclines being partial to Italian style. Very glad you're coming."[46] Although Edith McCormick requested a villa design, Platt would characteristically have thought of Italy in response to the lakefront site. Before his second visit, Mrs. McCormick wrote asking him to bring plans of High Court. She had seen the house published in the *Architectural Record* and felt it "was very interesting on a simple and modest basis."[47] In its early stages, Villa Turicum, as the McCormicks named their house, was loosely modeled on High Court, with a U-shaped plan and colonnaded courtyard overlooking Lake Michigan. Despite the clients' great wealth, they commissioned a relatively modest house at first and added to it and the grounds in stages over the next decade. In the end, however, the unselfconscious charm and simplicity of the Cornish precedent was overwhelmed and nearly forgotten.

117

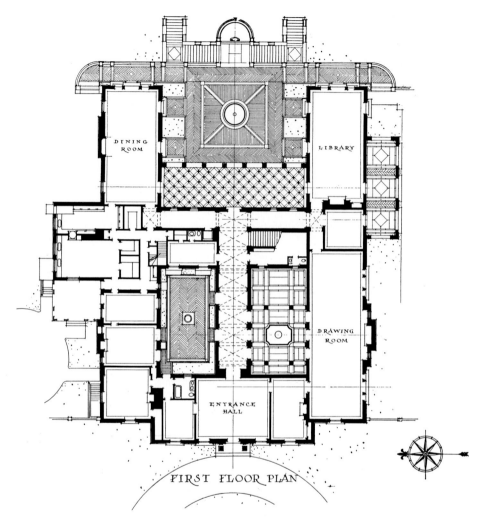

76. First floor plan, Villa Turicum, showing house as completed in 1911.

The approach to the McCormick house was through a large, semicircular, wrought-iron gateway and along a gently curving drive that straightened out as one drew near the house. A large service area with stables and kitchen and flower gardens was located north of the main drive and was reached by a separate service road. Before the house, Platt laid out a 300-yard-long greensward, anchored by four elms at the corners. As usual, upon reaching the entrance, one had to enter the house in order to experience the rest of the view of the estate (Figs. 75, 76). From the entrance hall, one perceived the first vista of the lake, straight ahead through the mass of the house. An axial corridor, flanked by an open and skylighted courtyard to left and right, led to a paved, three-sided court overlooking the lake (Fig. 77). Both an interior hallway and an exterior loggia crossed this axis, connecting the major public rooms on either side. To the north of the lakefront courtyard were the dining room and the kitchen, pantry and service facilities. On the south, the space corresponding to the dining room was filled by the library. The other components of the south facade were a small writing room and an enormous drawing room, all with a view of the formal gardens to the south.[48] Villa Turicum was representative of Platt's organizational approach in which the entrance (west), service (north), view (east), and gardens (south) extended from the house in four directions. Normally, the house would have been sited with the major rooms facing south and west for maximum exposure, but the desire to capitalize upon the lake view demanded a rotation in plan.

In architectural detail as in name, the influence of Italy reigned at Villa Turicum. On the entrance facade, a two-story, five-bay section

77. Courtyard at top of lakefront terraces, Villa Turicum.

119

projected from single-bay wings. Platt modeled the columned marble door surround on that of the Villa Mondragone in Frascati.[49] He kept other decoration minimal except for the first story window frames and balconies beneath the second story wing windows. Platt believed that the "Italian ideal is to have the exterior of the building very severe and to warm up as one goes in, and to use colors and materials as a foil for the severity of the exterior."[50] The warmth of color, texture, and ornament was apparent throughout Platt's interiors.

The most overtly Italian devices were the terraces from the rear courtyard of the house down to the water's edge; these were added to the property from 1910 to 1912 (Fig. 78). Platt created here a superimposition of elements from the gardens of the Villa d'Este at Tivoli and the Villa Lante at Bagnaia.[51] From the paved courtyard two flights of lateral steps descended to a grassed segmental terrace. Ramped steps continued down from the convex perimeter of this terrace to an alternating series of straight water staircases and lozenge-shaped stairs, ending in a swimming pool at the water's edge. Elsewhere, the gardens included a bowling green and a sunken or lily garden, and a polo field was developed at some distance from the house.

The McCormick estate, although it embodied the major theories behind Platt's designs, was not typical of his country houses. The scale was immense and the money available encouraged Platt to reproduce, more than adapt, the villas of Italy. With the exception of Eastover, Villa Turicum was Platt's most derivative design. To what extent the McCormicks influenced his work here is unknown. Certainly, the wealth and ambition of his patrons pushed Platt to unprecedented extremes and produced a house that received more attention than it merited. It was rather in projects such as Maxwell Court and Woodston, where Platt held tighter control of a more rational program, that his genius as a creator of country houses was most apparent.

In 1913, the year when most of the construction of Villa Turicum and its grounds neared completion, *The Works of Charles A. Platt,* a monograph surveying his architectural and landscape projects, was published. The *Architectural Record,* in reviewing the book, noted:

The fact that any publisher should find it a promise of profit in preparing so handsome, elaborate and costly a record of the work of a living architect is both a clear indication of the popularity and permanent value of certain phases of contemporary American architecture and an extraordinary tribute to the particular architect who has been the first selected for this work of distinction.[52]

The Works of Charles A. Platt, which was reissued in 1919 and in a reduced-scale student edition in 1925, inaugurated a new type of architectural book in America, the commercially produced photographic survey of a contemporary architect's career.[53] Among the most ambitious publications of this type was a four-volume monograph on McKim, Mead & White, which first appeared in 1915. The Platt book had a widespread influence throughout the profession, particularly the detail drawings. Geoffrey Platt recalls that these drawings "were a revelation to many of the architects of the time. It has been reported to me that the use of this book in numerous contemporary offices was intense. One architect told me that they called it 'the Bible.' "[54] In an era concerned with correct precedents, Platt's work became an accepted model itself.

But the publication of the monograph only continued a high level of visibility that Platt's work had enjoyed for over a decade. His designs

78. View of lakefront terraces, Villa Turicum.

had already been published in and praised by a wide variety of professional and popular periodicals.[55] This coverage was supplemented by the frequent publication of Platt designs in books on contemporary American architecture, especially those discussing domestic projects.[56] In fact, Platt's work was published as often as any of his contemporaries' and the appearance of the monograph is an indication of the architect's established national reputation which ensured the publishers that there was a market for the book.

The influence of the monograph and previous periodical and book publications of Platt designs extended to foreign interest in his work as well. The English periodical, *The Architectural Review,* noted with interest the appearance in 1913 of both Lawrence Weaver's *The Houses and Gardens of E. L. Lutyens* and the Platt monograph, calling these architects " the two most eminent exponents of domestic architecture in England and America respectively."[57] The reviewer continued by observing that " the name of Mr. Lutyens is perhaps more widely known among the general public than that of any other designer of private houses and the work of Mr. Platt is equally familiar to Americans."[58] In Germany, Werner Hegemann, writing in *Landhaus und Garten* (1907) and later in *Amerikanische architektur und stadbaukunst* (1925), pointed to Platt as the dominant figure in American domestic architecture.[59] And among the French, Jacques Gréber presented Platt as a leading domestic designer in his *L'Architecture aux Etats-Unis* (1920) and included the Platt monograph as one of only five books discussing "la periode contemporaine."[60]

The influence of Platt on contemporary practice in the United States clearly shows the power of the monograph and earlier publications of the architect's work. In Chicago, David Adler and Howard van Doren Shaw, the city's leading country-house architects, both demonstrated their admiration for Platt's work in their designs.[61] The example of Platt's house for the McCormicks at Lake Forest and of other published works led to Adler's Italian-villa-like projects from 1915 through 1931, both on the North Shore of Chicago and as far away as Fort Worth, Santa Barbara, and Honolulu, and to Shaw's Lake Forest commissions for Clayton Mark (1912), Edward L. Ryerson (1906 and 1912), and Donald R. McLenan (1914). In Detroit, Albert Kahn, who had executed the plans for the Yondotega Club Garden drawn by Platt in 1902, remained devoted to Platt to the extent of recommending him to the Russell Algers as architect for their Grosse Pointe house.[62] In Atlanta, one of the most ardent of Platt admirers was the popular Neel Reid who revealed his interest in the New Yorker's designs in several of his country

79. Entrance courtyard, Eugene and Agnes Meyer house,
Seven Springs Farm, Mount Kisco, New York, 1915–17.

or suburban house projects, including his own residence which he modeled closely after the Culver house of 1904 at Hadlyme, Connecticut.[63] These are only a few of the architects whose work Platt clearly affected. When the monograph appeared, Platt was fifty-two, at the height of his reputation, having achieved national prominence in yet another medium within a dozen years of his start as a professional architect.

Ironically, 1913 was also a year in which the conditions favorable to country-house architecture began to change. The enactment of the graduated income tax in that year placed the first restraints on previously uncontrolled American private wealth. Naturally, this law discouraged the costly construction, maintenance, and use of country houses. America's entry into the First World War and the decline of immigration in the 1920s, which had provided a ready servant class for country houses, further diminished the ability of many to perpetuate this life style.[64] Platt's success thus far had been based upon his country house and garden designs, but this aspect of his career began to decline in importance after the publication of the monograph and was replaced by other types of commissions in the years after the First World War.

To be sure, he continued to design country houses throughout his life. His projects of the later 1910s and 1920s were fewer in number and generally smaller in size. Yet the Westchester County estates of Eugene Meyer (1916–19) and William F. Fahnestock (1909–24) rivaled the scale of commissions from the first decade. The Meyer house, Seven Springs Farm, at Mount Kisco, was designed for Eugene Meyer, Wall

80. View from entrance hall to drawing room, Seven Springs Farm.

Street financier and later owner of the *Washington Post,* and for Agnes Meyer, a collector of Oriental art (Fig. 79). Platt was recommended to the Meyers by Charles L. Freer, for whom he was then designing the Freer Gallery of Art in Washington, D.C. Freer advised the Meyers, "if your taste in architecture runs in the direction of air, light, uncluttered space, simplicity and harmony of line . . . you couldn't do better in your choice of architect."[65] An indoor swimming pool and bowling alley suggest the size of the monumental house, yet the interiors were among the most restrained Platt ever designed (Fig. 80).

The clients' enthusiasm for the project was expressed well in a letter from Eugene Meyer to Charles Freer in September 1918:

It is modern, it is beautiful, and it is original in that it is not a copy of any style or structure. In as much as you had a very important part in it, I am sure you will get satisfaction as well as pleasure from seeing it.[66]

Platt would have liked this reaction. Although he always admitted the importance of precedents, he certainly did not think of himself as a revivalist architect. Agnes and Eugene Meyer were fully aware of revolutionary trends in European art, so that his use of the term *modern* here is somewhat self-conscious. Indeed, Agnes Meyer was currently writing for *291,* the avant-garde journal of art criticism, and the photographer Alfred Stieglitz was a close friend and frequent house guest (a series of his photographic murals was intended for Seven Springs Farm). The cool simplicity of the interiors of the Meyer house and the vaguely French character of the exterior make this commission one of the least style-conscious of Platt's designs. Although the Meyer house was not modern as that term came to be understood in the 1920s and 1930s, it was thoroughly an expression of its time, of Platt's philosophy of design, and of the ambitions of the clients.

If the Meyers were seeking a residence that reflected the "modern" spirit, William F. Fahnestock had commissioned a country seat that approached in extent its English and European precedents by including a full working farm and facilities for weekend shooting parties.[67] Although it has been demolished, the two other houses Platt designed for Fahnestock still exist: the interior remodeling (1922–24) of his New York town house, the north wing of the Villard houses at 457 Madison Avenue, and Bois Doré (1926–28), his summer house in Newport. Many of Platt's clients shuttled between town and country, but few of them enjoyed the additional luxury of a resort house, and no other patron commissioned Platt to design or alter all three. But the country place was the most interesting of his Fahnestock projects.

81. Entrance facade, William F. Fahnestock house, Girdle Ridge,
Katonah, New York, 1909–24.

82. Entrance porch,
Girdle Ridge.

83. Garden facade, Meredith Hare house, Pidgeon Hill,
Huntington, Long Island, New York, 1916–17.

84. Entrance porch,
Pidgeon Hill.

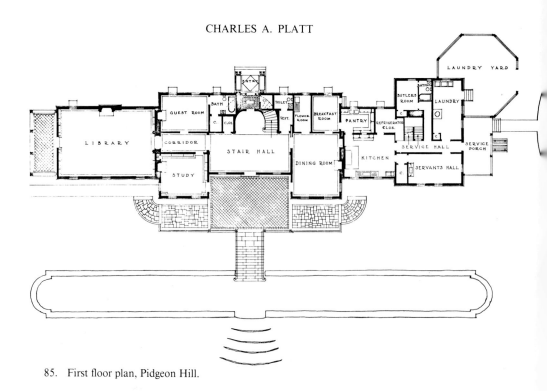

85. First floor plan, Pidgeon Hill.

Platt's skill in matching the character of a house to the requirements of a client are fully demonstrated by comparing Girdle Ridge, the
Fahnestock country house (Figs. 81, 82) with the roughly contemporary
project, Pidgeon Hill (1916–17), the residence of Meredith Hare (Figs.
83, 84) at Huntington, New York.[68] The Fahnestock and Hare houses
were somewhat similar in plan with columned entrance porches opening into central halls connecting to inset rear loggias (Fig. 85). The
differences in scale, materials, and image are more significant. The
Fahnestock house was stuccoed, three stories, and block-like in a manner similar to the Nichols house at Katonah. The Hare house was more
horizontal in its massing and covered with large, white-painted shingles,
typical of colonial Long Island. At Girdle Ridge, Platt projected the
image of the wealthy and aspiring New York gentleman in the crisp
geometry of the imposing mansion and manicured grounds. At Pidgeon
Hill, he suggested the more relaxed ambiance of the sports enthusiast
and outdoorsman in the regional vernacular forms of Long Island architecture and the more naturalized garden. Similarly, the entrance porches
of the two houses announce different intentions for life in the country
(see Figs. 82, 84).

Even after Platt's practice had clearly shifted to institutional,
commercial, and urban residential work, he continued to receive com-

missions for country houses. Indeed, one of his last major designs was a Dedham, Massachusetts, house for Mrs. H. Wendell Endicott, a daughter of Francis T. Maxwell, who was determined to have a Platt house of her own. But why did he have such unparalleled success as the architect of country places? His sensitivity to landscape, developed first as a painter, meant that Platt more than any of his contemporaries had a vision for each site and an ability to merge each building and its environment. Like many of the best architects of his generation, he believed in the careful study of past form but restricted himself to what he considered the most appropriate models for this building type, villas influenced by the Renaissance. Within this restricted vocabulary he achieved endless variety in the scores of country houses he built from coast to coast. The design principles he adopted in his earliest houses remained the basis for four decades of domestic commissions. Although he adhered to classical sources, he adapted these forms to the conditions of the early twentieth century and created designs of distinct character, elegance, and restraint. Each Platt house has a sense of self-confidence, an assurance of security, and a clarity of purpose. Of all his work as an architect, Platt was admired most by his generation, and should be remembered first by posterity for his country houses and their gardens.

5

City Buildings

URBAN COMMISSIONS comprised less than twenty percent of Platt's work, but they were a consistent and lucrative component of his career. They included private residences, apartment buildings and hotels, office and commercial structures, and public buildings and monuments. The vast majority of this work was done in New York City. And half of all his city jobs were commissioned by the Vincent Astor Estate Office, for which Platt worked from 1906 until 1932. These commissions included new construction, remodeling structures for new uses, and minor alterations. Although Platt designed many urban buildings of true distinction, his city work exerted a smaller influence on his contemporaries and often represented more routine design solutions than his country-house commissions. Just as he had derived his philosophy of domestic architecture from a study of the Renaissance villa, Platt based his city buildings — both residential and commercial — on the Italian palazzo, a model that was only partially adaptable to the multiple demands of his urban commissions. The palazzo model certainly inspired many of Platt's New York colleagues, but none adhered to this ideal with such loyalty as his.

His earliest city clients probably chose Platt because of his rising reputation as a landscape and country-house architect. In fact, his first job in town was a project intended to bring the fresh air and recreation of the country to city dwellers. Charles G. Schwab, steel millionaire, commissioned Platt in 1902 to design bathing and dining pavilions (Fig. 86), superintendent's and gardener's cottages, and lavatories for Richmond Beach Park, a large-scale public bathing-beach development on Staten Island.[1] Here Platt's Doric-columned, wood-and-stucco pavilions provided a familiar classical revival setting for the New Yorker's day at the

86. Dining pavilion, Richmond Beach Park, Huguenot,
Staten Island, New York, 1902.

shore. His designs reflected both the formality of his garden schemes and
the informality of his summer houses in New Hampshire.

Aside from this unique assignment, Platt's other early city
projects were town houses in Manhattan. In half of the cases, Platt either
had designed or would later design a country or resort house for these
urban clients.[2] Single-family dwellings were becoming comparatively
rare in Manhattan when Platt received his first commissions for that
building type. In the year 1890, 835 private residences were constructed
on the island at an average cost of $15,000. But by 1902, the number
reportedly had been reduced to 102 per year at an average price of
$64,000.[3] Not surprisingly, therefore, the number and scale of one-fam-
ily houses that Platt built in New York decreased with each decade.

Platt's first town house, located at 125 East 65th Street, was
commissioned by Frederick S. Lee in 1904. Both the situation and
Platt's solution made this house remarkable. Dr. Lee purchased two
brownstone residences at numbers 125 and 127 which he demolished for
the new house. Having the advantage of two lots, Platt devised a wider
and shallower building with fewer stories than the characteristic town
house. A contemporary single-lot residence in this neighborhood was
usually six stories high and 85 to 90 feet deep.[4] The Lee house was only
four levels plus a basement. It was 68 feet deep, thus allowing for a

131

garden at the rear of the property, a luxury and a relative novelty in New York town houses. In addition, he chose a dumbbell-shaped plan with a corridor and stairwells between the front and rear rooms flanked by lightwells, but he covered these air spaces with skylights to permit vertical and side lighting within the body of the building.

The facade of the Lee house projected considerably from the adjacent brownstones, because Platt used only three exterior steps and designed a vestibule of seven additional steps within the mass of the house (Fig. 87). This forward placement also suggested to Platt the traditional "English basement" formula, with a high wrought-iron fence

87. Entrance facade,
Frederick S. Lee house,
New York, New York, 1904.

132

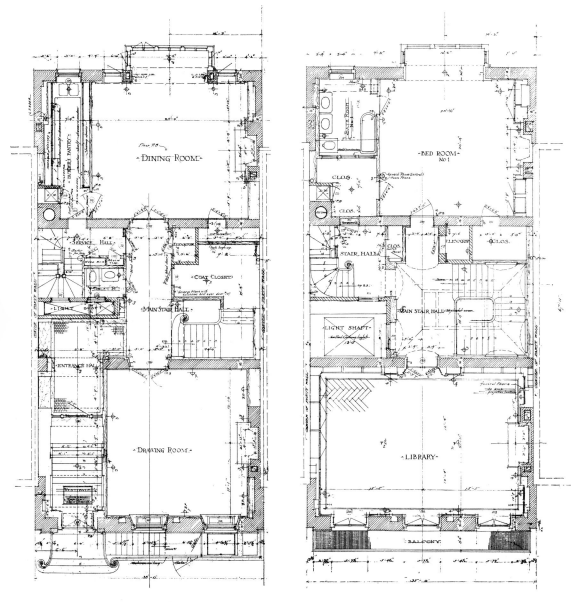

88. First and second floor plans, Lee house.

across the front of the property and a gate at the right opening onto a service stair to the basement. The slight asymmetry of the left bay entrance was overshadowed by the three large windows of the second level which centralized the overall elevation. The facade of dark red brick trimmed with limestone revealed clearly the hierarchy and function of interior spaces. Recessing every seventh row of bricks to resemble a rusticated first floor, Platt emphasized the importance of the second floor front library, the largest room in the house, by French doors opening onto a wrought-iron balcony.[5] The third level of bedrooms and the fourth floor of servants' rooms and a chemical laboratory for Dr. Lee were progressively decreased in height and embellishment.

133

The plan of the Lee house was unusual and innovative (Fig. 88).[6] On a cross axis, the entrance hall connected to the white-painted wood stairhall, served by an interior skylight. Platt's placement of the drawing room and dining room on the first level avoided the inconvenience of guests having to climb to a second level reception room both before and after dinner. Here the second floor library served as both an after-dinner withdrawing room and a more private living room for the family. Platt's ability to incorporate in his designs the social and personal customs of his clients was demonstrated in many of his residences, though it was especially apparent in the Lee house.

The most distinguished rooms in the Lee house were the library and dining room (Fig. 89). Both were paneled in dark wood and dually focused on a fireplace and a wall of large windows. The rectangular paneling was scaled to match the panes of glass in the windows so that a unified gridwork controlled the rooms. In the library, a beamed ceiling further reinforced this geometric organization. The glazed bookcases that covered two-thirds the height of all walls in the library also reflected the grid system. Nevertheless, it was not a heavy-handed or obvious solution. The simplicity of this scheme was well suited to the small proportions of a city residence.

He completed this architectonic approach in the choice and placement of furniture and decoration. The large baluster-legged table set in the center of the room, the armchairs balanced on either side of the fireplace, and the bust and candlesticks silhouetted against the wall above the mantel all perpetuated the gridwork scheme. Platt did not eschew pattern and color in his interiors, but he was careful to ensure that the decoration never overpowered the architecture itself. In comparison with many architect-designed interiors of the early twentieth century, the Lee house, and Platt's work in general, showed restraint in the choice and quantity of furnishings.

Platt solved the problems of a double town house in the building he constructed at 47–49 East 65th Street in 1907. The client was Mrs. James Roosevelt who lived in one half of the double residence and gave the other half to her son and daughter-in-law, Franklin and Eleanor Roosevelt. Whether Platt received this prestigious commission for any reason other than his growing reputation is not known. When completed in October 1908, the project had a total cost of $132,000, showing the expense of construction in Manhattan had continued to climb even when one remembers that two houses were built on this site.[7] As in the Lee project, Platt had two former brownstone house lots to work with, but the needs of the clients were radically different.

89. Library, Lee house.

Platt designed for the Roosevelts what appeared to be a single town house, five stories of brick and limestone over a high basement (Fig. 90). On the interior, the dwelling was divided vertically into two equal halves, but this was in no way indicated on the exterior. Platt repeated the vestibule device he had used at the Lee house, but here he placed the vestibule in the center and located doors to the right and left leading to the residences of Sara Roosevelt and of her children. As before, he emphasized the importance of the second story with a functional, wrought-iron balcony, limestone surrounds for the full-length windows, and a wide bandcourse above. The clients' model for this double town house was the Ludlow-Parish houses at numbers 6 and 8 East 76th Street, where in 1905, Eleanor had been given in marriage to her cousin Franklin by her uncle, President Theodore Roosevelt.[8]

135

90.   Entrance facade, Sara Roosevelt houses, New York, New York, 1907.

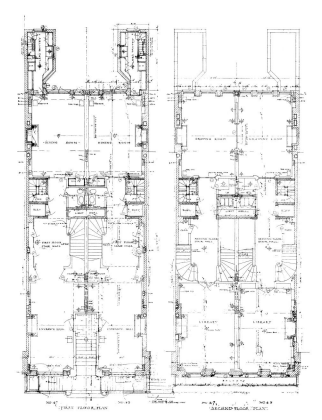

91. First and second floor
plans, Roosevelt houses.

The Roosevelt house floor plans represented a pairing of Platt's Lee town house plan with some unique variations (Fig. 91). Like most contemporary New York town-house plans, all of Platt's layouts for city dwellings could be divided into three equal sections: a front third for the most important and public spaces; a center section for stairwells, light or air shafts, and service or mechanical facilities; and a rear third for another major room. The Roosevelts' houses had a very open first floor arrangement. The entrance hall flowed into the stairhall where an open string staircase climbed the inside wall and a narrow passage, flanked by a service stairs, an elevator, and a lavatory, provided access to the dining room at the rear of the first floor.[9]

The second floor of each of the Roosevelts' houses had libraries in the front and drawing rooms at the rear. The roofs of the butlers' pantries at the back of the lot served as terraces from the drawing rooms. Sliding doors between the two drawing rooms and dining rooms permitted them to be combined for large-scale entertaining, a situation with which

137

Eleanor, like many new daughters-in-law, was not completely happy. The library in the house of Franklin and Eleanor was lined with shelves and cabinets for books and, consequently, required a mantel of heavier proportions than the one in Sara Roosevelt's library, which had no bookshelves. Otherwise, the two houses were treated identically in terms of interior architecture. Above the second floor, the staircases were transferred to the outside walls. A large central light well, shared by both houses, provided natural side illumination for the corridors of the upper floors. All bedrooms had an exterior window.

In addition to private commissions like the Lee and Roosevelt houses, Platt also altered town houses for rental purposes. The Vincent Astor Estate Office, for which Platt later did many large-scale city projects, commissioned him to remodel two brownstone residences at

92. Entrance facade, town house renovation for the Astor Estate Office, New York, New York, 1906.

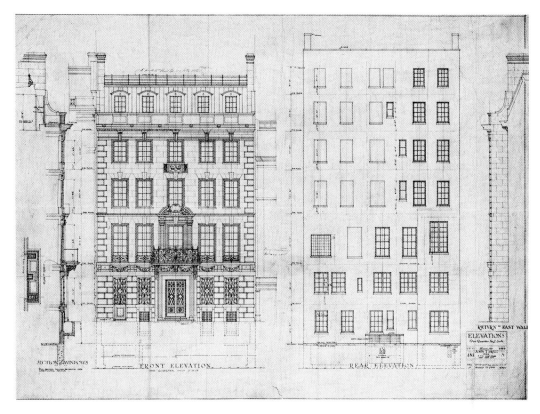

93.   Front and rear elevations, John T. Pratt house, New York, New York, 1915.

844 Fifth Avenue (1906) and at 7 East 65th Street (1911).[10] The client required additional space but wished, for financial reasons, to maintain the floor levels of the existing buildings. Platt solved the problems by bringing new facades forward, as he did in the Lee and Roosevelt houses, and by placing the entrance at the basement level, three steps down from the sidewalk (Fig. 92). He adapted the gridwork scheme of the Lee library for the facades of these town houses, using rusticated limestone and window muntins to create a uniform exterior pattern. Despite the speculative nature of these buildings, both Platt and the Astor Estate Office wanted first-class rental properties.

The largest New York town house Platt ever designed was a 1915 project located at 7 East 61st Street (Fig. 93). The client was John T. Pratt for whom Platt had built The Manor House at Glen Cove in 1909.[11] On a 46-foot-wide lot, Platt erected a five-bay, five-story dwelling with an ornately carved limestone facade. The fifth floor, reserved for servants' bedrooms, was set back 10 feet, concealing it from street-level view. The five bays of the second floor front lit an impressive library, while the same space at the back was divided between a dining room at the center and a serving pantry and breakfast room to either side. The number and variety of rooms in the Pratt house brought construction costs to almost $200,000. Despite the increased scale of this commission, Platt basically followed the formula he had established in earlier and smaller projects.

He continued to use this scheme of spatial organization in two New York town houses he designed in the 1920s.[12] Elements of the Lee and Pratt houses, for example, are evident in the 1925 town house for Henry S. Morgan. This elevation clearly projects the layering of service, entertainment, family bedrooms, and staff bedrooms from bottom to top of the facade. Perhaps more than any other building type, the New York town house showed Platt's habit of working out what he considered "the right" solution in early commissions and readapting it in succeeding projects. The development pressure in Manhattan further limited his design options as the cost of land and of construction reinforced the standard New York lot size and restricted elevation design to a single facade.

Outside New York, Platt only designed two town houses in Chicago. The character of these buildings revealed circumstances vastly different from his Manhattan commissions. The Arthur Meeker house, built in 1913 at 3030 Lake Shore Drive, was a freestanding house set on a large corner lot overlooking Lake Michigan.[13] The generous proportions and minimal decoration of its four-story brick facade were severe to the point of blandness. But the fenced formal garden behind and the stable and garage to the right make the complex unique among Platt's city residences. The largest by far of any of his town houses was his 1928 proposal for the city residence (Fig. 94) of Mrs. Edith Rockefeller McCormick, builder of Villa Turicum.[14] Never constructed (although working drawings, since destroyed, were made), this immense mansion was conceived by Mrs. McCormick to serve as her town house and, after her death, to be divided into a residence for the mayors of Chicago and a municipal art museum. Unfortunately, only this one elevation drawing survives to suggest the character of Platt's scheme. If built, the house would have rivaled the scale of its Renaissance palazzo models. But the atypical nature of these Chicago commissions bore little relation to the exacting requirements of the narrow lots and building codes that Platt worked under in New York.

As the cost of private residences continued to soar in New York City, the apartment house gained in popularity and respectability.[15]

140

Multiple housing had previously meant only tenements for the lower class. By the 1880s, there was increased interest in "the apartment, or 'French flat,'" reputedly imported from Boston "where the 'craze' had originated."[16] Also introduced in the 1880s in New York was the duplex apartment, which sought through its two-level arrangement to emulate the privacy of a single-family residence and also to differentiate itself clearly from the single-level apartments of lower-income tenements.[17] The establishment of citywide electric power in 1897 stimulated the installation of passenger elevators in apartment houses and abolished the generally observed height limitation of five stories.[18] Many buildings were syndicated or cooperative apartments where most residents purchased a share in the building.[19] By 1903, the *Architectural Record* could report that, "New York, or rather the Borough of Manhattan, is becoming more and more a city of tenements and apartment houses."[20]

94. Elevations, Edith Rockefeller McCormick town house project,
Chicago, Illinois, 1928.

95.   Street facades, Studio Building, New York, New York, 1905–6.

One of the interesting duplex apartment-house variants was the "studio building," designed for (and often by) artists to combine working and living accommodations. In 1905, Platt's first multiple-dwelling project was the Studio Building at 131–135 East 66th Street, a cooperative building of duplex apartments and a commission from an earlier country house client and real-estate developer, Frederick C. Culver.[21]

142

Since so much of apartment or tenement construction was solely the work of developers, architect-designed studio cooperatives were looked to as models of what well-conceived apartments could be. *Architectural Record,* in praising the quality of most studio buildings, observed that artists "naturally object to the impropriety and vulgarity of marble halls and the other stock-in-trade of the speculative builder," preferring "to keep the entrance of the building and its public spaces simple, substantial and quiet in appearance, like the entrance of the average apartment house in Paris."[22] The artists may have pioneered in commissioning cooperative, architect-designed apartment buildings, but other professionals and economic groups quickly followed their lead. By the time Platt designed his 66th Street building, there were several other studio apartment houses from which he could draw ideas, but his Studio Building was far more elegant in overall design and interior finish than any other New York example of this type and period.[23]

Platt's Studio Building was located at the northeast corner of Lexington Avenue and 66th Street on a lot that ran 100 feet on the avenue and 160 feet on the street (Fig. 95). The property was divided into two 100 by 80-foot halves with two entrances on 66th Street. The section at the corner was an L-shaped plan, while the eastern half was an inverted T, thus together creating two northern light courts (Fig. 96). Almost all apartments were duplex units with two floors of rooms equal to the 18-foot height of the studio space.[24] The T-shaped section was modeled on the plan of an earlier studio building on West 67th Street, with four north-lighted apartments per duplex floor.[25] In the L-shaped section, Platt was able to provide a proper northern studio light in one of the three apartments on each duplex level. However, there was a wide variety in size and number of rooms for all these apartments. Each studio was a full two stories, with a balcony view from the second-level hallway. With the exception of the bachelor apartments, each unit was a duplex with the public rooms on the first level and the sleeping rooms above. Two elevators and stairwells were positioned to serve three or four apartments on every second level.

If Platt relied partially upon earlier floor plans, he improved upon his precedents in other aspects of the building. Rather than the accepted developer's brick, Platt chose limestone as the building material and looked to the urban palaces of the Renaissance as his models. The overall massing was that of a rectangular block strictly contained by a deep projecting cornice. Platt stressed careful proportions, the solidity of the material, and the distribution of openings; the details that he featured were handled boldly but sparingly. Reiterated horizontal divisions, such as the rustication of the first three stories and the bandcourses above the third, fourth, sixth, and tenth levels, divided the wall into rectangular fields that belied the height of the building. Platt did not attempt a tripartite organization of his tall-building facades into a base, shaft, and capital format to resemble a classical column.[26] Rather, he used repeated devices to limit the height of the building and to relate it to the scale of the street. The articulation of the wall was reduced as it proceeded up the facade. Platt emphasized the scale of this building in

96. Typical floor plans, Studio Building.

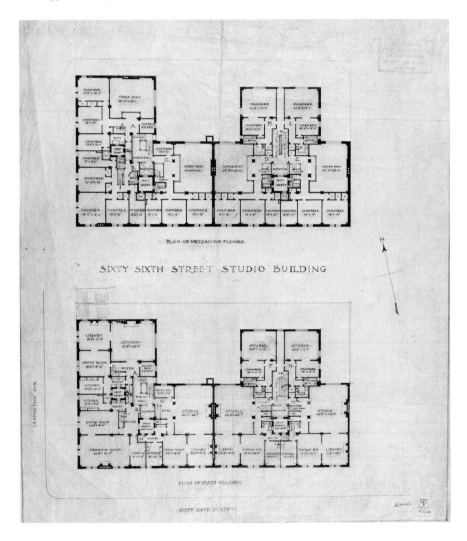

the three-story-tall columns and broken pediments of the entrances which served as a visual bridge between human proportions and the size of the entire building. The New York Tenement Law of 1901 limited the height of the building to only one and a half times the width of the street.[27] For legal purposes, therefore, the building fronted on the avenue, although the entrances were on 66th Street. Within these height restrictions, it was to the advantage of the developer and the cooperative owners for Platt to include as many floors as possible. He felt that the palazzo format best met both the financial and functional requirements and the aesthetic demands of city architecture.

Platt continued the restrained propriety of the exterior in the interior public spaces. The lobbies and lower halls were finished in plaster, scored and painted to resemble Caen stone like the Parisian apartment buildings he had known as a student. Since he was a personal friend of the developer and of many of the artist-tenants, Platt was commissioned to design interiors for several of the apartments.[28] The monumental simplicity of Platt's interiors was best shown in his own library-studio (Fig. 97). Here he emphasized the vertical space with high paneling around the base of the room and tapestries hung on the walls above, an oversized Renaissance mantel, and a brightly painted beamed ceiling that pulled the eye up to the full height of the room. The lavish treatment of Platt's and other studio spaces in the building shows that they were used more as ample drawing rooms than as painting studios.

Through the design of the Studio Building, Platt established a reputation as an innovative and accomplished architect of apartment buildings as well as of private residences. This reputation led to an invitation in 1906 from the Vincent Astor Estate Office to design the first of twenty-four residential and commercial projects. Platt received these commissions most likely through Nicholas Biddle, manager of the Astor Trust and brother of Ellen Biddle Shipman, Charles's friend and garden collaborator.[29] However the relationship began, Platt served for a quarter of a century as the architect for the estate office and frequently for the family too. This work provided a very healthy financial base for the operation of the Platt firm.

Increased activity for the estate office came after 1912, when Vincent Astor succeeded to the family fortune upon the death of his father in the sinking of the *Titanic*.[30] The Astors had made their money initially in fur trading and had augmented it in New York City real estate. Unlike his forebears, who had rented their property on long-term leases and remained indifferent toward conditions in the resultant slums, Vincent Astor sold his low-rent tenement holdings and invested

145

97.   Fireplace wall of library, Charles A. Platt apartment, Studio Building.

in construction of well-maintained commercial and middle- or upper-income residential structures.[31] Platt was the Astor executant in reshaping this real-estate empire. For example, at the request of the Astor Estate, Platt converted hotels to office buildings, including the Astor House Hotel in 1915 (at Broadway and Vesey Street), and, with Prohibi-

146

tion cutting further into hotel profits, the Knickerbocker in 1920.[32] At the same time, Vincent Astor tried to change the family image through Platt's designs for luxury apartment buildings. And for the Astor family, the range of Platt's commissions extended from laying out the gardens at Ferncliff (1916), the family estate in Rhinebeck, New York, to designing the interiors of the *Nourmahal* (1927), Vincent Astor's motor yacht.

Representative of the client's new real-estate investments was the construction in 1914–15 of the Astor Court Apartments on Broadway between 89th and 90th streets. The courtyard form of apartment building, of which Astor Court is a supreme example, was introduced to New York City as early as 1882 in the Dakota, Henry J. Hardenbergh's masterpiece on Central Park West.[33] Platt's building was located near two larger courtyard apartment houses — the Apthorp, designed in 1908 by Clinton & Russell for the competitive English branch of the Astor family, and the comparable Belnord, also designed in 1908 by H. Hobart Weekes.[34] All these buildings relied upon palatial scale and an ample central court for light and air. The architects of the Belnord and the Apthorp used their courtyards as *cours d'honneur,* providing a carriage entrance and limited landscape treatment. Platt devoted his courtyard solely to the garden. Both the estate office and Platt strove to produce a model apartment design that would provide "all the features of planning and convenience that are to be found in the isolated houses."[35] Platt's background as a country-house and town-house architect equipped him well to fulfill these demands. Intended for conventional upper-middle-income tenants, Astor Court presented a more comprehensive and complex program than Platt's earlier Studio Building.

Astor Court's plan comprised roughly half of a city block with more than a third of the lot devoted to the interior garden court (Fig. 98). It was a detached, U-shaped structure with its base along Broadway and its entrances at the midpoints of the side-street facades. A common sightline connected the two entrances with a fountain in the center of the lower section of the garden. The ground floor area along Broadway was assigned to small shops, both serving the needs of the tenants and capitalizing upon the business of the avenue. Platt necessarily segregated the commercial activity on Broadway from the residential entrances on the side streets in order to ensure the proper domestic character for the apartment dwellers.

In elevation, Astor Court more closely resembled the Studio Building (Fig. 99). Built of dark red brick over a two-story rusticated limestone base, it presented a cube-like appearance, appropriate for a structure covering half a city block. Platt treated the twelve-story eleva-

147

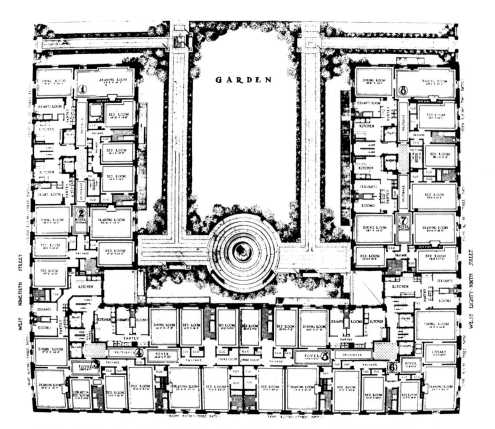

98. Typical floor plan, Astor Court Apartments, New York, New York, 1914–15.

tions as vast planes defined by the vertical lines of paired window bays and anchored by the horizontal stripes of a rusticated base, limestone bandcourses, and the deep shadow of the cornice, now constructed of wood and painted in bright colors. To suggest the domestic nature of the building, he dotted the facades with symmetrically placed balconies and heraldic emblems.[36]

A typical floor of the building contained eight apartments. There were four elevators and stairwell spines, each serving two living units per floor. All apartments included two or three bedrooms and one or two servants' rooms. Each had a dining room and drawing room, and the corner apartments on Broadway also included a library. A penthouse, the thirteenth story, contained thirty-two laundry cubicles, a few storage rooms, and dormitories for additional servants. As always, light and air were given careful attention. All rooms had windows to the exterior. Platt cut light courts into the interior angles of the U to create additional natural illumination at the building's widest points. The amenity of an interior landscaped courtyard indicated the architect's and the developer's commitment to the quality of life in this building. Astor Court represented the standard of upper-middle-income elegance and comfort that Platt sought to achieve uniformly for the Astor Trust.

In a more expansive manner, Platt and the Astor Estate Office created a costly residential neighborhood on East 86th Street and East End Avenue. Because of the developmental advantages of the extra-wide street, Vincent Astor began in 1929 to buy land in this formerly unfashionable area.[37] Between that year and his death, Platt designed three apartment structures and remodeled two town houses that gave new

99. Broadway facade, Astor Court Apartments.

prestige to these blocks near Carl Schurz Park.[38] The keystone of this development was a pair of nearly identical apartment buildings at 520 and 528–540 (later 530) East 86th Street, built in 1927–28. Freestanding structures on a U-shaped plan, both were reduced versions of Astor Court. Representative of a new level of luxury, there were only three carefully laid-out apartments per floor and only two on the penthouse level. Both were fifteen-story buildings, faced in limestone for the first

100.   Street facades, Astor Apartments, 120 East End Avenue, New York, New York, 1930–31.

150

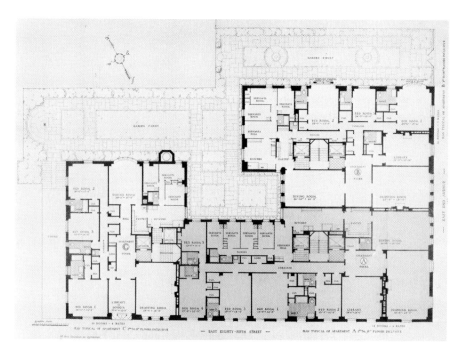

101. Typical floor plan, 120 East End Avenue.

two levels and in brick with stone trim above and planned around an interior garden court. Due to the regularity of the fenestration, the design of these buildings was indifferent. Only finely detailed entrance doors differentiated one unit from the other.

Within the same block, Platt created his last and most deluxe apartment building in 1930–31 at 120 East End Avenue, on the northwest corner of East 85th Street (Fig. 100). The eighteen-story building was faced in limestone, rusticated on the first two levels, and had inset loggias and bowed windows overlooking an interior court. This was the finest of all the Astor apartment buildings and was very carefully studied in plan and elevation. The plan contained three large apartments per floor (Fig. 101). The relationship of rooms was as thoughtfully arranged as those in Platt's country houses. The ceilings were 10 feet high, and there were many long windows to the floor with wrought-iron railings. Mandated by the New York Zoning Law of 1916, setbacks for the three upper stories eliminated the characteristic deep cornice and produced a design of great strength and elegance.[39] As a group, these Astor buildings established the Schurz Park and Gracie Mansion neighborhood as an exclusive residential district.

151

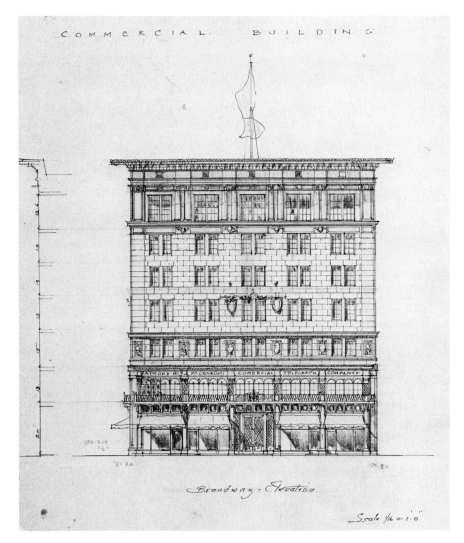

102.   Broadway elevation, commercial building study, New York, New York, n.d.
Drawing by G. T. Goulstone.

Most of the commercial buildings Platt designed were commissions for the Astor Estate Office as well. Characteristic of these projects was the undated, hypothetical design for a Commerical Building drawn for Platt by G. T. Goulstone (Fig. 102). The city palaces of the Renaissance were the obvious inspiration for Platt's commercial, as well as his apartment, buildings. And throughout his tall-building designs, he denied verticality through frequent horizontal divisions and emphasis on

152

wall surface. In Goulstone's drawing, the first two stories were extensively glazed to tie this area to the street, the repetition of multiple office floors was obscured by rustication, bandcourses, and carved panels, and the top was contained by a deep cornice, in the shadow of which he set large-mullioned glass walls framed by paired, applied columns. This element was loosely derived from the Palazzo Davanzati in Florence, to which an entire photograph album in Platt's office library was devoted and on which McKim, Mead & White had previously based both a commercial building and a branch of the New York Public Library.[40] Platt also used this device in 1911 for an Astor commercial building at 28–30 West 33rd Street, part of an Astor grouping of commercial real estate somewhat similar to the concentration of residential property on East 86th Street.[41] The Davanzati model allowed Platt to open up walls at the top of the building as well as in the display windows on the first floor.

Goulstone's proposed Commercial Building design was translated most closely into the Longacre Building (Fig. 103), an Astor Estate

103. Steet facade, Longacre Building, New York, New York, 1910.

153

Office project that Platt designed in 1910 for a site on the west side of Times Square between 43rd and 44th streets, subsequently the site of the Paramount Building. Lacking the Davanzati top, the Longacre Building did preseve the bottom floors of open fenestration, paired window bays, emphasis on wall articulation, and elaborate cornice that were the hallmarks of Platt's commercial schemes. As Royal Cortissoz commented, the Longacre Building was atypical for its neighborhood:

The obvious, easy expedient for an architect confronted by the task here involved was to frame a bold rococo design, robust enough to hold its own against the blare of Broadway in its most vicious mood. But Platt could not for the life of him have dabbled in turbid waters. He had to be himself. He had to be the man of pure taste, the man of perfect style. Hence the lonesomeness of the building in question.[42]

Cortissoz suggests here a critical problem for Platt's commercial architecture, indeed for his entire production: the unswerving adherence to an idealized model. His use of the Renaissance palazzo as the inspiration for a four-story town house, a block-long apartment building, a thirteen-story loft structure, or an office building on Times Square strained the credibility of reliance on select precedents.

Platt stated his somewhat pessimistic approach to tall building projects in one of his rare surviving comments on architecture, a 1914 lecture to architecture students at Harvard University: "Today, owing to the introduction of the skyscraper and all such innovations in architecture, the most beautiful building can be destroyed in its surroundings."[43] His lack of sympathy for the tall building as a type is not surprising considering his constant concern for the relationship of a structure to its environment. And his commitment to traditional forms of architecture denied him the expressive opportunities inherent in steel-frame construction. In the end, he probably was most in sympathy with his colleague Thomas Hastings, who concluded as early as 1894 that the artistic design of the skyscraper was impossible:

From the artistic point, it is admitted by almost everyone who has tried to solve the problem that the limitations are almost unsurmountable. The extreme height, tending to the treatment of every building as a tower, on the one hand, the exaggerated demand for light, which destroyed all possibility of wall surfaces which are requisite to the design of a beautiful tower and the impossibility, owing to fire laws and other regulations, of using even the structural features of the building to accentuate the design have resolved the problem into vain attempts resulting in absolute monotony, expressive only by its size or absolute decoration of wall surface.[44]

Like Hastings, Platt strove to contain verticality and to provide artistic interest through decoration of wall surface, as shown in three projects he undertook for the Hanna family in Cleveland, Ohio.

A fourteen-story office building was the first commission from Dan R. Hanna and one of the tallest structures Platt ever built. This 1911 project was the design of a home for the Leader-News Company (Fig. 104). The lot was 160 by 220 feet and was located on a southwest corner of Superior Avenue, a street of the surprising width of 120 feet. Because of a local ordinance, the Leader-News building could not exceed fourteen stories or 150 feet.[45] Thus, by requirement and opportunity, Platt was presented with a project that permitted him to design a structure of balanced horizontal and vertical proportions which could be seen from a sufficient distance to merit this attention.

Unlike the stressed solidity of his Studio Building and Astor Court projects, the Leader-News Building boasted a limestone skin suspended from a metal frame. Herbert Croly, reviewing the design for the *Architectural Record,* noted that the facades did not appear "fallaciously deep, strong and solid," but attempted "to be a real screen . . . built to enclose and define one side of a street."[46] Platt returned again to the rusticated limestone elevations of his earlier Astor residence. He arranged pairs of vertical bays of one-over-one sash. Although the size of the panes did not exactly match the scale of the blocks, Platt did create a mesh of small-scaled rectangles. Heavy bandcourses at the fourth, fifth, and twelfth stories wrapped the building like ribbons on a package, and the characteristic deep cornice — modeled on that of the Strozzi Palace in Florence — firmly capped the box (Fig. 105). In addition to the rustication, Platt placed heraldic devices at the even story levels to emphasize further the surface, nonstructural aspect of the wall. Finally, he revealed that the facade was a non-self-supporting screen by using slender, pressed metal colonettes to divide the ground floor display windows and to support visually the thirteen stories of stone above.

The street screen effect was continued in the plan as well. Platt chose an E-shaped plan with the E facing the adjacent building to the west on Superior Avenue, a common plan-type for tall buildings at that time. He thereby achieved both the continuity of street elevations and the necessity of interior courtyards for natural lighting. The elevator core was located near the 6th Street entrance or at the base of the center bar of the E. Thus, a building that appeared externally as a cube actually enjoyed successful cross ventilation and natural illumination.

Eight years after the Leader-News was completed, Dan R. Hanna commissioned two similar buildings in Cleveland to be named in honor

155

104.   Superior Avenue facade, Leader-News Building, Cleveland,
Ohio, 1911.

of his father, Senator Mark A. Hanna (Fig. 106). Superficially, the new
projects resembled the earlier one. Actually, the Hanna Building was
constructed in two sections. One at the corner of Euclid Avenue and East

14th Street was a full fifteen stories; a second, called the Hanna Building Annex, was attached by a second-story bridge and was located at the corner of East 14th Street and Prospect Avenue. The Annex was built to a height of eight stories but constructed so that later it could be increased to match the size of the adjacent building. Both structures were essentially two rooms deep with a central corridor paralleling the streets. Fourteenth Street diagonally intersected the avenues, producing an acute angle at Euclid Avenue and an obtuse angle at Prospect. Platt softened these forms by truncating the corners. The first floor areas of the interiors were occupied by a restaurant in the Hanna Building and by the Hanna Theater in the Annex, both spaces decorated in the style of Pompeiian murals. The Hanna Theater, like the Coolidge Auditorium that Platt built within a courtyard of the Library of Congress in 1925, was praised for its acoustical quality. Although Platt reused the totally rusticated facades of the Leader-News Building for the Hanna Building and Annex, he gave the wall greater emphasis and suggested a masonry-bearing function. The ground floor shopfronts were surmounted by splayed stone lintels, and the flat stone balcony above the second level

105. Cornice detail, Leader-News Building. Rendering by Schell Lewis.

157

106.   Street facades, Hanna Building and Hanna Building Annex,
Cleveland, Ohio, 1919.

increased the sense of weight. Both signaled a retreat from the architecture of screen to the architecture of supporting wall. This reversal was an
indication of a more conservative design approach in which the stress

was placed on masonry image rather than structural expression. Since Platt's interest throughout was the creation of traditional beauty, the expression of metal construction was of secondary importance.

Like his villa-derived country houses, the palazzo-inspired city buildings showed again the vitality that Platt could evoke from traditional forms, while at the same time demonstrating the limitations that a design philosophy dependent upon historical forms imposed on modern building types. Platt's ideal image of the Italian Renaissance urban palace reinforced his desire to control verticality and to design buildings effectively related to the human proportions of the street. Platt easily adapted this model for town houses and smaller commercial structures. In large-scale apartment buildings, such as the Studio Building and Astor Court Apartments, he managed to use elements from the palazzo to give these structures great dignity and domestic scale. The heavy cornice capping a masonry block was the general image that Platt conceived for his city commissions. Only under the constraints imposed by New York's Zoning Law of 1916 and in response to increasing height demands did Platt desert this formula in the large apartment buildings of the late 1920s and early 1930s. If he had ever received a commission for a truly ambitious skyscraper, he would obviously have had to abandon his prejudices against exaggerated verticality. But within the palazzo format, especially in his town houses and early apartment buildings, he created a restrained elegance in elevation, a sensitivity to place and scale, an attention to light and air within the mass of the structure, and an innovative and economical handling of plan.

6

Museums and Schools

AMERICA'S ENTRY into the First World War produced a brief hiatus in Platt's practice and marked a radical change in the nature and number of his commissions. Platt executed nearly as many projects between 1919 and the onset of the Depression as he had during the previous three decades combined. He achieved national recognition as an architect in his designs for the Freer Gallery of Art (1913–23), and in the 1920s his commissions were almost entirely for public buildings and monuments—museums, libraries, collegiate and private secondary-school buildings, memorials, fountains, and mausoleums. The ideas he had evolved for personal, domestic designs he now modified as the basis for corporate, public projects. However, the architectural philosophy that he had developed in the 1890s had lost its critical edge by the 1920s. He asked few new questions but remained convinced by his old answers.

Emboldened by the expanding economy of the pre-1929 decade, Platt's clients turned to institutions to embody and reinforce the social and cultural American status quo which the war in Europe had begun to challenge. But his patrons also became more cautious; more designs went unexecuted, alterations and minor additions became more common, competitions became more frequent as clients sought public and professional approval for their plans, and service as a consultant architect became an ordinary aspect of his practice.[1] Platt provided his clients with traditional symbols for the Protestant, Eastern financial and cultural establishment that was fighting to maintain the control it had firmly enjoyed before the war.

Death and patriotism were the natural preoccupations for Americans in the years immediately following the First World War. Although Platt's own war experiences were brief and inconsequential—he served from October 1918 until January 1919 as the representative of the United States Food Administration in Italy before returning in frustration over lack of Italian or American support—his commissions in the 1920s showed the scars the war had left on the general population. The most obvious indications were the tombstones and monuments Platt designed.[2] He received scores of commissions for personal mausoleums and gravestones, and while serving on the Commission of Fine Arts, he supplied in 1919 the official design for the Arlington Cemetery headstones.[3] For the American Battle Monuments Commission, he was the architect in 1927–29 of an American cemetery and chapel in Suresnes, France (Fig. 107).[4] The stone chapel, fronted by a tetrastyle Doric portico and later expanded in lateral wings added by Platt's sons, overlooked neat, symmetrical rows of crosses on a gently sloping site. Independently and in conjunction with the sculptors Daniel Chester French and Herbert Adams, Platt designed war memorials and monuments to American cultural and political heroes.[5] Platt generally provided the

107. Entrance facade, chapel, American Military Cemetery, Suresnes, France, 1927. Flanking loggias, end chapels, and forecourt added by William and Geoffrey Platt, 1952.

landscape and architectural setting for sculpture, such as the symbolic soldiers of Herbert Adams's First World War memorials at Winchester (1926) and Fitchburg (1927), Massachusetts, or the bust designed by D. C. French as the centerpiece of the Washington Irving Memorial (1927) at Irvington, New York. And at his clients' requests, he frequently incorporated memorials or patriotic imagery into the design of libraries, museums, and academic buildings.

Platt had begun to formulate his conception of public architecture in a major prewar commission from a close personal friend. For the most part, he controlled his clients and considered it his duty to educate them in the art of architecture. One exception was Charles Lang Freer, his continuing and sympathetic patron, who truly understood Platt's aesthetic ideas and provided numerous opportunities for their expression. Over the years following their meeting at Cornish in the early 1890s, Freer recommended Platt to friends and committees as the designer of LaSalle Gardens South (1897–99) and the Yondotega Club Garden (1902), both in Detroit, William G. Mather's Gwinn (1907–8) in Cleveland, and the McMillan Memorial Fountain (1908–11) in Washington, D.C.[6] After a successful career as an industrialist, Freer retired from business in 1900 and devoted himself to the study and collecting of art.[7] In 1906, he bequeathed his holdings of American paintings and Oriental art to the nation and agreed to erect a building to display them on the Mall in Washington. In 1913, Freer commissioned Platt to design his museum, which was begun in 1918, stood unfinished at the client's death the following year, and opened finally in 1923 to critical acclaim.

Early in 1913, Freer called Platt to a meeting at the Plaza Hotel in New York to invite his participation in the gallery project.[8] Unlike most Platt clients, Freer had definite opinions on architecture. In fact, he presented Platt with scores of hand-drawn plans and a list of buildings he considered possible models for the museum. Freer's first proposal was a 240-foot-square building with a large interior court and 50-foot-wide lateral wings for the Chinese and Japanese collections (Fig. 108). Freer noted on the page, "Study and storage in basement/Gallery & Exhibition rooms on Second Floor."[9] Other undated Freer variants showed rectangles with strangely scaled galleries, but nearly all with an interior courtyard and attached exterior gardens. More seriously considered by Platt were several five-part plans drawn by Freer (Fig. 109). In these the Chinese and Japanese collections were housed in flanking pavilions connected by passageways to the central block, which was reserved for American paintings. Among the extant renderings from Platt's office is

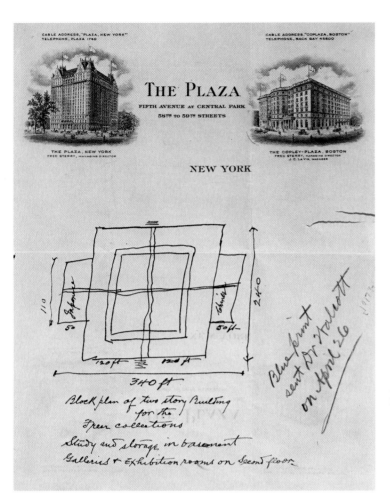

108. Charles L. Freer, 1913 proposed plan, Freer Gallery of Art, Washington, D.C., 1913–23.

109. Charles L. Freer, proposed plan, Freer Gallery, n.d.

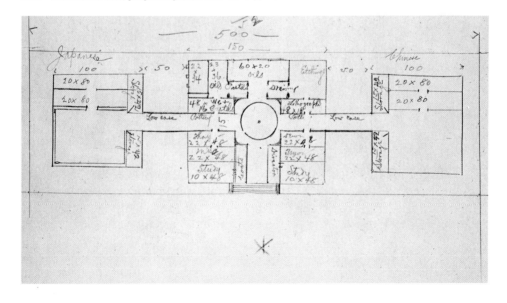

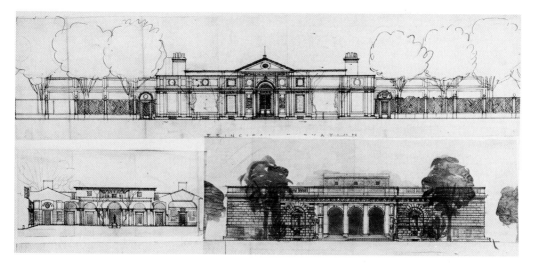

110.   Elevation and section studies, Freer Gallery, ca. 1915.
Rendering by Schell Lewis.

one that could be an elevation derived from these five-part plans (Fig. 110, top).[10] Although Platt eventually drew the exhibition spaces into a unified block, he preserved the important interior courtyard and Freer's original ideas for use of the basement and main floor.

Less useful and more surprising were Freer's suggestions for the appearance and stylistic model for the building. He considered a wide spectrum of sources but was most strongly drawn to sixteenth-century English manor houses.[11] He seemed strangely oblivious of the incongruity of these picturesque structures to the box-like simplicity of his plans.[12] Given the nature of Freer's pioneering Oriental collection, it was logical for him to consider Eastern influences as well. On one plan he scribbled, "let light in some places come from above and some low down as in Japanese houses."[13] His architect, however, firmly rejected all of Freer's elevation suggestions.

Platt realized that a classical vocabulary was essential for the building's location on the Mall. Concurrently with designing the Freer Gallery, Platt served from 1916 to 1921 on the Commission of Fine Arts, the body responsible for the development of the capital's public areas.[14] Thus, he was acutely aware of the Freer Gallery's relation to the future scheme for the Mall. The Senate Park Commission Plan of 1902 had established uniform sightlines for location of buildings along the Mall and had specified for major public buildings a monumental classicism, "the general style of architecture adopted when the Capitol and White

House were built."[15] Platt personally supported these guidelines. Freer had little choice but to accept his architect's advice.

After signing a contract for the Freer Gallery on December 30, 1913, the Platt office embarked upon one of its longest and most intensely studied commissions. Schell Lewis, Platt's renderer, recalled spending a full year personally reworking elevations for the museum, a luxury provided partially by the lucrative and repetitive nature of the Astor Estate projects at this time.[16] One of the reasons for these changes was uncertainty as to the gallery's site.[17] The exact location had to be accepted by Congress and that action was useless until Freer was ready to make a financial commitment. During most of 1914, sites on the north side of the Mall, near the Natural History Museum, were under consideration. By year's end, the size of the gallery had been reduced and its present location suggested. Because of sightlines established by the Senate Park Commission, also known as the McMillan Commission, Platt was now restricted to a building 290 by 180 feet.

A second problem was Freer's failing health and the question of his financial capabilities.[18] At the start of 1915, Freer had been ordered by his doctors to go to California for rest. Although publicly thought to be suffering from tuberculosis, Freer had congenital syphilis, which over the next four years would destroy his mind and then take his life. Concerning Freer's financial situation, in October 1915 it appeared that construction of the museum, then estimated at $1,250,000, would have to be delayed because there was no market for Freer's Parke, Davis Drug Company stock. Eugene Meyer, New York financier, knew Freer through his wife Agnes Meyer, also a collector of Oriental art, and he offered to buy this stock, which forced the Parke, Davis partners to acquire what Freer wanted to sell to avoid any "Wall Street" involvement.

In May 1916, plans for the gallery were approved by all the requisite Washington commissions, but Platt informed Dr. Charles Walcott, Smithsonian Secretary, that he was still studying the design.[19] As late as July 27, 1917, Platt made a visit to Freer's Detroit home to review the objects that would be displayed in the museum.[20] When construction finally began the following year, the building had been in the planning stages for five years. The First World War now caused shortages in men and materials that increased the cost and delayed or halted construction periodically.[21] Ten years after the architect and client began discussions, the Freer Gallery of Art was finally opened to the public.

As erected, the Freer Gallery demonstrates the successful interac-

111.   Entrance facade, Freer Gallery.

tion of architect and client. The building took the form of a one-story block on a high basement with a central colonnaded courtyard closest to the southern side of the mass (Fig. 111). Platt designed fully rusticated granite facades, capped by a balustraded parapet, except for the smooth ashlar, triple-arched porch which greeted visitors from the Mall. Elsewhere he superimposed rusticated arches on a rusticated wall with a wave-patterned bandcourse appearing between the arches at the level of the gallery floor. Below the bandcourse were windows to illuminate the basement study and storage areas. Above the bandcourse, the blank wall expressed the exhibition area behind. The allocation of functions, which Platt so effectively revealed on the exterior, followed the wishes that Freer had consistently voiced from their earliest discussions of the gallery.

If Freer influenced the basic spatial composition, Platt alone established the appearance of the building. Its conceptual sources were the city gates and palaces of the sixteenth-century Veronese architect, Michele Sanmicheli, whose work Platt had encouraged Freer to visit as early as 1894.[22] As Platt's painter friend, Kenyon Cox, wrote to his son

166

Allyn while the gallery was under construction: "[Platt] finds Sanmicheli the most inspiring of Italian architects . . . with all his taste there's a real robustness and inventiveness about Platt."[23] Sanmicheli's muscular forms were especially appropriate models for Platt in designing a small building on the Mall, since the gallery would have to compete for attention with much larger neighbors. Gone were Freer's English manor house ideas; Platt's devotion to the Italian Renaissance carried the day.

Within, the gallery continued the dialogue between Platt and Freer. Running east and west, two major cross-axis halls were connected by four smaller corridors, two within the body of the building and two under the arcades flanking the courtyard (Fig. 112). The central open space served both a visual and a functional or climatic purpose. Freer

112. First floor plan, Freer Gallery.

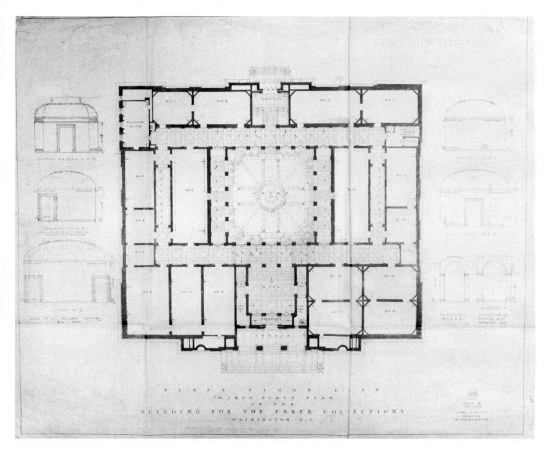

113.   Exhibition room, Freer Gallery.

conceived of the area as a quiet retreat for students to contemplate the objects they had seen. Because of the damp and humid climate of Washington, Platt considered the courtyard essential for increased air circulation for the sake of both the art and the visitors.[24]

Platt devoted the entire main floor to exhibition rooms, all lighted from above (Fig. 113). Because of his background as a painter, he was fanatical in his concern for natural illumination. He even went so far as to have a full-scale model of a typical exhibition gallery built on the roof of his office building in New York. He then borrowed some of the Freer paintings and objects that later would be exhibited so as to determine the effectiveness of his skylights.[25] The natural illumination was supplemented by artificial lighting within the skylight, and there were movable canvas louvers to control the intensity of natural light. Thus, he created a system in which the strength or type of illumination could be altered according to external conditions.

The visitor to the Freer Gallery is astounded by the unexpected world Platt and Freer created. The exterior is severely sophisticated. Unlike its more pompous marble neighbors, the Freer conveys immediate composure and invites the viewer to study the subtle but complex intertwining of facade elements — wall, arch, window, and bandcourse. On the Mall approach the arched central motive directs the visitor into the building. One is welcomed by the intricate paneled vestibule ceiling, the only concession to Freer's English manor house interest, which pulls the visitor's eye up to the level of the courtyard. A transitional moment of animation is soon left behind for an atmosphere of solemnity and quiet. The extreme austerity of the interior architecture and the omnipresence of light heightens the collections. The Freer is a museum where one is quickly lost in thought, unconscious of the setting. The courtyard echoes with the drip of water from the central, basin fountain, and one can easily imagine the early days of the museum when peacocks inhabited this retreat. The introspective mood of the interior was exactly what Freer had envisioned. Platt achieved it with his characteristic understatement and reserve. The Freer Gallery was one of Platt's greatest successes for two reasons: the rigid classicism of the Mall provided the perfect environment for the proper and poised elevations, and the art-for-art's-sake spirit that guided Freer in assembling and displaying his collections exactly matched Platt's intentions for the building as a work of art.

The Freer Gallery is one of the finest examples of those turn-of-the-century institutions created to exhibit personal collections. The relevant precedents would certainly include McKim, Mead & White designs for small museums and libraries, from the Walker Art Gallery (1891–94) at Bowdoin College through the more comparable and exquisite J. Pierpont Morgan Library (1902–6) in New York City.[26] Platt's Freer Gallery shares with both these buildings the image of a single-story fortress with windowless walls and an arched central entrance. In plan, the Freer represents the popular courtyard-type museum, such as Cass Gilbert had designed in his polychromatic, Renaissance-inspired Allen Memorial Museum (1917) for Oberlin College.[27] To serve academic needs, Gilbert created a covered courtyard with a library superimposed on the artificially lighted galleries, while Platt could emphasize the exhibition purposes, providing natural illumination from above and placing library, study, and service areas below. Among the museums that the Platt design team visited for technical concerns in preparing the Freer plans was the Henry Clay Frick residence in New York, designed by Carrère & Hastings in 1911 and eventually altered by John Russell Pope in 1935 when it became a public museum. While the Freer and Frick buildings are similar in scale and intention, the pompous French classicism of the Frick has, as John Canaday has observed, a certain *arriviste*

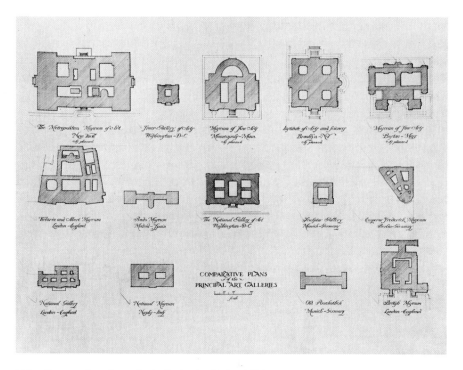

114. Comparative plans of principal art galleries, 1924.

quality when compared to the quiet dignity and confident repose of the Freer.[28] Hopefully, the underground additions to the Freer, currently under construction on the east side of the building, will not alter the Gallery's special qualities.

On May 14, 1923, soon after the opening week of the Freer Gallery, Smithsonian Secretary Walcott wrote to Platt praising his design for the building and expressing his wish that "we had as fine a building for the National Gallery of Art."[29] Walcott's enthusiasm for Platt's work convinced the Smithsonian Board of Regents to raise $10,000 privately in 1924 for plans of a National Gallery to be prepared; they hoped that Platt's scheme would encourage Congress to appropriate the necessary monies to build it. Platt had foreseen this possible opportunity. He had been appointed to the National Gallery of Art Commission in June 1921, but he tendered his resignation the following December, explaining, "if the question of erecting a building to house the possessions of the National Gallery of Art comes up, I should like to be considered as *architect* for the building."[30] When the occasion arose three years later, Platt was ready.

In preparing his designs for the National Gallery, Platt felt the need to revisit the major museums of Europe. With his architect-student son, William, as his secretary and draftsman, Platt traveled in May and June 1924 to London, Paris, Madrid, Berlin, Munich, Florence, Rome, and Naples.[31] Although he compiled comparative information on the plans of the museums in each city, his real objective was to study proportion, the shape of galleries, and the essential treatment of lighting (Fig. 114). From this observation, he evolved a design for the National Gallery that could be built in stages, as funds became available (Figs. 115, 116). The plan was laid out around a large central garden court and four flanking light courts.[32] Unlike the enclosed, monastic character of the Freer, Platt's National Gallery would have been open and welcoming, with large exterior windows ringing the first floor and a projecting monumental portico at the Mall entrance, similar to those on several

115. Elevation and sections, preliminary study, National Gallery of Art project, Washington, D.C., 1924.

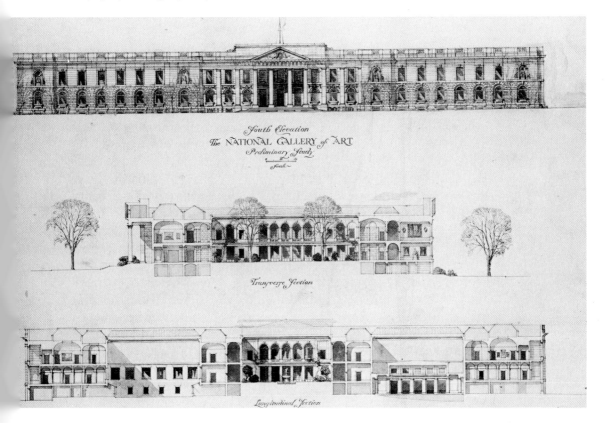

171

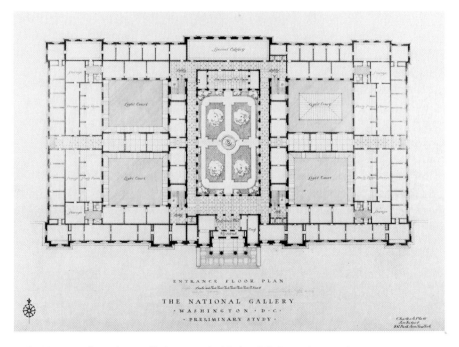

116. Entrance floor plan, preliminary study, National Gallery of Art project.

Platt country houses. His stated intention in the National Gallery was to design a functional and well-lighted art museum, not an ornate palace for the nation's treasures. In avoiding the temptation of a domed central rotunda, Platt showed his general commitment to function over ceremony.

Unfortunately, the Platt plans did not provide the anticipated incentive for a Congressional allocation. As Secretary Walcott had feared, the construction of a National Gallery would, like the Freer, have to await a private benefactor. When that patron, Andrew Mellon, did emerge, Platt had died and the design of the National Gallery was entrusted to John Russell Pope. The publicity that both the Freer and the National Gallery projects generated, however, ensured Platt's reputation as a museum architect and brought him six other gallery commissions during the decade.[33] The scale of these projects varied greatly, starting with the small, shingled gallery Platt designed in 1920 for the summer art colony at Old Lyme, Connecticut (Fig. 117). Most of these museums, both the proposed and executed designs, combined top-lighted galleries, a blank-walled exterior of brick or stone, and a monumental entrance portico—all ideas tested in the Freer and National

172

117.   Lyme Art Gallery, Old Lyme, Connecticut, 1920–21.

118.   Second floor plan, Clark Wing, Corcoran Gallery of Art,
Washington, D.C., 1925–28.

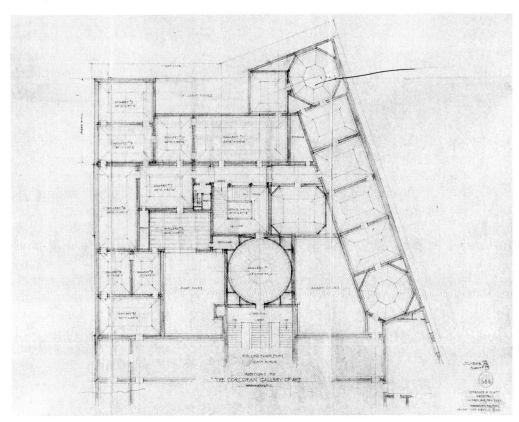

173

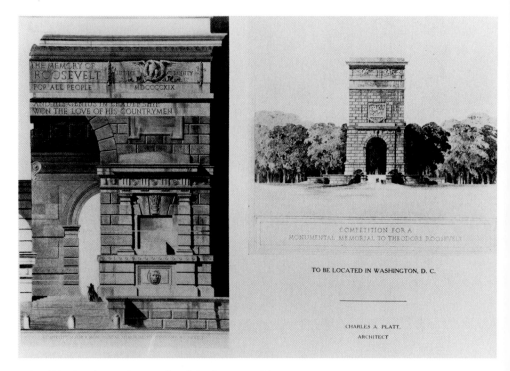

119.   Side elevation and composite of details, competition entry,
Theodore Roosevelt Memorial, Washington, D.C., 1925.

Gallery schemes. The most elaborate program Platt executed was the
Clark Wing for the Corcoran Gallery of Art (1925–28) in Washington,
D.C. (Fig. 118). He had to integrate his major addition with Ernest
Flagg's 1897 building, while maintaining an independent environment
for the display of Senator Clark's diverse collection. This new wing is an
extension of the original building along E Street. Platt served as the
architect of the Clark Wing in the fullest sense of the word, advising the
gallery director on the acceptance of the collection, selecting works to be
exhibited, making recommendations on the restoration and conserva-
tion of objects, designing the building, and supervising the installation.[34]
In the Clark, Lyme, Lyman Allyn Museum in New London, Connecticut, and other contemporary projects, Platt always maintained the same
balance between appropriate, quiet dignity and careful planning and
natural lighting.

Related to the museum projects in Washington was an entry Platt
submitted to the 1925 competition for a monument to Theodore Roosevelt (Fig. 119).[35] He proposed a monumental triumphal arch to be

located at the far end of a large rectangular reflecting pool; it was to be on axis with the White House and at approximately the site of the present Jefferson Memorial. As in his Freer designs, Platt turned to the city gates of Sanmicheli for a muscular, rusticated vocabulary appropriate to Teddy Roosevelt.[36] John Russell Pope's design was premiated from a field of eight competitors but was never constructed.[37] Competitions for public buildings and monuments were common at this time, but the Roosevelt Memorial was the only one Platt entered. He did so because his son, William, had recently joined the office and was enthusiastic about the project. To explain his reticence about competitions, Platt once stated, "My colleagues say I can't win prizes any more. Painters say I'm an architect and architects say I'm a painter."[38] More importantly, he felt he could not produce a fully satisfactory design without direct consultation with a client from the inception of a commission. But his keen sense of analysis made him a frequent choice as a juror in competitions.[39]

Although the museum commissions may have brought Platt the most national recognition, academic projects actually consumed the largest part of his time and energy during the last fifteen years of his life. Including the design of buildings and campus plans for private secondary schools, colleges, and universities, institutional commissions provided a more uniform and profitable basis for the office. These jobs also gave Platt the opportunity to utilize his talents as a landscape planner and architect on a large scale. In essence, he expanded the formula he had devised for country-house design to encompass multiple interrelated buildings set within a controlled landscape. Courtyards and greenswards necessarily replaced flower-planted terraces as the vocabulary was increased in scale. And as in his domestic commissions, Platt oversaw all aspects of his projects down to the placement of furnishings and the design of bookplates. He even suggested curriculum changes to bring the arts into a more central focus in the life of the schools.

As early as 1902, Platt had written to the Johns Hopkins University in Baltimore, offering his services in the formulation of expansion plans for the institution.[40] Nothing came of the suggestion, but from 1919 until 1933 he served with John Russell Pope and Grosvenor Atterbury on the Homewood Advisory Board that supervised the development of the new suburban campus of Johns Hopkins.[41] Unlike his colleagues, however, Platt never designed buildings for the school, but only advised on the work of other architects. He also served as the consulting architect for Dartmouth College (1926–31) and for the River Campus of the University of Rochester (1926–33).[42] At Rochester, he

120.   Campus plan, University of Illinois, Urbana, Illinois, 1922.

developed, in collaboration with the Olmsted Brothers, a master plan for
a completely new facility. Again, Platt designed no specific buildings
but, working very closely with the local executant architects, Gordon &
Kaelber, he left his imprint on the Rochester campus by supporting the
choice of an architectural image derived from regional Greek Revival
forms and by stressing the need to plan from the start for large-scale
future development.

More representative of Platt's work as an institutional architect was his continuing affiliation with the University of Illinois at Urbana-Champaign. After considering four nationally recognized architectural firms, the Board of Trustees appointed Platt on December 13, 1921, "to act as architect for the Agriculture Building and to study the general campus plan."[43] The university had long been conscious of the need for planning. In 1906, Frederick Law Olmsted, Jr., had made basic recommendations for campus development which were carried further by the 1912 Burnham Campus Plan Commission, headed by architect Daniel Hudson Burnham. Four subsequent schemes were developed by James M. White, resident architect of the university, and by Holabird & Roche of Chicago.[44] While inheriting certain features from these earlier plans, Platt advanced a comprehensive master plan for the university's next twenty years and for its ultimate development.

In submitting his 1922 master plan Platt accepted a campus meridian, or central axis, established by Olmsted and the general subdivisions recommended by Burnham (Fig. 120).[45] The earlier portion of the campus consisted of a north-south mall that had gradually evolved from the more picturesque scheme of random placement begun in the 1870s. In the first decade of this century, campus planners and architects began to propose a tree-lined greensward flanked by classical revival buildings, a scheme predictable for the state that had hosted the 1893 Columbian Exposition and had seen the birth of the City Beautiful Movement. But Platt's major development was located south of and separate from the old campus, further away from town, and was balanced along a new east-west mall on land then used for agricultural research, military parades, and recreation. He convinced the Board of Trustees to begin laying out roads and walkways and to plant trees on this land in preparation for rapid campus expansion.

Between 1913 and 1923, the university experienced a quadrupling in enrollment, so Platt was encouraged to design compact building units. He devised varying combinations of four T- and U-shaped buildings to create interior courtyards and to present their long facades on malls and walkways (Fig. 121). In the "ultimate" plan for the university, Platt proposed malls crossed by diagonal avenues that could be extended indefinitely into the farmland south of the campus. Ferrucio Vitale, Platt's landscape collaborator here, observed: "The plain of Illinois upon which the University is built dictated to Charles Platt a formal plan, the grandeur of which will be realized more and more as additional structures are built."[46] This scheme, the closest Platt ever came to urban planning, showed his admiration for the L'Enfant plan of Washington

177

121.   General proposal for grouping and massing of buildings,
University of Illinois.

and possibly Burnham's plan of Chicago. Respect for the Platt scheme
was best demonstrated when the 1960s addition to his library was placed
underground so as not to destroy the strength and clarity of his landscape
plan. As with most Platt designs, the plan for the University of Illinois
was a resolute conception that was intended not to be altered easily.

In elevation, too, Platt determined a campus plan. The trustees
were eager to establish an official style for university buildings. Since
Platt found no appropriate local or campus traditions on which to base
the design of new buildings, he imposed an architectural vocabulary of
English Georgian, which was consistent with the formality of his plan
and could be expanded easily to accommodate the needs of differing
departments and programs. His choice of the Georgian stylistic model
(Fig. 122) paralleled much academic architecture of the 1910s and
1920s, including the new Homewood Campus of the Johns Hopkins
University for which Platt was currently serving as an architectural
consultant. Also, a red brick Colonial Georgian mode had been chosen
for most recent architecture at Harvard University, where Platt's third
son was a student at this time and where Platt served as a juror in the
1924 competition for the new Harvard Business School complex.[47]

178

122. Entrance facade, Building for Architecture and Kindred Subjects,
University of Illinois, Urbana, 1926–27.

123. Gateway between Building for Architecture and Commerce Department
Building, University of Illinois, Urbana.

Much like the architects of the 1893 World's Columbian Exposition, Platt dictated a uniform building material and cornice height.[48] All new construction was to be of red brick with limestone trim, three-and-a-half stories high (or the equivalent cornice level), with gray slate, hipped roofs, and tall chimneys. He provided for further coherence by the use of segmental lintels for the second-story windows of classroom buildings, limestone niches, and wrought-iron fences and gateways between buildings (Fig. 123). Platt designed the campus buildings to emphasize long, uninterrupted facades which were complemented by terraced plantings and allees of uniform trees. In both landscape and architecture, Platt celebrated the infinite horizontality of the Illinois prairie, countered only by the rhythmic march of his tall chimneys.

124. Entrance facade, University Library, University of Illinois, Urbana, 1924–29.

125. Longitudinal section, Study for Library, Urbana, n.d. As built, the catalogue room, shown as a domed space at the center of this drawing, took the form of a clerestory-lighted nave flanked by lower aisles behind column screens.

Among the dozen buildings Platt built in Urbana was one that particularly demonstrated his talents as an institutional architect. After the Agriculture Building, the University Library was Platt's second and largest project for the school (Figs. 124, 125). It was built in three stages in 1923, 1925, and 1927 at a total cost of $1,750,000.[49] Contrary to the accepted practice of making the library an axial campus landmark, complete on all four sides, Platt placed his building on one side of a mall and left open land behind it for phased additions.[50] The main eastern elevation, masking the public areas of the building, was 300 feet long and two-and-a-half stories high.

The tall arched windows of the second level corresponded to the main reading room, a space that occupied the entire width of the facade. Within, Platt provided this room with natural illumination from four sides by cutting light courts into the mass of the building. The location of the reading room resembled that of Charles McKim's Boston Public Library (1888–95) and the inspiration for it, Henri Labrouste's Bibliothèque Ste.-Geneviève (1843–50) in Paris, as well as the more recent Widener Library (1915) by Horace Trumbauer at Harvard University and the Detroit Public Library (1921) by Cass Gilbert.[51] To approach this impressive space one entered the first floor through one of three rusticated limestone archways into a lobby equal in depth to the reading room above. Two monumental staircases at the rear of the lobby ascended left and right to a wide hall between the reading room at the front and the card catalogue and delivery room behind (Fig. 126). The upper levels of the stairwells were decorated by four mural maps, the

181

work of Platt's close friend, Barry Faulkner.[52] The catalogue and delivery room occupied the second floor of a wing extending west, perpendicular to the main reading room and flanked by light courts to the north and south. Behind the delivery desk at the west were the bookstacks designed as a self-supporting metal skeleton and erected in advance of the masonry walls. Because of the long, exposed west elevation, Platt placed 5-inch-thick reinforced concrete slabs on alternate levels of the bookstacks that acted as "diaphragms to equalize wind pressure throughout the entire structure."[53] So, when periodic expansions of storage area were required, the west wall could be removed without affecting the stability of the bookstacks and without requiring auxiliary bracing in the stack additions. Despite its adherence to tradition in building form, the Platt office provided its clients with thoroughly modern solutions to structural and technical problems.

All of Platt's designs for the University of Illinois between 1922 and 1928 were executed in cooperation with campus architect, James M. White. As early as 1907, the trustees had established the office of

126. View from the stair landing into catalogue room and delivery desk, University Library. To left and right are mural maps painted by Barry Faulkner.

182

Supervising Architect to foster uniformity in campus buildings.[54] White worked well and closely with Platt and easily adopted the latter's style. Platt served as the designer for the library, agriculture, and architecture buildings and collaborated with White on two gymnasiums, an armory, a dormitory, a building for the Commerce Department, the university hospital, and the president's house. Although the burden of design responsibility gradually shifted from Platt to White, both men were fully involved in every project. The collaboration allowed Platt to avoid frequent trips to Illinois but reduced the profits from these commissions. Even after the university ceased to require Platt's services, White and his successors continued to follow the guidelines of the master plan for nearly twenty years, as Platt had envisioned.[55]

The culmination of Platt's career, and of many of the ideals of the 1920s, was his development of Phillips Academy, Andover, Massachusetts. Here he had an institutional commission, yet he worked with the backing of a strong and determined patron. The program of the school and of Platt's buildings stressed an awareness of history and tradition. He sought to create a humanizing environment and showed a sensitivity to local architectural precedents. Most importantly, at Andover Platt had nearly total control of an environment—the campus plan and landscape, individual buildings and their contents.

In September 1921, the school first contacted Platt to begin consideration of a master plan for development in collaboration with Guy Lowell, the academy's architect, and the Olmsted Brothers, landscape designers.[56] Phillips Andover had purchased a few years earlier the grounds and buildings of Andover Theological Seminary, on the eastern side of Main Street, across from the academy. After a successful building and endowment fund campaign in 1919–20, the academy planned a major expansion and looked to the higher ground of the adjacent seminary property as the likely location. In 1920, Guy Lowell advised the school, "It is the modern theory of college planning that important buildings should turn their faces to the center of college life, the campus, and not the outside world."[57] He recommended that a new inward-looking group of buildings be constructed to the east of Main Street as the focus for future development. When Platt was consulted the following year, he evidently supported this philosophy and helped determine the location of the quadrangle, which was the organizing unit in his own later work.

Platt remained in an advisory position for several years. Guy Lowell designed Samuel Phillips Hall (1920), the major classroom building at the head of the new quadrangle, but with Platt's collaboration and landscaping. After the election in 1923 of Thomas Cochran as an academy trustee, the stage was set for Platt to provide direction. Cochran was a J. P. Morgan partner, a childless widower with boundless enthusiasm, who devoted his energies and fortune to the school. Cochran wanted the country's best colonial revival architect for the academy and recommended Platt as Lowell's replacement.[58] Platt was concerned that he not offend Lowell and insisted that Lowell be consulted on this change. Lasting until 1932, Platt's involvement included a complete reorganization of the campus, the design of seven new buildings, and the demolition, moving, or alteration of other structures.

When Platt succeeded to the unofficial position of academy architect, he inherited the former seminary campus as his primary stage for the expansion of Phillips Academy. Andover Theological Seminary was founded in 1808 to train Congregational clergy and shared for nearly a century its Board of Trustees and some of its physical plant with adjacent Phillips Academy.[59] When the seminary established an affiliation with Harvard University and moved to Cambridge in 1908, the academy purchased its grounds and buildings. In addition to Guy Lowell's recently completed Samuel Phillips Hall, the new campus contained a chapel, a recitation building, two dormitories, and several houses when Platt began his work. The seminary structures included Phillips Hall (1809) and Bartlett Hall (1821), four-story, brick boxes flanking Bartlett Chapel (1818), a classroom and assembly building of similar scale and materials, fronted by a pedimented pavilion and topped by a mid-Victorian tower. These three compatible structures were sited along a slight plateau facing west. Intended as the focus for a new quadrangle, Guy Lowell's 1920 classroom building had been placed behind the center structure, which was renamed Pearson Hall. The seminary chapel (1875), a polychromatic Gothic design by the Boston firm of Cummings & Sears, was located north and west of the three original buildings overlooking a fenced campus crossed by elm-lined walks. Platt admired the quiet dignity of these buildings, but his reverence did not inhibit his determination to improve upon all that he now saw (Fig. 127). He ultimately demolished the Gothic Revival chapel, moved Pearson Hall, and removed the fourth stories of the two dormitory buildings.

In a period of renewed national pride, Cochran and Platt emphasized the American roots of Andover. Cochran, after reading Claude Moore Fuess's history of Andover, *An Old New England School,* embarked upon a campaign to capitalize on the rich heritage of the academy. He convinced the trustees to name new buildings after national heroes who had attended or somehow been associated with the school.[60]

184

Likewise, Platt designed his new buildings to harmonize with the style of earlier structures on the campus. Charles Bulfinch had designed one of the oldest extant academy buildings, Pearson Hall (1818), and it suggested the formal vocabulary for Platt's Andover work. Beyond that, Cochran purchased objects that had been owned by honored alumni, including their portraits (or copies he commissioned), to give the school a feeling for the richness of its history.

Platt inspired Cochran to conceive and execute his image of an "Ideal Andover" both in terms of physical setting and of intellectual and cultural advantages (Fig. 128). A master of the academy remembered Platt's role in convincing Cochran that beauty should be stressed in the boys' education. He paraphrased Platt:

Why not surround them with the very best in architecture and nature and fine arts? Why not a bird sanctuary, a really fine library, a topnotch art gallery, a good Colonial church with an organ? Why not a few broad vistas, some lawns and terraces, even some notable lectures and concerts—all instruments of culture? I'd like to try my hand at it.[61]

Cochran was soon consumed by Platt's vision and provided the funds and the power to realize these aspirations.

Typical of Platt's influence and of the scale on which these two men plotted was a July 11, 1928, letter from Cochran to James C. Sawyer, the academy's Treasurer:

On the way down on the train yesterday afternoon Mr. Platt painted the following picture, which he described as a very interesting one to dream over:
1 — Eliminate the West wing of Phillips Inn by destroying it when the improvements on the Inn are made.
2 — Close Bartlett Street, as we discussed.
3 — Move the Headmaster's house toward Phillips Inn, occupying as part of the required space the property acquired by closing Bartlett Street.
4 — Build a new chapel on a line opposite with the memorial tower and parallel with Main Street.
5 — Erect a stone wall along Chapel Street in front of the Headmaster's house and the new Chapel, extending the wall to Main Street and down Main Street one block.
6 — Build a Phillips Memorial gateway on Bartlett Street between the two stone walls. Make it a significant gateway, but not an arch.
7 — Build an art gallery on the site where we had planned to build the new chapel.[62]

Amazingly, all of these ideas and more were accomplished. Platt and Cochran, by the time of this letter, had already been radically rearrang-

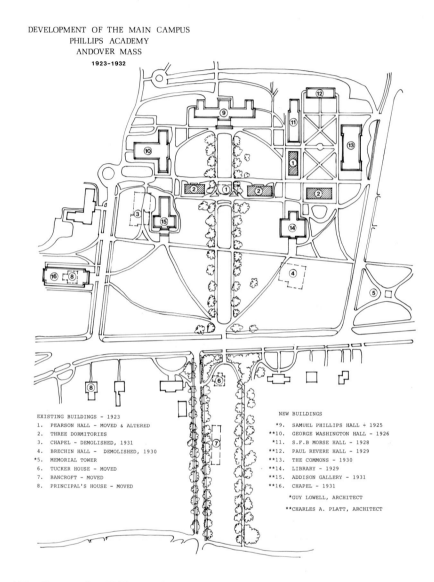

DEVELOPMENT OF THE MAIN CAMPUS
PHILLIPS ACADEMY
ANDOVER MASS
1923-1932

EXISTING BUILDINGS - 1923
1.   PEARSON HALL - MOVED & ALTERED
2.   THREE DORMITORIES
3.   CHAPEL - DEMOLISHED, 1931
4.   BRECHIN HALL - DEMOLISHED, 1930
*5. MEMORIAL TOWER
6.   TUCKER HOUSE - MOVED
7.   BANCROFT - MOVED
8.   PRINCIPAL'S HOUSE - MOVED

NEW BUILDINGS
*9.   SAMUEL PHILLIPS HALL + 1925
**10. GEORGE WASHINGTON HALL - 1926
*11. S.F.B MORSE HALL - 1928
**12. PAUL REVERE HALL - 1929
**13. THE COMMONS - 1930
**14. LIBRARY - 1929
**15. ADDISON GALLERY - 1931
**16. CHAPEL - 1931

*GUY LOWELL, ARCHITECT

**CHARLES A. PLATT, ARCHITECT

127.   Campus plan, Phillips Academy, Andover, Massachusetts, 1922–31, showing buildings extant before Platt began his work and the changes he made in the campus. The original Phillips Hall (1809) was renamed Foxcroft Hall in 1925; Bartlett Chapel (1818) was renamed Pearson Hall (1908), and moved in 1924.

ing the school. Two years earlier, Cochran had commissioned a scale model of the academy, complete with proposed new construction.[63] He used this device to convince his fellow trustees of the merit of Platt's ideas and as an aid in visualizing the result.

186

All of the development was on the eastern side of Main Street and was divisible into three major areas. The Great Quadrangle stood on the highest ground, well removed from the street. It was dominated by Lowell's Samuel Phillips Hall on the east and included the two early-nineteenth-century dormitories on the west, a new administration building by Platt on the north, and the relocated Pearson Hall and a new science building on the south. To the south of this complex was the Junior Quadrangle with dormitories on the east and west ends and Platt's Commons (1930) at the south. Between Main Street and both quadrangles, Platt opened the Lawn, or Front Green (Fig. 129), with key monuments positioned on its north, east, and south sides. In 1922, Guy Lowell had designed the Fuller Memorial Tower which stood to the

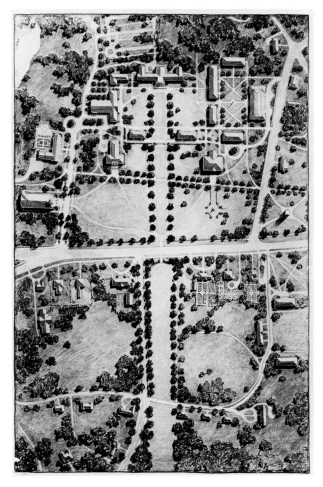

128. Plan for
The Ideal Andover.

187

129. Front Green, Phillips Andover, showing from left to right:
Cochran Chapel (1930–31), Addison Gallery of American Art (1929),
and Oliver Wendell Holmes Library (1928–29).

south of the Green. To balance this spire, Platt placed his new chapel at
the north end and designed a steeple of comparable height and scale. On
the east were his new art museum and library, each fronted by a pedimented portico. The Front Green presented the image of the school and
was laid out to give an impressive survey in one glance. A major tree-
lined allee (Fig. 130) extended west from Phillips Hall, crossing the Great
Quadrangle and the Front Green, and connecting the new section of the
school with the older campus across Main Street and the hills in the
distance. Platt's plan was so complete that all subsequent buildings have
been constructed behind or beyond his scheme.

 Despite a basic axial arrangement, Platt maintained a degree of
informality in the positioning of the academy buildings, a feeling he
perpetuated in the structures themselves. In contrast to the uniformity of
his designs for the University of Illinois, Platt gave his Andover projects
individual and differing characters. Yet, he unified them by consistently
using Dover River red brick trimmed with Deer Isle granite and Indiana

limestone, supposedly in the style of Charles Bulfinch. Actually, only one of Platt's designs showed specific references to Bulfinch; most were simply based on colonial or English Georgian buildings of sympathetic scale and material. The canopy of arching elms and the low, rough granite walls successfully merged these new buildings with their land-

130. Vista to western hills from Samuel Phillips Hall, Phillips Andover.

131. Entrance bay, Oliver
Wendell Holmes Library,
Phillips Andover, 1928–29.
Rendering by Schell Lewis.

scape and quickly gave them the appearance of having stood on this site for a century.

Platt's new buildings predominate throughout the campus. George Washington Hall (1925) was his first Andover commission. Located at the north end of the Great Quad, it was a three-story administration building with the school auditorium extending to the rear. In the Junior Quadrangle, Platt built Paul Revere Hall, a four-story, gambrel-roofed dormitory, and The Commons, a dining hall complex decorated with murals by Barry Faulkner.

On the Front Green, Platt balanced the Oliver Wendell Holmes Library (1928–29) and the Addison Gallery of American Art (1929) on either side of the vista facing west. Inside and out, the library showed the exacting attention to detail for which the Platt office was famous (Figs. 131, 132). And for the gallery Platt and Cochran conceived of a building that would be "an artistic gem, set in a place on the academy grounds that would be ideal in every standpoint."[64] The plan of the gallery included library, study, and storage areas in the basement, in a manner similar to the Freer Gallery; side-lit exhibition rooms on the first floor (Fig. 133); and sky-lit galleries on the top level. The mere existence of a substantial art gallery at a secondary school was unique then and is still rare today. Cochran restricted the collections to objects produced by native or naturalized Americans, continuing the patriotic idealism of his overall Andover plan. And Platt continued to exert his comprehensive influence on the life of the school in the paintings and objects he selected for the gallery.

The Chapel was Platt's most prominent structure and, fittingly, was a memorial to Cochran's family (Fig. 134). On the exterior, Platt

132.   Reading room, Holmes Library.

191

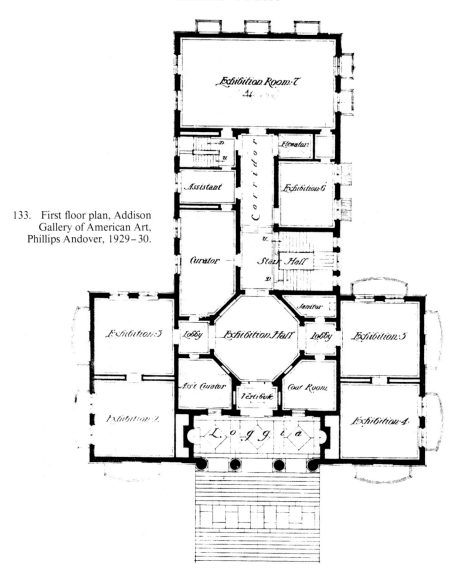

133. First floor plan, Addison
     Gallery of American Art,
     Phillips Andover, 1929–30.

combined ideas from American buildings to create the desired traditional effect. He modeled the porch on Bulfinch's Lancaster Meeting-
house (1816–17), Lancaster, Massachusetts, and superimposed on it a
tower reminiscent of Philip Hooker's Second Presbyterian Church
(1813), Albany, New York.[65] For the interior (Fig. 135), Platt was forced
to turn to English prototypes, as explained in a letter between two
trustees:

Stearns [the Headmaster] has wanted a warm interior, not the white paint and clear light of Bulfinch. Accordingly Platt has turned to the London churches, with large pillars and colored glass. These latter churches, however, were built for a wholly different use from ours, a liturgical and largely musical service in which the sermon was totally negligible. I have my doubts whether the type is not directly inconsistent with our uses, and whether we have not got to turn to the New England type and then make Platt warm it up as much as he can.[66]

But a London church of the Wren period it remained inside. The nave

134.   Cochran Chapel, Phillips Andover, 1930–31.

was a coffered barrel vault supported by arches on columns. The aisles were lighted by large arched windows of tinted glass that reinforced the warmth of fumed oak woodwork and stippled light brown walls. Because of the conflicting stylistic and ecclesiastical demands, the Cochran Chapel was not a fully integrated design. However, Platt's success in creating a coherent plan for the entire academy overshadowed any dissatisfaction with the chapel project.

Because of the success of the Andover expansion, Platt became involved with other New England preparatory schools, notably Deerfield Academy in Deerfield, Massachusetts.[67] He was commissioned in 1929 to oversee an extensive building campaign for the academy through the intercession of both Frank D. Cheney, his cousin and a Deerfield trustee, and Thomas Cochran. In fact, Cochran believed so implicitly in Platt's ability that he provided the funds to terminate a relationship with the previous academy architects, Perry, Shaw & Hepburn. The Georgian red brick and limestone Academy Building (1930), Gymnasium (1930), and Science Building (1932) continued the aca-

135.   View down nave, Cochran Chapel.

136.   G. T. Goulstone, tombstone for
Charles A. Platt, East Cemetery,
Manchester, Connecticut, 1933.

demic formula Platt had developed for both Illinois and Andover. Although he made recommendations for the campus plan and additional buildings, the Depression and his death occurred before his ideas could be implemented. However, his successor firm, William & Geoffrey Platt, continued to oversee compatible campus development through the 1950s.

The completion of the chapel signaled the end of the Platt-Cochran years at Andover. The Depression discouraged further construction and the benefactor soon died. These preparatory-school buildings were the last major designs of Platt's career before his own death on September 12, 1933 (Fig. 136). In general, the institutional commissions, with the exception of the Freer Gallery, were rarely published and exerted no significant influence on American architecture of the 1920s. But the art museums and academic buildings are as clear statements of Platt's architectural philosophy as any of his designs. The qualities that characterized his influential country houses and gardens of the prewar period are restated with a confidence that reveals no self-doubt about changes in American architecture or society. Today, Platt's surviving gardens have been reduced to lawns; only a handful of his country houses are being used and maintained as he envisioned; his town houses have generally been converted to institutional facilities. Of all Platt's works, it is his public buildings as a group that best approximate the character and use that Platt intended. For the museum visitor at the Freer or the Lyme Art Gallery and the student at Illinois or Andover, the resolute sense of purpose and calm repose of his buildings and land-scapes still speak lucidly of the aspirations and convictions of Charles A. Platt (Fig. 137).

137.   Photograph of Charles A. Platt in 1923.

196

Epilogue

PLATT CREATED buildings and gardens that reflected the economic and social conditions of early twentieth-century American wealth, but his philosophy of art is as valid and instructive today as it was in his lifetime. Although he rarely wrote about architecture or granted interviews, his few published statements and, more importantly, his 250 completed commissions demonstrated his point of view: first, that design should begin from a knowledge of the past, creatively adapting the best of our inheritance to the needs of the present; second, that any design must be derived from and fully interrelated with its setting; third, that the elements of a design must be restricted to those that clearly emphasize and reinforce the larger spatial and organizational framework; and finally, that the creation of beauty must be the ultimate purpose of all art — for Platt, a beauty based on symmetry, a coherence and hierarchy of parts, and a system of visually interlocking forms. While the issues of historical precedents, integration of building and site, and reduction of design elements can be seen as characteristic of the best work of his generation, Platt was unique in basing his approach to all these concerns upon a broad artistic commitment to his ideal of beauty.

To modern eyes, Platt's world and his art can often seem softly focused, especially as originally described by words like *elegance, charm,* and *beauty* — words that usually are avoided today. And his life may seem somewhat placid, undisturbed by the Russian Revolution, the new literature, or the Armory Show — all of which he surely condemned, but by which he was only passingly affected. Platt supported and was supported by the corporate, capitalist establishment from which he had emerged and whose ambitions he understood and fulfilled. The patrons that he served embraced the concept of a genteel culture, in architecture and in life generally. And his unruffled, unquestioning acceptance of the dominant society was certainly one reason for his rapid success as an architect.

But beyond the economic and social context, Platt's designs must be understood and evaluated by the precise criteria that he established for himself. His search for universal architectural ideals pushed him to create forms of self-confidence, consistency, stability, and refinement. Thus, there is often an unapproachable, thoroughly resolved quality to his work. Platt seems to have both posed the questions and provided the answers, intending to leave no room for debate. When at his best — in the gardens of Faulkner Farm, the country houses for Francis Maxwell or Marshall Slade, the Freer Gallery, or the general scheme for Phillips Academy — Platt created designs of great distinction and striking visual appeal that will always merit admiration and study. These and many other commissions are surely equal to the exacting standards that Platt set for himself in all phases of his life as an artist.

A MEMOIR by
Geoffrey Platt

Note: Charles A. Platt married Eleanor Hardy Bunker in 1893. They had five children: Sylvia (1895–1912), William (1897–1984), Roger (1898–1948), Geoffrey (1905–85), and Charles (b. 1913). William and Geoffrey became architects and joined their father's firm. Roger was a rancher in Colorado for some years before returning to New York City where he was a teacher at St. Bernard's School for the rest of his life. Charles also started the rancher's life and lived in the West until he retired recently to live in Cornish, New Hampshire.

MY FATHER was a fortunate man. He had talents to which he could give full expression and he received full recognition for them in his lifetime.

His career was unique. Born in 1861, he rapidly established his reputation in etching and painting early in the 1880s. By the mid-1890s he had begun landscape design, and by 1900 he had become an architect. He continued in this career until his death in 1933. Throughout his life he continued to paint and he was an artist in all that he did.

I was only dimly aware of C.A.P.* for many years. The business of bringing up the five children was left to our mother. She was a romantic and warmhearted person who believed that the role of the artist's wife was to give him complete devotion and support so that he could concentrate all his energies on his work. She had been cruelly deprived of this role when her first husband, Dennis Bunker, the painter, died after only three months of marriage. In C.A.P. she found complete fulfillment. His health was not the most robust (he had a strong tendency to bronchial infection), and the demands of his professional life were great. Her care during his illnesses and her constant concern for the saving of his energies were essential for his great accomplishments.

---

* He was known to many friends and associates as C.A.P., so this designation will be used here.

My first recollection of him was as a kindly man with a beard, an august person known as "Fard" (the family name for him). It was only in my early adolescence that I really began to know him. I think he was waiting until he could carry on a conversation with me. At any rate, he never remonstrated when I hurled my rapidly growing self into valuable antique chairs thereby producing frequent sinister cracking noises. He revealed himself to be a calm, humorous, and sympathetic person. He was genial and could be very funny, but he was self-absorbed, not generally loquacious, and not given to expressions of emotion. He had many friends to whom he revealed all these qualities. He also particularly enjoyed the companionship of ladies and their presence brought out his most attractive characteristics. When he talked to you he made you feel your importance to him and if he wanted to make a point, he would do so in a positive and succinct manner. He didn't impose his convictions on anyone unless it was appropriate. Nor did he boast about his work in any way. If asked which of the buildings he had designed he liked most, he would invite the questioner to make his own choice. To strangers, he might appear formidable. He was a strong presence. His blue eyes seemed cold and his taciturnity forbidding, but this impression could fall away and reveal a charming, interested, and vital person. Underneath it all was an artist of profound intensity.

In appearance, C.A.P. was slight and of medium height. He had a flowing mustache, a small beard, a full head of hair, a ruddy complexion, and bushy eyebrows which he raised and lowered individually or together. This gesture was very effective in conveying his reaction to what had just been said or done, and was more expressive than words.

He always dressed meticulously in his own style. An early portrait of him at the age of twenty-three, when he was an art student in Paris, shows him in a black suit with a vest and gold chain, stiff collar and tie, looking more like a banker than an art student. He always had his suits tailor-made, and favored tweeds and suits of one color. His appearance was elegant and distinguished. He wore a hat and carried a cane. I remember particularly a winter coat lined with mink and with a mink collar. Mother wore a fur coat of some lesser animal.

He had been brought up in intellectual surroundings. Although his formal schooling had ended at age seventeen, he was a very cultivated man. He read a great deal all his life, mostly history, biography, and memoirs, as well as a great deal of French literature. He read lots of fiction—such widely diverse authors as Anatole France, Trollope, Mark Twain, Conan Doyle, and Wodehouse—and took particular pleasure in detective stories. He did not read any books of a philosophical or speculative nature, and he was not interested in either philosophical talk or conjectural conversation. It is clear that his theories on art and architecture were not developed conceptually, but rather through observation and experience.

My father's many years abroad contributed to his intellectual makeup. He spoke French fluently and Italian less so. Many words and phrases from those languages (*simpatico, ça va,* and the like) cropped up in his conversation. C.A.P. had been taught to play the piano as a boy and loved music. He went to the opera and concerts regularly and as often as possible to musical comedies, where he could be found doubled up by belly laughs, enjoying his favorite comedians, Leon Errol and W. C. Fields.

His demeanor was deceptive. He never seemed to hurry but if you walked with him you found yourself working hard to keep up. His pace got him along faster than the apparent determined walker's; he seemed to scoot. There were times when he could show sustained periods of energy. In 1924 his son William went abroad with him to study the arrangement and lighting in museums. The daily trips through the museums, carried on at a rapid pace, were exhausting to William, then a young man of twenty-seven, but not to C.A.P.

He loved games of all kinds. They were his greatest form of relaxation. There were two-handed games: piquet (a French card game), backgammon and its French counterpart known as jacquet, casino, and poker, but most of all bridge. He thought it essential to play for a stake no matter how small, and he played all his games with fierce concentration to win. He also loved golf and I played with him a lot. It was at this time that we really became companions. He was not a big hitter but was very crafty on and around the greens. I am told that when he was younger and played tennis, he had a wicked underhand serve. Croquet (a game requiring great subtlety and skill) was played on the lawn in Cornish, with the English set of big mallets and high, narrow wickets. There were many fierce battles, particularly when Paul Manship, the sculptor, was on hand.

When he traveled, testing new dishes at famous restaurants was a major interest. We never went to a restaurant with him without his appearance causing a great flurry of activity, with excellent results. This interest in food caused Mother to see to it that the family cooks outdid themselves. He loved wine and took a particular pleasure in choosing just the right one for the meal. When we were all growing up in the twenties, Prohibition was in full swing. There wasn't any wine but in one way or another there was an adequate supply of liquor. We did indeed

201

mix gin in the bathtub in the New York apartment. C.A.P. liked his Martinis three to one, and he also liked Orange Blossoms. He limited himself to two drinks before dinner. His sons thought the glasses too small and the drinks too few but that was his regime.

Mother was careful to hold down entertaining. They would either dine alone, or with a good friend, or with a couple for bridge afterward. Their simple social life was due in part to C.A.P.'s frequent absences supervising his work all over the country, and to his winter travels abroad. There were occasional dinner parties, but my parents hardly ever went out to large affairs. In Cornish C.A.P. used to work in the studio until he heard the noon whistle from Windsor, then for a game of jacquet or backgammon before lunch with Barry Faulkner, the mural painter, or whoever else was around. The afternoon was spent on the golf course or the croquet lawn. Dinner then with family or friends was usually followed by cards.

C.A.P. had histrionic ability which was demonstrated at an early age. Emily Cheney Learned wrote of one of his visits to Manchester when he was a boy: "Charles was always amusing and witty. We recall his coming to visit our school dressed like a country parson and making 'a few remarks' to the rest of us. The remarks consisted of the alphabet recited many times with expressive oratory and gestures: it seemed tremendously funny to us children." In the early days in Cornish there used to be many charade parties in which he took an active part. He was a great raconteur and his stories were all told with dramatic effect. C.A.P. also used to sing for us children the "Owl and the Pussycat" which he did with great expression.

C.A.P. was a sensitive and imaginative person with people. He was direct and he got along very well with artists, contractors, artisans, workmen, businessmen, children, ladies, and government officials. He was gregarious in a sense. While he was not a hail-fellow-well-met, he loved to be with his friends either alone or in small groups. The men that I knew who came to the house frequently were Royal Cortissoz, the art critic of the *Tribune*; Willard Metcalf, the painter; Ingalls Kimball, the typographer; and, in Cornish, Paul Manship and Barry Faulkner. For many years Barry spent a great part of the summer with us. C.A.P. liked to lunch or dine at his clubs in New York: the Coffee House where Frank Crowninshield, editor of *Vanity Fair,* and Harrie Lindeberg presided; and the Century, where there was an architects' table which often included John Russell Pope, William Kendall, and Henry Bacon. Before he moved his office to midtown, he would frequent the Players Club, which also had an architects' table. He knew most of the architects and painters of his time in New York and, of course, all the artists and intellectuals in Cornish.

He and Stanford White were great friends and C.A.P. turned to White for help when he designed one of his first houses [see Chapter 2]. The families were intimate and Mother was a real help to Mrs. White after her husband's tragic death. Lawrence G. White, their son, was devoted to C.A.P. and was a great friend of all of ours.

He was interested in younger artists and architects and was generous with his advice and assistance. If they were painters or sculptors he would give them commissions if he could or buy some of their works. He knew the painter George Bellows as a young man and bought a painting from him. The Addison Gallery at Andover offered a large sum for this in 1929, but C.A.P. would sell it only for the price that he had paid Bellows. Another case in point was Ellen Shipman, a friend and neighbor in Cornish, who had come on bad times. (Her husband was an unsuccessful playwright.) C.A.P. thought she had talent, apparent in her lovely flower garden and the way she had decorated her house. He encouraged her to take up landscape gardening, giving her drawing instruments and passing on to her all that he knew on the subject. When she had gained some proficiency, he had her do many of the planting plans for his gardens. This launched her career and she became one of the finest landscape gardeners in the country.

As the artist controls the complete production of his painting or sculpture, so C.A.P. was fortunately able to do the same in his practice of architecture. He considered the design of a house or a building, its setting, and its furnishings to be an indissoluble whole. It was unusual that one person could provide his clients with this complete service, but he did throughout his career.

He had all the qualities of mind of an artist: sensitivity to colors, shapes, textures, and to the world about him — the sky, trees, clouds, weather. But he had intellectual capacities beyond these that particularly equipped him for the direction of his talents to architecture.

He was blessed with an uncluttered mind. It was forceful, precise, and capable of intense concentration on any artistic project that presented itself, whether an etching, a painting, a garden, or a building. He had a basic sense of order and the right solution always seemed to come to him instinctively.

As an etcher and painter he could give full rein to this artistic decisiveness on paper and canvas, but when it came to landscape design and architecture he had clients whom he had to convince. His success lay in his ability to do so. These qualities of mind also enabled him to

203

develop from an artist to an architect, with all the responsibilities of organization and the business abilities that the profession required.

It has always been a matter of interest, indeed of amazement, how C.A.P. became an architect without the usual professional training. Once I asked him how he had learned to be an architect and he said, "I learned by trying it on the dog." This was something of an oversimplification. Before he formally became an architect, he had designed and built some ten houses and several large gardens, learning a lot in the process.

The fact that this well-known painter and landscape architect had turned his hand to architecture without formal training caused misconceptions in many minds. Some thought of him as a dilettante who dabbled in architecture. No matter what they thought, by about 1900 he had begun to develop his office organization and his unique design process. While he had a full understanding of all the technical aspects of building, his capable staff relieved him of the technical execution and left him free for the basic conception and design and the final development of all the other elements of the "villa" — the landscape design and furnishings. He organized his own time, too. He never went to his office at night or on holidays or Sundays, preferring to work at home if need be.

Basic to the design process was his architectural library. This contained two hundred volumes, mostly of the Italian and French Renaissance, and English seventeenth and eighteenth century, as well as the classic ancient sources, such as Vitruvius. These books provided a vocabulary perfectly natural to C.A.P. and his designers, who molded the material in their own way. Whatever detail or design they found relevant to the project at hand was only a starting point. It was studied exhaustively, modified, and adapted to be a part of the new composition. The process was creative. The fitness of detail, its scale and its freshness, together with C.A.P.'s perfect sense of proportion gave all his houses and his buildings their distinctive character.

The period when C.A.P. was designing is categorized by some as "Eclectic" and is frequently misunderstood. It has been assumed to mean that details and whole designs were simply lifted without thought from books and applied to the building at hand. For most of the capable architects of the time, nothing could have been further from the truth.

The Platt office was considered in the profession to have the highest standards in the quality of its drawings, the nature and completeness of its details, and the perfect construction of its buildings. It has been said that the office was run like a studio. This is true of the amount of study given to details in drawings and models. But primarily it was a professional office, organized to produce the results desired and controlled by the artist and architect who created it.

C.A.P. had capable business and technical assistance, and the office worked well; it made money from the beginning. Of course there were good years and poor years. There are no extant account books to detail this, but I can testify that we all lived extremely comfortably in New York and Cornish, did everything that we wanted to, and had everything that we needed, all within reason. In 1925, C.A.P. told my brother William that he seemed to be able to earn not less than $50,000 a year — a considerable sum in those days. In addition to his annual earnings he had been able to accumulate considerable savings. Sadly, almost all was lost as a result of the crash of 1929, when he attempted to rescue his brother John who was overextended in the stock market.

Because C.A.P. designed the house, the gardens, and the interior furnishings, he undertook a prolonged relationship with his clients. Practically all his work with them was done in person. No letters or memoranda have survived and I don't believe there were many of them. His clients in his great days of house building from 1900 until World War I were often people of undeveloped taste, lacking the sophistication and knowledge that came later in the century. For the most part they had made fortunes in finance or industry and were eager to establish family estates in the European tradition which would be handed down for generations. Some of his clients were of more limited means, but C.A.P. was always able to produce designs appropriate for each situation.

He stated his views once on the basic relations between the architect and his client:

It depends on the combination of the client and the architect what is accomplished. Some architects have said that a house is the portrait of a client, and there is no doubt that a good deal of the personality of the client may go into the house; but I believe it is the architect's business to express the ideals of the client, mixed with the architectural ideals of his own time.

He never talked about his individual clients, so we can only assume that these intimate and long relationships were happy ones. There is no record of a project, once begun, being abandoned through disagreement. He was a charming man, confident in his abilities, and it must have been a joy to work with him. After they had accepted the general design with normal give-and-take, his clients had complete confidence in him. It has been said that C.A.P.'s influence on his clients was almost hypnotic, but it appears that there were occasions when it may not have been. In a lecture at the Harvard School of Architecture in 1914

205

he said,"At times we are very much annoyed at the client for forcing us to do things which we think impossible of artistic expression; yet, in this way we accomplish some of the best things of our work. That has been my experience." C.A.P. once told me, "If a client claims credit for an idea in the house that you have just done for him, give him the credit whether he deserves it or not."

In 1915 he moved his offices from 24th Street to 101 Park Avenue. These were on the seventeenth floor, and above it he had built a penthouse studio in which there was no telephone, enabling him to get away from his desk and the pressures in the office. Many architectural problems were solved while he was painting. He often brought his clients here for relaxation after they had been working on plans in the office. In 1923, Mrs. Tiffany Blake of Chicago, a trustee and chairman of the selection committee for the University of Illinois, came to New York to interview four architectural firms. Besides C.A.P. the others were McKim, Mead & White, Delano & Aldrich, and John Russell Pope. After talking for some time in his office, he invited Mrs. Blake to see what he was working on in the studio. We do not know whether it was this experience of the artist that tipped the scales in his favor, but he got the job.

His wide practice required a great deal of travel around the country to see clients and projects. In addition, he would make trips regularly to Europe in midwinter to acquire furnishings for his clients. They relied on him to fill their houses with rugs, tapestries, wallpapers, wall brocades, chairs, tables, sideboards, mirrors, *objets d'art*, bric-a-brac, paintings, sculpture, lamps and lighting fixtures — in fact, everything that was needed to have a completely finished interior. This included appropriate fountains, statuary, and other ornaments for the garden. He went mostly to France and Italy and his trips were systematic and well arranged. He had agents in Paris and in Rome who handled all the details of negotiation, packing, and shipping.

Needless to say, he had definite convictions of what was appropriate and a well-defined taste. My brother William accompanied him on a buying expedition to Rome at one time and described the experience as follows:

He had the system down pat. He had an Italian agent who did the actual buying. He didn't have time to haggle. With C.A.P.'s visual memory and imagination, he'd go through a building full of antiques. He'd look at a room and choose what he wanted. There was no fuss over prices. He always looked for interesting things of no particular style, for things which fitted, not for a period piece.

206

Reproductions were made of many of the pieces of furniture, such as tables and chairs, that he liked particularly and he used them again and again in various houses.

C.A.P.'s interest in younger architects naturally included brother William and me. After taking his degree at the Columbia architectural school, William entered C.A.P.'s office in the fall of 1924. As I had announced at the age of four (1909) that I was going to be an architect, I considered William an interloper. He worked in the drafting room under C.A.P.'s watchful eye, and he was rapidly given as much responsibility as he could take. In due course, he was handling complete house projects and dealing with the clients, thus relieving C.A.P. of part of this heavy load. When C.A.P. turned a job over to him, he left him entirely alone to do the work. In time William began to get his own jobs and had a separate office with his own draftsmen. C.A.P. wanted him to develop independently. In addition to his personal work he participated in various capacities in a number of the main-office projects. I entered the office in the summer of 1931. The effects of the Depression were already being felt and work had all but dried up. C.A.P. had nurtured my early decision to be an architect by urging me to keep my options open. When I was about to go to Harvard, he advised me to get as broad an education as possible — good for an architectural career, but leaving me uncommitted. When it came time to go to Columbia for training, he said an architectural education would be a good experience even if I decided not to be an architect. Anyway, I went through with my original determination.

One might have expected during the years that Bill and I were growing up as architects that we would have been sitting at C.A.P.'s feet while he imparted to us great words of wisdom on art and architecture. But that was not his way. We learned by watching him go about his work and observing the results. After his death in 1933 we followed in his footsteps but only in our basic approach to design. We knew that every design was a whole, that every building must become a natural part of its site, and that the interior and its surroundings must be knitted together. The economic pressures after the Depression forced us to use every advantage the site held as one could no longer afford retaining walls, terraces, and formal gardens. We knew that every detail of the design must be exhaustively studied and shaped for its particular part in the composition. We may have lacked his powers of concentration in achieving rapidly the one and only solution, but when we did finally get it, we knew it was right. We have never regretted the legacy of prolonged and detailed study, but the economics of carrying out this design procedure in modern times did not seem to work as profitably in our office as it had for C.A.P. He never counted the cost of this essential study; nor did we.

On January 1, 1933, C.A.P. announced the formation of the firm of Charles A. Platt, William and Geoffrey Platt; at the time there was absolutely no work in the office. He died in September of that year. In January 1934, the firm of William and Geoffrey Platt came into being. We felt that it was important to establish our own identity and we knew that was what he would have wished.

Where we lived was of the greatest importance to all of us. In 1906, when I was a year old, the family moved into an apartment on the tenth and eleventh floors of 131 East 66th Street, a just-completed building that C.A.P. had designed. Most of the rooms were well-lit from the southern exposure provided by the low roof of the Church of St. Vincent Ferrer. The main feature of the apartment was a great two-story room with an enormous north window. Its dimensions were 24 by 28 feet with a 19-foot ceiling. The room was monumental but not the least bit intimidating. Its design and furnishing were Italian Renaissance in feeling and scale: dark wood wainscot, antique red brocatelle above, tapestries, huge stone mantel, bronze statue, chandeliers, painted beam ceiling, herringbone floors, Oriental rugs, big upholstered furniture. Everything in the room seemed just right for its place. It was a wonderful place for parties of all sizes, yet was comfortable to be in alone.

C.A.P. had a study on the lower floor in a wing to the north. There was an enormous chair equipped for taking naps, a long drafting table under the north window, and a desk, bookcases, and a record player with C.A.P.'s collection. A bridge table hid in a closet. The room was important to him as a retreat.

In the summer we lived in the house in Cornish, New Hampshire, that had evolved from its original status as a bachelor's studio in 1890 (enlarged in 1904 and again in 1909) to a roomy, comfortable family house. All the main spaces — entrance hall, parlor, dining room, and porch — faced south and were flooded with light, looking over the garden and the view down the Connecticut River Valley in the distance. The ground fell away from the main floor level, and both the parlor and the dining room had big triple windows reaching to the floor. This device bound the rooms, the view, and the garden together. At the west end of the house was a large open porch, called "the Piazza." One saw the view and Mt. Ascutney from there through Greek Doric columns. C.A.P. had his studio up the hill above the house. So he had a retreat, as in the apartment and at the office. Here he could paint, or putter, or work on his architecture.

There are several things to be said about the house in Cornish that apply to all of C.A.P.'s houses. His clarity of mind produced plans that were orderly, direct, and logical. One knew just where one was and turned with delight to savor the relationship of one space to another space, to the house, and to the outside. The proportions of the rooms were in perfect scale with the house, and their detail had a subtle fitness that gave each room its own character. In addition, the furniture, the decoration, and the paintings and objects in the various rooms were just right for their place. In its simplest terms, there was a rightness about everything that gave one a strong sense of comfort and serenity. The design of the outside of the house was very simple, and so was the design of the garden. No one element predominated over the other—they all took their place within the whole. So here we have this wonderful "place," house, garden view, all of a piece and a joy to live in.

The apartment was sold in 1934, and Mother moved to Cornish where she lived until her death in 1953. The house is more active than ever, being inhabited now by C.A.P.'s children, grandchildren, and great-grandchildren. It is withstanding a more intense use than ever was intended but is handling it with great equanimity. The house is full of his paintings and etchings and other of C.A.P.'s favorite things—a glorious inheritance for all of us!

Notes

INTRODUCTION

1. Royal Cortissoz, "Charles A. Platt, F.A.I.A. Etcher, Landscape Painter, Landscape Architect, Mural Painter and Architect," *Pencil Points* 14 (November 1933), 481. Reprinted from *The New York Herald Tribune,* September 15, 1933.

2. Barry Faulkner, "C.A.P. A Narrative Written for His Family," n.d., 1, Platt Office Papers, Geoffrey Platt, Bedford, N.Y. (hereinafter called Platt Office Papers).

3. Thomas E. Tallmadge, *The Story of Architecture in America* (New York: W. W. Norton & Co., 1927), 268.

4. G. H. Edgell, *The American Architecture of To-Day* (New York: Charles Scribner's Sons, 1928), 135–36, 248–49.

5. Wayne Andrews, *Architecture, Ambitions and Americans* (New York: Harper & Brothers, 1947), 200–201.

6. Henry-Russell Hitchcock, *Architecture. Nineteenth and Twentieth Centuries* (Baltimore: Penguin Books, 1958), 399.

7. *Monograph of the Works of Charles A. Platt. With An Introduction by Royal Cortissoz* (New York: Architectural Book Publishing Co., 1913), ix.

CHAPTER 1

1. Charles Moore, "Charles A. Platt," *Dictionary of American Biography* (New York: Charles Scribner's Sons, 1935), XV, 1–2.

2. G. Lewis Platt, *The Platt Lineage* (New York: T. Whittaker, 1891), 142. I am indebted to Henry Hope Reed, Jr., who did much of the genealogical research on Platt's forebears in the 1950s.

3. "William Barnes Platt," *Encyclopedia of Contemporary Biography of New York* (New York, 1878), I, 175.

4. "Charles H. Adams," *Encyclopedia of Contemporary Biography of New York* (New York, 1878), I, 208. Platt did not like his uncle, however, and always signed and called himself Charles A. Platt.

5. Charles Henry Pope, *The Cheney Genealogy* (Boston: C. H. Pope, 1897), 199 and passim.

6. William E. Buckley, *A New England Pattern. The History of Manchester, Connecticut* (Chester, Conn.: Pequot Press, 1973), 87ff.

7. For further information on Charles Platt's artist great-uncles, see: R. P. Tolman, "John Cheney," *Dictionary of American Biography* (New York: Charles Scribner's Sons, 1939), III, 52–53; and Harold V. Faulkner, "Seth Wells Cheney," *Dictionary of American Biography* (New York: Charles Scribner's Sons, 1937), III, 55–56.

8. Ednah Dow Cheney, *Memoir of John Cheney, Engraver* (Boston: Lee and Shepard Publishers, 1889), 50.

9. Ibid., 49.

10. "Memorial of John H. Platt," delivered at the Century Club, n.d., not paginated, Platt Office Papers.

11. Democratic Committee of Westchester County, New York, *Civil and Political Record of the Hon. Waldo Hutchins, M.C.* (New York, 1882). This brochure was part of an attempt to get Hutchins nominated as a gubernatorial candidate.

12. "Memorial of John H. Platt," op. cit.

13. Letter, Emily C. Learned to Charles Moore, November 8, 1933, Library of Congress, Manuscript Division, Charles Moore Papers, General Correspondence, Box 8, not paginated.

14. "Memorial of John H. Platt," op. cit.

15. Moore Papers, op. cit. Emily Learned continued to describe the active and social qualities of the Platt home: "It was characteristic that the boys had upper and lower bunks in their rooms. Herbert Putnam, Guy Waring, and the Lamberts were among those who used to congregate in that upper room." Information on the Platt family residence can be found in *Trow's General Directory of the Boroughs of Manhattan and Bronx, City of New York* (New York, 1861 continuing). During Charles Platt's first nine years, the family moved rather often: 1861–62, 155 East 19th Street; 1863, 96 East 19th Street; 1864, Long Island; 1865, 40 East 41st Street; 1866–67, no listing; 1868–69, Staten Island; 1870 forward, 90 Lexington Avenue. John Platt's office, however, remained at 40 Wall Street throughout Charles's life.

16. Interview, Geoffrey Platt, with author, May 16, 1977.

17. "John H. Platt," obituary, *New York Times,* August 8, 1886. For biographical information on Bryant, see: Allan Nevins, "William Cullen Bryant," *Dictionary of American Biography* (New York: Charles Scribner's Sons, 1937), II, 200–205. John Platt handled the copyrights for Bryant's poems and was an executor of his estate. New York Public Library, Manuscript Division, Bryant-Godwin Collection, contains two letters from John Platt concerning the copyright of Bryant's work: (1) to George H. Putnam, March 12, 1880; and (2) to Parke Godwin, June 23, 1880.

18. *The Century Association Year-Book* (New York, 1975), 7.

19. Letter, Charles Platt to his family, June 29, 1882, Platt Office Papers.

20. Letter, Charles A. Platt to Royal Cortissoz, June 10, 1913, Yale University, Beinecke Library, Cortissoz Papers, Platt Letter File.

21. Moore Papers, op. cit.

22. "An Industrial Experiment at South Manchester," *Harper's New Monthly Magazine* 45 (1872), 836–44.

23. Ibid., 840.

24. For an illustration and discussion of the Cheney Block, see: Henry-Russell Hitch-

cock, *The Architecture of H. H. Richardson and His Times* (rev. ed., Cambridge, Mass.: M.I.T. Press, 1961), 164ff. and pl. 43. The design for an addition to the Cheney Block was published in 1877.

25. Ibid., 161-63. The Rush Cheney project was designed in 1876, and the house for James Cheney in 1878. Because of White's success in detailing the William Watts Sherman house, 1875, Newport, Hitchcock thinks that White was given control of the similar Rush Cheney commission. When James Cheney actually built a house a few years later, he turned to White again.

26. One cousin remembered that Charles's parents were worried because he would not study and spent his hours in school staring out the window, absorbed in his own thought. Letter, Mrs. Clifford Cheney to Henry Hope Reed, Jr., October 4 (no year), 2, Platt Office Papers.

27. Letter, Alice G. Melrose to author, October 29, 1976.

28. Eliot Clark, *History of the National Academy of Design, 1825-1953* (New York: Columbia University Press, 1954), 90.

29. For further information on these artists, see: John Dennison Champlin, Jr., ed., *Cyclopedia of Painters and Paintings* (New York: Charles Scribner's Sons, 1913), I, 211 and 268; IV, 436.

30. Lois Marie Fink and Joshua C. Taylor, *Academy: The Academic Tradition in American Art* (Washington: Smithsonian Institution Press, 1975), 59.

31. Marchal E. Landgren, *Years of Art: The Story of the Art Students League of New York* (New York: R. M. McBride & Co., 1940), 21.

32. Richard Murray, "Painting and Sculpture," in *The American Renaissance 1876-1917* (Brooklyn, N.Y.: Brooklyn Museum, 1979), 155.

33. Letter, Charles A. Platt to John H. Platt, Nov. 25, 1884, Platt Office Papers.

34. See also: Ulrich Thieme and Felix Becker, "Stephen Parrish," in *Allgemeines Lexikon der Bildenden Kunst* (Leipzig: Verlag von E. A. Seemann, 1932), XXVI, 256.

35. Frank Weitenkampf, *American Graphic Art* (New York: Henry Holt & Co., 1912), 10.

36. Ripley Hitchcock, *Etching in America: With Lists of American Etchers and Notable Collections of Prints* (New York: White, Stokes & Allen, 1886), 13.

37. In 1883, Platt was visited by the illustrator Joseph Pennell who was passing through Paris on his way to Italy to prepare illustrations for an article on Tuscan cities by William Dean Howells. Platt had previously rejected an offer from *Century* magazine to provide etchings for this article, and wrote to his parents withering comments about Pennell: "He looks upon art in the light of business and talks about it in that way . . . " (CAP to family, 1/28/1883, Platt Office Papers; see n. 42 below).

38. S. R. Koehler, "The Works of American Etchers. XXV-. Charles A. Platt," *American Art Review* 2, pt. 2 (1881), 156.

39. Interview, William Platt with author, April 13, 1978.

40. For a fuller analysis of Platt's position in the etching revival, see: George E. Downing, "American Etching (c. 1875-1900). Studies in Relation to its Background in the Nineteenth Century Theory and Practice of Art," (Ph.D. diss., Harvard University, 1946).

41. Hitchcock, *Etching,* 76-80.

42.　The years 1882–86 are fully recorded in the letters written by Platt to members of his family. These have been preserved and are located with the Platt Office Papers. They have been transcribed and amount to 166 single-spaced, typed pages. Unfortunately, the only other sets of correspondence consist of a small number of letters between Platt and his wife in 1900–1902 and memoranda, telegrams, and letters from a few months Platt spent working for the Food Administration in Italy during the First World War. Because the Paris letters are a major source of information for these student years, they will be abbreviated in the Notes by use of CAP (Platt) to family member, date. In some cases, the letter took the form of a journal entry and was not addressed to anyone, thus: CAP journal, date. The quotations from Platt's letters have not been altered, nor has [*sic*] been inserted after errors, unless necessary for clarity.

43.　CAP to father, 11/10/1882: "I shall send home by way of the [J. D.] Warings some water-colors to be sent to the exhibitions and so forth and I hope that now that I am away the sale of my etchings will not stop." He was spending his days at this time experimenting with watercolors. For lists of what Platt exhibited in New York from 1882 onward, see the New York Etching Club and National Academy of Design catalogues. Charles was having success in Paris too. CAP to family, 11/24/1882: "Colonel Waring brought a friend of his in to look at my work. Major Forester, an English gentleman from Hampshire . . . he was so favorably impressed that he has bought four of my pictures." Two days later, Platt reported the sale of a sketch to another man, making his income from art work $380.00 for this unusual week.

44.　CAP to father, 5/29/1882.

45.　CAP journal, 8/10/1882.

46.　Theodore Child, "Frank Myers Boggs," *The Art Amateur,* August 1884, 54.

47.　For information on the Dutch School, see: David Croal Thomson, *The Brothers Maris* (London: The Studio, 1907), vii–viii; and Max Eisler, *Josef Israels* (London: The Studio, 1924), 5.

48.　CAP to family, 11/5/1883. The more important of the painters Platt visited were Jacob Maris (1837–99) and Joseph Israels (1824–1911). Maris had been trained in the studio Hébert in Paris and exhibited at the Salon from 1862 to 1872. In the latter year, he moved to The Hague and developed a reputation for marine landscapes with a Barbizon flavor: Thieme-Becker, "Jacob Maris," *Lexikon* (Leipzig: Verlag von E. A. Seemann, 1930), XXIV, 113–14: and Thieme-Becker, "Joseph Israels," *Lexikon* (Leipzig: Verlag von E. A. Seemann, 1926), XIX, 255–61.

49.　CAP to family, 6/5/1883.

50.　On December 9, 1882, Platt recorded in his journal:
> I am at present working on some sketches with a view to a largish picture for the Salon. It is the custom over here to do a Salon picture the first thing after getting back from the country, then you get the criticism of everyone before it is sent in. My subject is some boats at low tide in the Harbor of Trouville. The tide is running out and the boats are leaning up against the quay, in the distance are some dark buildings, a bridge, and a night sky reflected in the water. It's a stunning subject, was not easy to treat large. I shall do my best but if it is not a success, I shall not send it to the exhibition.

He later reported to his parents that the canvas was a little larger than 5 by 3 feet, which he feared they would think too big, but which he felt was smaller than most at the Salons. By the end of January 1883, it was nearly finished, and Boggs promised to bring friends for a critique. When the subject disappears from his letters and a trip is planned for May, it is obvious that the harbor view had not met with critical approval.

51. CAP to family, 4/19/1884.

52. CAP to family, 5/13/1884. There are no entries for Platt in the catalogue for the 1884 Salon: *Explication des ouvrages de peintres . . . exposés au palais des Champs-Elysees. Le 1er mai 1884* (Paris: E. Bernard, 1884). The *Art Amateur* and other American art periodicals make no mention of Platt in reviews of the Salon.

53. CAP to family, 12/25/1884. In this letter, Platt also gives a full report of his daily schedule and the geographical relationships of Julian's, his studio, and his residence.

54. CAP to father, 11/25/1884. Charles also calms his father's fear that he might want to settle in Paris permanently, but Platt reminds him that Eastman Johnson stayed in Paris for ten or eleven years: "Don't let any of your Academician friends, whom you meet at the Century, scare you into thinking that I will lose all capacity to treat American subjects. The sort of training that one gets here is of the purest kind, it teaches each man to study nature himself and to avoid mannerism in every way."

55. CAP to family, 5/28/1885.

56. "The Prize Fund Exhibition," *Art Amateur,* June 1885, 5, 24.

57. Letter, Platt to Cortissoz, op. cit. For information on Beaux-Arts education, theory, and influence, see: Arthur Drexler, ed., *The Architecture of the Ecole des Beaux-Arts* (New York: Museum of Modern Art, 1977), passim.

58. David Walker, "Sir John James Burnet," *Edwardian Architecture and its Origins,* ed. by Alistair Service (London: Architectural Press, 1975), 197.

59. CAP to mother, 7/23/1882.

60. When Platt met Frank Myers Boggs, he was impressed by the fact that his new friend "does all his pictures out of doors from nature and never works in a studio at all" (CAP journal, 8/12/1882).

61. CAP to family, 4/19/1884. Platt was describing paintings he had seen in Dresden following a visit to Uncle Charles Adams and family in Berlin.

62. CAP to family, 2/23/1885.

63. Royal Cortissoz, "Introduction," *A Monograph of the Works of Charles A. Platt* (New York: Architectural Book Publishing Co., 1913), iv.

64. Herbert Croly, "The Architectural Work of Charles A. Platt," *Architectural Record* 15 (March 1904), 242.

65. CAP to family, 10/19/1885.

66. CAP to mother, 2/8/1885.

67. Charles C. Burlingham, *Aunt Annie. Annie C. Hoe Platt, 1852–1887. A Sketch* (privately printed, 1957), passim.

68. CAP to mother, 2/8/1885.

69. Journal of Mrs. Stephen Parrish, Feb. 16, 1886, typescript, Platt Office Papers.

70. Letter, Geoffrey Platt to author, March 20, 1978.

71. CAP to family, 3/7/1886.

72. Charles C. Burlingham, "Reminiscences of Charles A. Platt," manuscript, Platt Office Papers.

73. Letter, Platt to Cortissoz, op. cit.: " . . . returning here in '87, I then was elected a

member of the Society of American Artists, and later an Associate of the National Academy of Design." For a discussion of the Society of American Artists, see: Fink and Taylor, *Academy,* 79–89.

74. The Century Association, Minutes of the Committee on Admissions, 1875–1897, 1887, not paginated, and *The Players* (New York: 1890), 9. The painter, George Henry Hall, and the publisher, Charles Collins, proposed Platt for membership in the Century; the painter, Thomas W. Dewing, and the architect, Stanford White, proposed Platt for membership in The Players.

75. Concerning Platt's activities in the summer of 1887, see: Letters, Dennis Bunker to Joe Evans, August 5, 14, September 16, and October 13, 1887, Archives of American Art, Washington, D.C., Dennis Bunker Papers. The following year, Bunker reported to Evans from England: "I've not been to see Miss Terry, but Platt went the other night with Campbell. . . . Platt has gone off to Holland, went last night." Letter, Dennis Bunker to Joe Evans, June 18, 1888, ibid. On September 11, 1888, Bunker again reported that Platt had sailed for America two days before. For information on Joe Evans, see: Charles C. Burlingham, *Joe Evans 1851–1898* (New York: by the author, 1949), passim.

CHAPTER 2

1. For a fuller discussion of Platt's work at Cornish, see: Keith N. Morgan, "Charles A. Platt's Houses and Gardens for the Cornish Colony," *Antiques* 122 (July 1982), 117–29.

2. Platt performed the following work for these sculptors: (1) for Saint-Gaudens, Platt handled the 1905 alterations of the pedestal for "The Puritan" in Philadelphia. That same year Platt advised on outdoor furniture, and his office conducted a topographical survey of the Saint-Gaudens property in Cornish. After the sculptor's death, Platt served as president of the Saint-Gaudens Memorial, a position subsequently held by his son and grandson. Letter, Augustus Saint-Gaudens to Charles Platt, May 4, 1905, Saint-Gaudens Papers, Dartmouth College Library. (2) After the death of Henry Bacon, Platt became French's assistant for architectural and landscape matters. These projects included: Russell Memorial, 1927, Greenfield, Mass.; Henry White Tablet, 1927–28, National Cathedral, Washington, D.C.; St. Mihiel Monument project, 1926; and the Washington Irving Monument, 1927, Irvington, N.Y. (3) Platt designed Herbert Adams's house in Plainfield and he collaborated with him on: World War I Monument, 1927, Fitchburg, Mass.; World War I Monument, 1926, Winchester, Mass.; and the McMillan Memorial Fountain, 1910–13, Washington, D.C.

3. The best discussion of gardening in Cornish is found in: Frances Duncan, "The Gardens of Cornish," *The Century Magazine* 72 (May 1906), 3–19.

4. Hugh Mason Wade, *A Brief History of Cornish, 1763–1974* (Hanover, N.H.: University Press of New England, 1975), 52.

5. Duncan, "Gardens of Cornish," 14.

6. The Platt house was enlarged as Platt's needs and family expanded. A large drawing-room wing was added on the eastern end in 1904, and the house assumed its present form by 1912. The only recent study of Platt's work as a landscape architect is found in: Norman Newton, *Design on the Land. The Development of Landscape Architecture* (Cambridge, Mass.: The Belknap Press of Harvard University Press, 1971).

7. For information on Annie Lazarus, see: Eduard Jacob Heinrich, *The World of Emma Lazarus* (New York: Schocken Books, 1949), 208–10 and passim.

8. Letter, Charles A. Platt to Stanford White, August 29, 1890, New-York Historical Society, Stanford White Papers, Platt Letter File. As built, the wings of High Court were a full two stories.

9. *A Monograph of the Works of McKim, Mead & White, 1879–1915* (rev. ed., New York: Benjamin Blom, 1973), 63, pl. 38.

10. The most comprehensive discussion of these important houses is: William C. Shopsin and Mosette Glaser Broderick, *The Villard Houses. Life Story of a Landmark* (New York: Viking Press in cooperation with the Municipal Art Society of New York, 1980). See also: Leland Roth, *McKim, Mead & White, Architects* (New York: Harper & Row, 1983), chap. 3.

11. Aymar Embury, "Charles A. Platt. His Works," *Architecture* 26 (August 1912), 142.

12. H. Edward Nettles, "Charles Eliot Norton," *Dictionary of American Biography* (New York: Charles Scribner's Sons, 1937), XIII, 569–72.

13. Charles Eliot Norton, *Notes of Study and Travel in Italy* (Boston: Ticknor and Fields, 1860).

14. Letter, Frederick Law Olmsted to Charles Eliot Norton, January 30, 1892, Library of Congress, F. L. Olmsted Collection, Letterpress.

15. Ibid.

16. Letter, Frederick Law Olmsted to William Platt, February 1, 1892, Library of Congress, F. L. Olmsted Collection, Letterpress. Also cited in Laura Wood Roper, *FLO. A Biography of Frederick Law Olmsted* (Baltimore: Johns Hopkins University Press, 1973), 433.

17. Letter, Charles A. Platt to Royal Cortissoz, June 30, 1913, Yale University, Beinecke Library, Cortissoz Collection, Platt Letter File. The long letter from which this quotation is taken was evidently written in response to questions raised by Cortissoz in preparation for his introduction to the Platt monograph. Platt gets the chronology confused, stating that William was a member of the Olmsted office when Charles returned from studying in Paris and that the brothers made their trip in 1888.

18. The itinerary for the Italian tour, taken from the labeled photographs in the "Italian Gardens" album at the Century Club Library included: (1) the Colonna Gardens; (2) the Quirinal Gardens; (3) Villa Aldobrandini, Rome; (4) Villa Medici, Rome; (5) Villa Mattei, Rome; (6) Villa d'Este, Tivoli; (7) Villa Aldobrandini, Frascati; (8) Villa Mondragone, Frascati; (9) Villa Muti, Frascati; (10) Villa Borghese, Rome; (11) Villa Albani, Frascati; (12) Villa Falconeri, Frascati; (13) Villa Conti, Frascati; (14) Villa Farnese, Caprarola; (15) Villa Lante, Bagnaia; (16) the Boboli Gardens, Florence; (17) Villa Medici, Castello; (18) Villa Medici, Poggio a Cajano; (19) Isola Bella, Lago Maggiore; and various squares and urban gardens in Palermo, Florence, and Genoa.

19. Charles Henry Pope, *The Platt Genealogy* (Boston: C. H. Pope, 1897), 409. William Barnes Platt was born May 16, 1868, and was twenty-four at the time of his death.

20. *World's Columbian Exposition. Revised Catalogue, Department of Fine Arts* (Chicago: W. B. Conkey & Co., 1893). Platt exhibited two paintings, "Winter Landscape" (#283) and "Early Spring" (#293), and showed seventeen etchings (#2360–76), primarily French and Dutch landscapes. He received bronze medals for both painting and etching (pp. 14–15), the bronze being the only class of medal awarded.

21. Barry Faulkner, "C.A.P. A Narrative Written for His Family," n.d., 1, Platt Office Papers.

22. Ibid.

23. *Garden and Forest* 5 (November 2, 1892), 528. *Garden and Forest* was "conducted" by Charles Sprague Sargent, director of Harvard's Arnold Arboretum, from 1888 to 1897. The death of William A. Stiles, editor for much of the journal's ten-year history, was announced in the October 6, 1897 issue, and publication ceased with the end of the calendar year. The periodical is the best indicator of current ideas during this important period for the developing landscape profession.

24. *Garden and Forest* 6 (August 2, 1893), 322. A review of Platt's July article in *Harper's Magazine* can be found in *Garden and Forest* 6 (July 5, 1893), 290.

25. Ibid.

26. Harper & Brothers and Charles A. Platt, April 17, 1893, Columbia University Library, Special Collections, Harper & Brothers Collection, Charles A. Platt File. The contract was altered from originally 2,000 to 1,000 additional words.

27. Platt, *Italian Gardens,* not paginated.

28. Ibid.

29. Ibid.

30. When the material appeared in book form, Charles Eliot mounted a critical attack in *The Nation:*

> The text of the book is very handsomely printed with wide margins, but consists of the briefest notes. Even if it is "taken purely as supplementary to the illustrations," as we are asked to take it, it is unsatisfactory. For the fairly-to-be-expected elucidation of the plates, plans (as well as fuller notes) are sadly needed, yet only one is provided. . . . Evidently our author is not acquainted with W. P. Tuckermann's "Die Gartenkunst der Italienischen Renaissance-Zeit," published in 1884, and containing some twenty cuts, some twenty ground-plans and cross-sections of Renaissance villas (*The Nation* 57 [December 1893], 491).

Eliot's criticisms were accurate, but Platt's purpose was in no way historical. He was still a painter and was interested in recording the qualities of the gardens as they had survived and not in the academic reconstruction of their original form.

31. For a description of the debate in England, see: Mark Girouard, *Sweetness and Light. The 'Queen Anne' Movement 1860–1900* (Oxford: Clarendon Press, 1977), 152ff.

32. For a brief discussion of the American interest in Italian gardens, see: David R. Coffin, "Introduction," in *The Italian Garden. First Dumbarton Oaks Colloquium on the History of Landscape Architecture* (Washington: Trustees for Harvard University, 1972). In addition to the books mentioned in the text, the following are notable early works on the Italian Renaissance garden, published in the United States: Julia Cartwright, *Italian Gardens of the Renaissance and Other Studies* (New York: Charles Scribner's Sons, 1914); and Harold Donaldson Eberlein, *Villas of Florence and Tuscany* (Philadelphia: Dodd, Mead & Co., 1926). Also important are American publications of English works and translations of Italian writings on Renaissance gardens.

33. Edith Wharton, *Italian Villas and Their Gardens* (New York: Century Co., 1905), 12. See also: R.W.B. Lewis, *Edith Wharton. A Biography* (New York: Harper & Brothers, 1975), 116–21.

34. Wharton, *Italian Villas,* 5.

35. Platt exhibited "Clouds" at the 1894 show of the Society of American Artists and was awarded the Webb landscape prize of $300. See: Letter, Thomas W. Dewing to Charles L. Freer, March 6, 1894, Freer Papers, Freer Gallery of Art, Washington, D.C.

36. Joan Platt, 1895–1904, 1, manuscript biography of Charles A. Platt, Platt Office Papers.

37. Croly was an important early supporter and publicist of Platt's work as an architect and garden designer through his articles and editorials in the *Architectural Record.*

38. Letter, Charles A. Platt to Royal Cortissoz, July 24, 1913, Yale University, Beinecke Library, Royal Cortissoz Collection, Platt Letter File.

39. Interview, Geoffrey Platt with author, June 29, 1981.

40. For documentation on the Eliot proposals for Faulkner Farm, consult the letters from Eliot to Charles F. Sprague in the Frederick Law Olmsted Papers, Manuscript Division, Library of Congress, Washington, D.C., Letter Book Volumes 38–43 (index to letters at the front of each volume).

41. Obituary of Charles F. Sprague, *New York Times,* January 31, 1902, 9:5.

42. According to existing records, Platt had not visited this renowned villa on any of his Italian tours. He certainly could have known it through the drawings of Percier and Fontaine or through Edouard André's book, *L'art des jardins,* which he purchased at about this time.

43. Barr Ferree, *American Estates and Gardens* (New York: Munn & Co., 1904), 289. Ferree offers a brief discussion of both the Hunnewell and Gardner gardens with multiple illustrations.

44. For information on the work of Carrère & Hastings, see: Curtis Channing Blake, "The Architecture of Carrère & Hastings," (Ph.D. diss., Columbia University, 1976), passim. Hastings discussed his plans for Indian Harbor in: Thomas Hastings, "Architectural Gardens," *Garden and Forest* 9 (June 17, 1896), 241.

45. The Freer-Dewing correspondence, Freer Gallery, Archives, passim.

46. Letter, Charles L. Freer to Thomas S. Jerome, November 17, 1900, Freer Papers, Letterpress. Freer also states here that Platt "is an intimate friend of Stanford White, Dewing and the New York gang."

47. Letter, Charles L. Freer to Frank J. Hecker, 1894, Freer Papers, passim.

48. Letter, Thomas L. Dewing to Charles A. Freer, July 21, 1897, Freer Papers, Letterpress.

49. Letter, Charles L. Freer to William G. Mather, June 28, 1898, Freer Papers, Letterpress.

50. As a result, their business relationship did not end amicably. On June 27, 1899, Freer wrote to Hecker: "I am sorry Platt finally went into court and somewhat surprised that he did not accept the offer you made his lawyer." Letter, Charles L. Freer to Frank J. Hecker, June 27, 1899, Freer Papers, Letterpress.

51. In explaining the design for Log Cabin Lands to his client, Eliot wrote: "The public grounds and all the streets are, by this plan, made curvilinear, in accordance with the expressed desires of your manager and your associates. The central public grounds shown on this plan are those which have already been conveyed to the city of Detroit. Several additional smaller open spaces are planned for different parts of the estate." Eliot to the Honorable T. W. Palmer, April 29, 1895, Olmsted Associates Papers, Vol.

40, # 101, Library of Congress, Washington, D.C. For a discussion of the Olmsted plans for Roland Park, see: Norman Newton, *Design on the Land*, 468–71.

52.   For an historical overview of American country clubs, see: C. D. Platt, "Country Clubs. A Thesis in Landscape Architecture 10," (master's thesis, Harvard University, 1924); the country club of Brookline is discussed on pp. 65–66.

53.   Letter, Charles Platt to Eleanor Platt, February 19, 1900, Platt Office Papers.

54.   Letter, Charles Platt to Eleanor Platt, October 14, 1900, Platt Office Papers.

55.   Letter, Charles Platt to Eleanor Platt, December 21, 1900, Platt Office Papers.

56.   Ibid.

57.   Ibid.

58.   The Clark garden was the subject of a 1980 master's thesis at the University of Connecticut by Judith A. Huhn.

59.   Pliny the Younger, *Letters*, trans. by William Melmoth (Cambridge, Mass.: Harvard University Press, 1940), I, 381–83. The excerpt from a letter to Domitius Apollinaris, Book V, vi, sounds the most like Glen Elsinore:

> [there is a] long portico, containing many divisions, one of which is an atrium, built after the manner of the ancients. In front of the portico is a terrace divided into a great number of geometrical figures, and bounded by a box hedge. . . . The whole is fenced in with a wall masked by box trees, which rise in graduated ranks to the top. Beyond the wall lies a meadow that owes as many beauties to nature as all I have described does to art. . . . At the extremity of the portico stands a grand dining room, which through its folding doors looks upon one end of the terrace; while beyond there is a very extensive prospect over the meadows up into the country.

60.   Charles A. Platt, "Villa," in *A Dictionary of Architecture and Building*, ed. by Russell Sturgis (New York: Macmillan Co., 1901), III, 905–6.

61.   Ibid., 906.

62.   Ibid.

63.   Ibid., 1004.

64.   Guy Lowell, *American Gardens* (Boston: Bates & Guild Co., 1902), introduction, not paginated.

65.   *Trow's General Directory of the Borough of Manhattan and Bronx, City of New York* (New York: Trow Publishing Co., 1897–98 and 1898–99).

66.   Until Platt moved his office to 26 East 20th Street in 1901, he used the landscape architect stamp for his books. Afterward, his stamp included his address but no occupation.

67.   Platt, "Villa," 1004.

CHAPTER 3

1.   Letter, Geoffrey Platt to author, June 30, 1984.

2.   Charles A. Platt, "Foreword," in R. W. Sexton, *Interior Architecture. The Design of Interiors of Modern American Homes* (New York: Architectural Book Publishing Co., 1927), not paginated.

3.   Harvard Lectures, Platt Office Papers. Platt was reluctant because of his native shyness. As he wrote in the introduction to a draft of the lecture notes, "when Prof. Warren wrote me last year asking if I would undertake three lectures . . . my first inclination was to decline, writing him that I had always avoided appearing in the light of a teacher on the ground that I had no capacity in that direction."

4.   Platt's correspondence with his family during his student years in Paris, 1882–87, and his letters to his wife from Rome in 1918–19, when he directed the U.S. Food Administration in Italy, are two major groups of personal papers that have survived. The family has a small number of other letters, and there is some correspondence to and from Platt in the papers of his friends and clients.

5.   For information about Americans trained at the Ecole, see: James P. Noffsinger, *Influence of the Ecole des Beaux-Arts on the Architecture of the United States* (Washington, D.C.: Catholic University Press, 1955), and Richard Chafee, "The Teaching of Architecture at the Ecole des Beaux-Arts," in Arthur Drexler, ed., *The Architecture of the Ecole des Beaux-Arts* (New York: Museum of Modern Art, 1977). Also, Richard Chafee, "Richardson's Record at the Ecole des Beaux-Arts," *Journal of the Society of Architectural Historians* 36 (October 1977), 175–88, gives a clear depiction of the nineteenth-century American experience at the Ecole.

6.   The most recent comprehensive study of Hunt is Paul R. Baker's *Richard Morris Hunt* (Cambridge, Mass.: MIT Press, 1980).

7.   Henry-Russell Hitchcock, *H. H. Richardson and His Times* (New York: Museum of Modern Art, 1936; rev. ed., Cambridge, Mass.: MIT Press, 1961), and Marianna Griswold van Rensselaer, *Henry Hobson Richardson and His Works* (Boston: Houghton Mifflin Co., 1888) remain the basic guides to Richardson and his architecture. Also of merit is Jeffrey Karl Ochsner, *H. H. Richardson. Complete Architectural Works* (Cambridge: MIT Press, 1982).

8.   Leland M. Roth, *McKim, Mead & White Architects* (New York: Harper & Row, 1983) is the most comprehensive analysis of the work and influence of this dominant late-nineteenth-century firm.

9.   A. D. F. Hamlin, "The Battle of Styles," *Architectural Record* 1 (March 31, 1982), 265–75, and (June 30, 1982), 405–13.

10.   Ibid., 265.

11.   Ibid., 272.

12.   Ibid., 275.

13.   Ibid.

14.   Herbert Croly, "The Works of Charles A. Platt," *Architectural Record* 15 (March 1904), 181.

15.   Ibid.

16.   Ibid., 182.

17.   Eyre stayed only one year at MIT, so he was the least affected by Ecole-inspired teaching of the four who attended architectural schools.

18.   For Cram's opinion on the Ecole, see: Ralph Adams Cram, "The Case Against the Ecole des Beaux-Arts," *American Architect and Building News,* 54 (December 26, 1896), 107–10.

19.   Curtis Channing Blake, "The Architecture of Carrère & Hastings," (Ph.D. diss.,

Columbia University, 1976), provides the fullest recent treatment of this firm's work.

20. Thomas Hastings, "Modern Architecture," in Ralph Adams Cram et al., *Six Lectures on Architecture* (Chicago: Chicago Art Institute, 1917), 98.

21. "Mr. Thomas Hastings on the Evolution of Style," *American Architect* 97 (February 9, 1910), 71.

22. Cass Gilbert, "The Greatest Element of Monumental Architecture," *American Architect,* 136 (August 5, 1929), 141.

23. See chap. 6.

24. Hastings, "Modern Architecture," 98–99.

25. Memorandum, Geoffrey Platt to the author, December 17, 1981. The story was recounted to Geoffrey Platt by Mrs. Lloyd Garrison, to whom Wright made the comment at a dinner party.

26. Interview, Henry Hope Reed, Jr., with William Platt, n.d., Platt Office Papers.

27. Reported to the author by Robert Schutz, Jr. Mr. Schutz's father commissioned Platt to design his Hartford, Connecticut, residence in 1907, as did Mr. Schutz's close friend, William G. Mather, in Cleveland, Ohio. Both Mather and Schutz were members of the Board of Trustees of Trinity College when a new college chapel was under consideration, and they naturally thought of Platt as the architect. A Gothic Revival chapel was ultimately designed by Frohman, Robb & Little in 1932.

28. Letter, Charles A. Platt to Royal Cortissoz, August 2, 1920. Yale University, Beinecke Library, Royal Cortissoz Papers, Platt Letter File.

29. Geoffrey Platt, conversation with the author, March 12, 1984.

30. Ralph Adams Cram, *Church Building. A Study of the Principles of Architecture in their Relation to the Church* (Boston: Marshall Jones Co., 1924), 1.

31. Ibid., 2.

32. Charles A. Platt, "Country Houses: Italy," Harvard University Lecture, February 12, 1914, Platt Office Papers, 2.

33. Cram, *Church Building,* 1.

34. Ibid., 43.

35. For modern appraisals of these architects, see: Douglass Shand Tucci, *Ralph Adams Cram. American Medievalist* (Boston: Boston Public Library, 1975) and Richard Oliver, *Bertram Grosvenor Goodhue* (New York and Cambridge, Mass.: The Architectural History Foundation and MIT Press, 1983).

36. Platt, "Country Houses: Italy," Harvard lecture, 3.

37. Out of 224 executed commissions, 126 were residential projects.

38. Betsy Fahlman's "The Architecture of Wilson Eyre," (master's thesis, University of Delaware, 1977), provides the only thorough study of Eyre's career, although Fahlman is preparing a monograph with the assistance of Edward Teitelman.

39. Julian Millard, "The Work of Wilson Eyre," *Architectural Record* 14 (October 1903), 284.

40. Platt, "Country Houses: Italy," 10.

41. Interview, Henry Hope Reed, Jr., with Schell Lewis, August 23, 1958, Platt Office Papers.

42. Ibid.

43. "Two eminent domestic architects: A comparison," *Architectural Review* 35 (March 1914), 61–63.

44. Letter, Charles Platt to Royal Cortissoz, June 30, 1913, Yale University, Beinecke Library, Cortissoz Papers, Platt Letter File.

45. Of course, the office personnel changed frequently between 1900 and 1933, with the exception of certain key individuals. George T. Goulstone and Francis L. Henderson, the engineering specialist, were members of the Platt team from the turn of the century onward. Schell Lewis joined the office around 1907 and remained there until he established a private practice as a renderer in the late 1920s. In the years just prior to the First World War, the staff assumed the size and organization it would maintain until Platt's death. The discussion of the design stages and personnel responsibility comes from discussions with both William and Geoffrey Platt.

46. Goulstone was a Canadian who worked for Platt from 1900 to 1933. Given the quality of the drawings that Goulstone produced from his earliest days in the Platt office, it can be assumed that he had worked previously for a Canadian architect, but no information on Goulstone's training or previous employment has survived.

47. Schell Lewis was a New Hampshire native and a nephew of Fred Waite, Platt's Cornish contractor. He started with Platt as an office boy but quickly showed exceptional skill at model making and rendering. He obtained his knowledge of architecture from practical experience in construction and from working with Platt.

48. Jerauld Dahler, "Charcoal Studies from the Office of Charles A. Platt," *Architecture* 31 (1915), 125–39, 147–61 discussed Lewis's rendering techniques.

49. Interview, Henry Hope Reed, Jr., with Schell Lewis, 1958, 2, Platt Office Papers.

50. Memorandum, Geoffrey Platt to author, July 1981.

51. This full-scale model of a Freer gallery became the office drafting room. Unfortunately, the Architects' Building, 101 Park Avenue South, where the Platt office was located at this time, was demolished in 1980.

52. Interview, William and Geoffrey Platt with author, April 13, 1978.

53. Memorandum, Geoffrey Platt to author, July 1981.

54. Harvard lecture, n.d., Platt Office Papers.

55. For a complete listing of the books in Platt's office library, see: Keith N. Morgan, "The Architecture and Landscapes of Charles A. Platt," (Ph.D. diss., Brown University, 1978), 315–41.

56. For varied views of the changing nature of American society during Platt's lifetime, consult: Richard Hofstadter, *The Age of Reform. From Bryan to F.D.R.* (New York: Vintage Books, 1955), and Robert H. Wiebe, *The Search for Order, 1877–1920* (New York: Hill and Wang, 1967).

57. William Herbert [Herbert Croly], *Houses for Town and Country* (New York: Duffield & Co., 1907). See especially pp. 3–4 and chap. 3.

58. Herbert Croly, *The Promise of American Life* (Cambridge, Mass.: The Belknap Press of Harvard University Press, 1965), 445. Originally published in 1909 by The Macmillan Co.

59. Interview, Henry Hope Reed, Jr., with William Platt, n.d., Platt Office Papers.

CHAPTER 4

1. Charles Downing Lay, "An Interview with Charles A. Platt," *Landscape Architecture* 2 (January 1912), 127.

2. For a general discussion of the economic considerations of the period, see: "The Performance of the American Economy Since 1860" in *The Growth of the American Economy,* ed. by Harold F. Williamson (New York: Prentice-Hall, 1944), 751–80.

3. Mark Girouard, *The Victorian Country House* (Oxford: Clarendon Press, 1971), 55. See also: Clive Aslet, *The Last Country Houses* (New Haven and London: Yale University Press, 1982), passim.

4. A. Lawrence Kocher, "The Country House: An Analysis of the Architect's Method of Approach," *Architectural Record* 62 (November 1927), 337.

5. For historical and cultural background on the country house movement, see: Peter T. Schmitt, *Back to Nature. The Arcadian Myth in Urban America, 1900–1930* (New York: Oxford University Press, 1969), chaps. 2 and 5. Schmitt does not differentiate between the country house development of the first two decades and a general move to suburbia.

6. "Over the draughting board—American Country Life and Art," *Architectural Record* 6 (January 1902), 112. The two new magazines alluded to were *Country Life in America* and *House and Garden.* In general, the author concluded that "the summer hotel is being supplanted by the country house."

7. James J. Fink, *The Car Culture* (Cambridge: MIT Press, 1975), 18.

8. For comments on the westward migration of the country house movement, see: A. C. David, "New Phases of American Domestic Architecture," *Architectural Record* 26 (November 1909), 311 and passim.

9. Platt's post-1913 domestic practice was by no means insubstantial. Although he averaged only three to four projects each year, he designed five houses in 1916. During the war years of 1918–19, he had no domestic jobs, and from 1920 until his death he was responsible for only thirteen country residences.

10. I am indebted to Geoffrey Platt for invaluable assistance in organizing and analyzing information on Platt's country houses, office, and library.

11. Charles A. Platt, "Foreword" in *Interior Architecture. The Design of Interiors of Modern American Homes* (New York: Architectural Book Publishing Co., 1927).

12. Barry Faulkner, "C.A.P. A Narrative Written for His Family," n.d., 6, Platt Office Papers.

13. "Performance of the American Economy," op. cit., 757–58 and 754 (fig. 2). A chart of Platt's country house projects reflects, but does not mirror, the business activity graph from 1900 to 1913. The crisis of 1903 caused a brief leveling in domestic commissions but the trend was reversed the following year when Platt had the highest number of country house projects of any year in his career. The 1907 crisis caused a more severe drop in Platt's activity, and the mild recession of 1910–11 reduced to zero the number of new jobs.

14. Commissions from the Cheney family included: Clifford D. Cheney (1904), J. Platt Cheney (1905–6), Frank J. Cheney, Jr. (1901), Mary Cheney (1900), J. Davenport Cheney (1905), and Phillip Cheney (1927–29).

15. As early as 1894, Platt had mentioned in a letter to Stanford White that he wanted

to show him a "scheme for an entrance to the Cheneys" (Letter, Charles Platt to Stanford White, August 12, 1894, New-York Historical Society, Stanford White Papers, Platt Letter File). Since Frank Cheney's house was the first family project Platt undertook, it is possible that the commission was under consideration seven years before the design was completed.

16. For further information on the library and the Maxwell family, see: George S. Brookes, *Cascades and Courage. The History of the Town of Vernon and the City of Rockville, Connecticut* (Rockville: T. F. Rady and Co., 1955), 270–74.

17. Interview, Mrs. Priscilla Maxwell Endicott with Henry Hope Reed, Jr., August 6, 1957, Platt Office Papers. "He started the plans, then held up for two years when he went abroad because he was ill. A frail man."

18. Ibid.

19. James Kornwolf, *M. H. Baillie Scott and the Arts and Crafts Movement. Pioneers of Modern Design* (Baltimore: Johns Hopkins Press, 1972), 34–71, discussed the influence of the English Arts and Crafts designers on American architects. Baillie Scott's work was published first in the United States in: C. Howard Walker, "Art Nouveau," *Architectural Review,* January 1904, 13–20. By this time, Voysey's work was also appearing in magazines like *House and Garden* and *House Beautiful;* see David Gebhard, *Charles F. A. Voysey, Architect* (Los Angeles: Hennessey & Ingalls, Inc., 1975), 88ff.

20. *American Architect and Building News,* 93 (April 29, 1908), 145.

21. "The Country Place of George L. Nichols, Esq.," *Architectural Record* 29 (April 1911), 310–17.

22. Two good articles on fireproof construction were: Benjamin A. Howes, "Architectural Development in Reinforced Concrete Houses," *Architectural Record* 25 (May 1909), 340–58; and M. M. Sloan, "The Architectural Treatment of Concrete Structures," *Architectural Record* 29 (May 1911), 401–6. The latter proposed new structural and ornamental forms appropriate to concrete.

23. The relationship of Sylvania to its site was noted by one architectural critic who recalled the respect "our fathers showed . . . in dotting the valley with domesticated Parthenons." "The House of Mr. John Jay Chapman at Barrytown, N.Y.," *Architectural Record* 24 (September 1908), 207.

24. Slade's sister, Emily, was a sculptor in Cornish, and Platt was building houses concurrently for both siblings. For illustrations and a description of the Emily Slade residence, Dingleton House, see: "A Cornish House and Garden," *Architectural Record* 22 (September 1907), 288–98. The initial construction of Woodston totaled $74,813.05 in 1907, but extensive alterations to the house and grounds were made in 1913 (Bills, January 11, 1907 and February 8, 1913, Platt Office Papers, Miscellaneous Architectural Services). For further information on Woodston, see: "The House of Mr. Marshall Slade at Mount Kisco, New York," *Architectural Record* 22 (September 1907), 260–71.

25. *Catalogue of an Exhibition of Etchings and Dry-Points by C. A. Platt at Frederick Keppel & Co., June 4 to June 29, 1907,* Introduction by Mrs. Schuyler van Rensselaer (New York, 1907), not paginated: "In the great *art of omitting,* Mr. Platt is in truth accomplished, and this is what gave his prints their simplicity, their harmony, their breadth, and unity of effect — what made it impossible to pick flaws in them as we could in more poetical and fervid work of Mr. Parrish."

26. "Colonial Architecture," photograph album, Century Association, Platt Library.

Platt seems to have purchased the photographs used later in: Frank Cousins and Phil M. Riley, *The Colonial Architecture of Philadelphia* (Boston: Little, Brown & Co., 1920), Pl. XIII. In a 1914 lecture, Platt showed a slide of the Wyck House and stated, "That to me suggests every kind of beauty in the country house." Lecture, Harvard, Platt Office Papers, 12.

27.　John Cordis Baker, ed., *American Country Homes and Their Gardens* (Philadelphia: House & Garden, 1906), 42–50.

28.　"Slade House," op. cit., 261–62.

29.　George Palmer formed an important collection of American decorative arts, which was sold to Mrs. Russell Sage and is now in the Metropolitan Museum of Art. The sale of his furniture provided funds to build the Palmer Chemistry Building at Northfield School, Northfield, Massachusetts, which Platt designed in 1926. Other Platt projects with which Palmer was involved included gates for the Cedar Grove Cemetery in New London and buildings at Connecticut College, where Palmer was a trustee. For Connecticut College Platt designed Palmer Library (1922) and Fanning Hall (1929–30). Platt was also the architect of the Lyman Allyn Museum of Arts (1928–30) located adjacent to the Connecticut College campus.

30.　William G. Mather, owner of Gwinn, recommended Platt as an architect to Robert H. Schutz. Schutz and Mather were fellow trustees of Trinity College in Hartford.

31.　Platt's first scheme for a nine-bay, two-and-a-half-story residence was rejected by Schutz with admonitions that he was not building Versailles. Interview, Robert H. Schutz, Jr., with author, August 17, 1975.

32.　"Schedule of Contracts and Extra Work for J.T. Pratt, Esq., Glen Cove, N.Y., December 1, 1911," Platt Office Papers.

33.　Now demolished, Timberline was a large and elegant house which cost $169,929 to construct (Platt Office Papers). Although Platt designed the formal gardens, Olmsted Associates was responsible for the landscape planning beyond the environs of the house (Olmsted Associates Collection, B221, #3250, Library of Congress, Washington, D.C.).

34.　Lecture, Harvard, op. cit., 8. This statement was made in discussing the McCormick House at Lake Forest, Illinois. For a comparative discussion of these three houses, see: Phil M. Riley, "The Spirit of the Renaissance on the Great Lakes. Three Modern Mid-Western Homes, designed by Charles A. Platt," *Country Life* 12 (September 1912), 28–30.

35.　As early as June 28, 1898, Charles L. Freer had recommended Platt's work to William Mather (Letter, Charles L. Freer to William G. Mather, Freer Papers, Freer Gallery of Art, Washington, D.C.). Mather had asked the landscape architect Warren Manning to help him select a house site, and Manning may also have recommended Platt as the architect (Letter, James D. Ireland to author, February 14, 1977). Manning served as the landscape architect for the more informal gardens located across Lakeshore Boulevard.

36.　The White House is prominently illustrated in Platt's photograph album on Colonial American architecture now at the Century Association.

37.　Charles Freer was a friend of the Alger family and may have recommended Platt for this commission.

38.　For biographical background on Mr. and Mrs. McCormick, see: "Harold Fowler McCormick," in *The National Encyclopedia of American Biography*, XXXV (New York: James T. White & Co., 1940), 9–10; and "Edith Rockefeller McCormick," in *The*

National Encyclopedia of American Biography, C (New York: James T. White & Co., 1930), 149.

39. Letter, Harold F. McCormick to James Gamble Rogers, August 28, 1906, Harold F. McCormick Papers, State Historical Society of Wisconsin, Madison, Wisconsin. I am indebted to Mark Nickerson for assistance with material from the McCormick Papers. James Gamble Rogers (1867–1947) was a successful Beaux-Arts architect, best known for the Harkness Memorial Quadrangle (1930) at Yale University.

40. Ibid.

41. Henry-Russell Hitchcock, *In the Nature of Materials. 1887–1914. The Buildings of Frank Lloyd Wright* (New York: Da Capo Press, 1976; 1st ed., 1942), 47.

42. Grant Carpenter Manson. *Frank Lloyd Wright to 1910. The First Golden Age* (New York; Reinhold Publishing Co., 1958), 202:
> "The story of the rejection of the McCormick design has never been fully revealed. It has been suggested that it was Mrs. McCormick who refused it, saying that her mode of life simply could not be suited by a Prairie House. In any case it was she who suddenly went to New York in August, 1908, and placed the commission for the house which she eventually occupied in the hands of a master of traditional architecture, Charles Augustus [*sic*] Platt, who gave her a handsome Italian villa that is as knowing a piece of archeology as can be seen in the Middle West. That it was erected upon the ruins of the Chicago School was, for him, unimportant."

A search in the Harold Fowler McCormick Papers, State Historical Society of Wisconsin, has produced no new information on the change in architects.

43. Ibid., 201.

44. Lectures, Harvard, op. cit., 2. Leonard K. Eaton, *Two Chicago Architects and Their Clients: Frank Lloyd Wright and Howard Van Doren Shaw* (Cambridge, Mass.: MIT Press, 1973), compares the patronage patterns for Wright and for Shaw, a Chicago architect whose work was heavily influenced by Platt. Although Eaton's book is flawed by an obvious bias for Wright and his middle-class clients in comparison with Shaw and his wealthier patrons, he does provide a composite of a typical Shaw client that could be applied equally to Platt's situation:
> [He is] a businessman born into sufficiently favorable circumstances so that his parents can give him some degree of higher education . . . he will normally be concerned with manufacturing, processing, or commercial paper . . . [and] with the expansion of the market. . . . When he builds a house, money is not a major problem. . . . His wife will come from the same social and economic background. . . . In the house-building project he will take the lead in working with the architect, while she will be in charge of furnishing the interior. . . . Because the family is quite sociable, the program of the house is likely to stress spaces for entertaining and guest rooms. . . . In short, the house should be a proper setting for the upperclass life of its owner [pp. 178–79].

45. I do not know whether Platt ever saw the plans Wright had developed for the McCormicks.

46. Telegram, Harold F. McCormick to Charles A. Platt, May 22, 1908, McCormick Papers.

47. Letter, Harold F. McCormick to Charles A. Platt, May 29, 1908, McCormick Papers. The clients were eager to restrict the first building campaign to a $50,000 house.

48. Villa Turicum was designed in three sections: (1) 1908, comprised the U-shaped

court facing the lake; (2) 1910–11, consisted of an E-shaped plan added to the base of the U, thus creating the two interior courtyards; and (3) 1917–18, never executed, would have included two wings added on the west, forming an entrance court; the northern one would have contained bedrooms, the larger southern one was designed for a music room and an art gallery surrounded by loggias.

49.   Platt based the entrance on the portal of the Palazzo delle Ritirata at the Villa Mondragone, Frascati. See: Carl L. Franck, *The Villas of Frascati 1550–1750* (London: Alec Tiranti, 1966), 63, fig. 58. Platt also borrowed the dragons from fountains at this Frascati villa to ornament the water staircase at Lake Forest.

50.   Lectures, Harvard, op. cit., 3.

51.   Platt greatly admired both the Villa Lante ("the most complete example of the Italian villa") and the Villa d'Este ("if one could study but a single villa in Italy, this should be the chosen one"). Charles A. Platt, *Italian Gardens* (New York: Harper & Brothers, 1894), 13 and 71.

52.   Herbert Croly, "The Architect's Library," *Architectural Record* 35 (January 1914), 89. Croly continued: "Numerous monographs on contemporary architects have been printed both in architectural and other periodicals; but this is the first book devoted exclusively to the work of any one designer."

53.   There are at least two earlier publications that are somewhat similar in nature. Marianna Griswold van Rensselaer's *Henry Hobson Richardson and His Works* (Boston: Houghton Mifflin Co., 1888) was a comprehensive biography of Richardson and analysis of his architecture published two years after his death. In 1912, the year before the Platt monograph appeared, the architects Albro & Lindeberg privately printed a monograph on their work entitled *Domestic Architecture.* The Platt book differs from both earlier publications in being a collection of photographs, drawings, and architectural details produced for the use of other professionals by a commercial publisher for profit. *A Monograph of the Works of McKim, Mead and White* (New York: Architectural Book Publishing Co., 1915) was an expansion of the Platt model, which was subsequently used for photographic monographs on most of the East Coast architects of the 1910s and 1920s.

54.   Letter, Geoffrey Platt to author, December 11, 1983.

55.   These included *Architectural Record, American Architect and Building News, Architectural Review, House and Garden, House Beautiful, Harper's Magazine, The Century Magazine, The Nation, The National Architect, Architecture, Brickbuilder, Landscape Architecture, Arts and Decoration,* and *Country Life in America.* For the citations to specific articles on Platt in these periodicals, consult: Keith N. Morgan, "The Architecture and Landscapes of Charles A. Platt (1861–1933)," (Ph.D. diss., Brown University, 1978), 356–68.

56.   Ibid., 344–56, is a list of books in which Platt's work is illustrated or discussed.

57.   "Two eminent domestic architects: A comparison," *Architectural Review* 35 (March 1914), 61–63.

58.   Ibid., 61.

59.   Hermann Muthesius, *Landhaus und Garten* (Munich: F. Bruckmann, 1907), 199 and 216, and Werner Hegemann, *Amerikanische architektur und Stadtbaukunst* (Berlin: Ernst Wasmuth, 1925), 142.

60.   Jacques Gréber, *L'Architecture aux Etats-Unis. Preuve de la Force d'Expansion du Génie Français* (Paris: Payot & Cie., 1920), 68–72.

61. For Adler, see: Richard Pratt, *David Adler. The Architect and His Work* (New York: M. Evans & Co., 1970), p. 15 and passim. For Shaw, see: Leonard K. Eaton, *Two Chicago Architects and Their Clients* (Cambridge, Mass.: MIT Press, 1969), 147, 186, 188, and 193.

62. W. Hawkins Ferry, *The Buildings of Detroit. A History* (Detroit: Wayne State University Press, 1968), 224.

63. James Grady, *The Architecture of Neel Reid in Georgia* (Athens: University of Georgia Press, 1973), passim.

64. Thomas Gold Frost, *A Treatise on the Federal Income Tax Law of 1913* (Albany: Matthew Bender & Co., 1913), 2: "In order to avoid any attack upon the constitutionality of future income tax laws, the sixteenth amendment to the United States Constitution was adopted early in the year 1913."

65. Merlo J. Pusey, *Eugene Meyer* (New York: Alfred A. Knopf, 1974), lll.

66. Letter, Eugene Meyer to Charles L. Freer, September 17, 1918, Eugene Meyer Collection, Manuscript Division, Library of Congress, Washington, D.C. Even less influenced by historical models was a country retreat Platt had completed for Charles L. Freer in 1917 at Great Barrington, Massachusetts. For illustration and further discussion of the Freer Bungalow, see: Keith N. Morgan, "The Patronage Matrix. Charles A. Platt, Architect, Charles L. Freer, Client," *Winterthur Portfolio* 17 (Summer/Autumn, 1982), 129–31.

67. The "Little Farm" at Girdle Ridge included a dairy barn, hog pen, pig pen, ice house, pheasant run, laundry, and garage, all designed by Platt between 1913 and 1923.

68. For a full description of the Hare estate, see: Herbert Croly, "Pidgeon Hill, Residence of Meredith Hare, Esq., Huntington, L.I., Charles A. Platt, Architect," *Architectural Record* 47 (September 1920), 178–91.

CHAPTER 5

1. The property is now occupied by St. Joseph's-by-the-Sea High School, and the buildings have been demolished.

2. Platt's town house clients for whom he designed a country residence were: Frederick S. Lee, Woodstock, Vt., 1906–8; George L. Nichols, Katonah, N.Y., 1906; William Fahnestock, Katonah, N.Y., 1909–24, and Newport, R.I., 1926–27; Harold McCormick, Lake Forest, Ill., 1908–18; and John T. Pratt, Glen Cove, N.Y., 1901–11. For further information on these commissions, see the List of Buildings, Gardens, and Projects.

3. Herbert Croly, "The Contemporary New York Residence," *Architectural Record* 12 (December 1902), 704.

4. "The House of Frederick S. Lee, New York City," *Architectural Record* 20 (November 1906), 427.

5. The balcony has since been pulled closer to the facade because of building codes.

6. For a survey of contemporary town houses, see: Croly, op. cit., or Montgomery Schuyler, "The Small City House in New York," *Architectural Record* 7 (April 1899), 357–88.

7. Contract Records, October 27, 1908, Platt Office Papers.

8. "Sara Delano Roosevelt Memorial House," New York City Landmarks Preservation Commission, September 25, 1973, Number 2, LP-0702. See also: Eleanor Roosevelt, *This Is My Story* (New York: Harper & Brothers, 1937), 152; and Joseph P. Lash, *Eleanor and Franklin* (New York: W. W. Norton & Co., 1971), 160.

9. In essence, Platt's solution was a combination of his ideas for the first level of the Lee house and that of a narrow town house he had remodeled for Norman Hapgood the previous year. For information on the Hapgood house, see: "The House of Mr. Norman Hapgood, East 73rd Street, New York City," *Architectural Record* 18 (July 1905), 8–13. Hapgood's remodeled house was much smaller than the Roosevelt residences, but it was similar in the ground floor arrangements. The entrance hall had an alcove for coats and a fireplace that gave it the feeling of a reception room. A triple-arched screen separated this area from the stairwell and from a narrow hallway leading to the dining room at the rear.

10. Both houses have been demolished. For information on 844 Fifth Avenue, see: "Residence, 844 Fifth Avenue, New York City," *Architectural Record* 21 (June 1907), 174–77.

11. The Pratt town house was Platt's most expensive city residence, costing $177,858.67. Contract Records, September 12, 1917, Platt Office Papers.

12. Platt's two 1920s town houses were located near each other in New York City and were similar in design, both being three bays wide, five stories tall, and built of brick with limestone trim: George L. Nichols, 108 East 37th Street, 1920; and Henry S. Morgan, 34 East 36th Street, 1925–26; both New York City.

13. When built, the Meeker house was located in a rather sparsely populated area that has since become densely built up. The residence was so prominent that it gave the neighborhood its unofficial name of Meekerville. See: Arthur Meeker, Jr., *Chicago With Love. A Polite and Personal History* (New York: Alfred A. Knopf, 1955), 68–69; and "Mrs. Meeker, Civic Leader 50 Years, Dies," *Chicago Daily News,* November 21, 1948.

14. Interview, William Platt with author, July 29, 1981.

15. The architectural press frequently reported statistics comparing house and apartment building construction in Manhattan. For example, see: A. C. David, "A Co-operative Studio Building," *Architectural Record* 14 (October 1903), 233. The earliest type was a five-floor building on a single lot with one apartment per floor.

16. "Apartment Buildings," *American Architect and Building News* 76 (June 28, 1902), 97.

17. For a discussion of the duplex apartment in New York, see: Robert A. M. Stern, "With Rhetoric: The New York Apartment House," *Via* IV (Cambridge, Mass.: University of Pennsylvania Graduate School of Architecture and MIT Press, 1980) 80ff.

18. David, op. cit., 234.

19. For an example of an early cooperative apartment building, see: D. Arnold Lewis and Keith N. Morgan, *American Victorian Architecture* (New York: Dover Press, 1975), II. 29, 87, and 149.

20. David, op. cit., 233.

21. The Studio Building was a commission for Frederick S. Culver, a real estate promoter; Culver had married Anna Osgood, for whom Platt had designed a country house at Hadlyme, Connecticut, in 1902.

22. A. C. David, "Co-operative Apartment House in New York," *Architectural Record* 24 (July 1908), 11.

23. David, "Co-operative Studio," 236. According to David, earlier studio buildings were erected at 57th Street and Seventh Avenue, 14th Street and Sixth Avenue, and 25 West 67th Street, but he neglected to provide the names of these buildings, their architects, or their dates. Stern, "With Rhetoric," 81, also mentions "the Bryant Park Studios, 80 West 40th Street, designed around 1900 by Charles Rich."

24. There is a bank of duplex apartments without studio rooms in the southeast corner of the building.

25. David, "Co-operative Studio," 233. The Studio Building which influenced plans for the 66th Street structure was located at 25 West 67th Street. It was designed by Sturgis & Simonson, and the cooperative was organized by Henry W. Ranger, the landscape painter.

26. For an analysis of tall-building design solutions, see: Winston Weisman, "A New View of Skyscraper History," in *The Rise of An American Architecture,* ed. by Edgar Kaufmann (New York: Praeger Publishers, 1970), 119 and passim. Platt's "skyscrapers" were never more than eighteen stories tall. Their design was closest to Weisman's Phase IV, but Platt developed a more horizontal-block format.

27. David, "Co-operative Apartment House," 1. Certain earlier studio buildings, such as the one on West 67th Street, had been in violation of the tenement height law. It was necessary to erect a twelve-story building for financial success, but a structure of that height had to be built on an avenue to meet the tenement law, thus increasing the cost of the land.

28. Platt designed or altered the apartments for Howard C. Hart, Percy Kent, Theodore F. Luling, F. S. Culver, Gordon Grant, H. O. Taylor, John W. Woolsey, Otis Skinner, C. F. Schallcross, "Mrs. Thaw," and himself.

29. Interview, Duncan Harris with Henry Hope Reed, Jr., February 28, 1958; and Interview, Mrs. Montgomery Angell with Henry Hope Reed, Jr., January 22, 1958, Platt Office Papers. Nicholas Biddle came to the Astor Trust in 1903–4 as adviser to Vincent's father and remained as manager until his death in 1923.

30. "Vincent Astor," obituary, February 4, 1959, *New York Times,* 33:3. Vincent Astor's parents were Colonel John Jacob Astor and Ava Lowie Willing. They were divorced in 1909; he married a woman the age of his son and she became Lady Ribblesdale. Vincent inherited a fortune of $87.2 million, of which $63 million was in real estate.

31. For a discussion of Vincent Astor's real estate ventures, see: Lucy Kavalier, *The Astors. A Family Chronicle* (London: George G. Harrap & Co, 1968), 232–35; and Harvey O'Connor, *The Astors* (New York: Alfred A. Knopf, 1941), 330–40.

32. The Knickerbocker had a bar which was decorated at Platt's suggestion with the famous King Cole mural by Maxfield Parrish. When the hotel was altered, the painting was lent to the Metropolitan Museum. When prohibition was ended in 1933, the painting was placed in the St. Regis Hotel (then owned by the Astors) in the newly decorated King Cole Bar. Memorandum, Geoffrey Platt to author, September 1983.

33. For a discussion of the courtyard apartment building type, see: Stern, "With Rhetoric," 88–90. Hardenbergh's Vancolear apartment building of 1879 should actually be credited as the first use of the French-derived courtyard formula, but the Dakota popularized the scheme. However, it was not until after 1900 that courtyard apartment houses were constructed regularly in New York.

34. O'Connor, *The Astors,* 336.

35. "The Development of the Apartment House," *American Architect* 110 (November 29, 1916), 335. The author continued: "It is not to be wondered that this type of dwelling is rapidly superseding the house with its many cares, fewer conveniences and large expense of maintenance."

36. Contemporary critics felt that Platt had achieved a degree of domesticity in the facades of his apartment buildings.

37. O'Connor, *The Astors,* 335.

38. In addition to the three apartment buildings mentioned in the text, Platt remodeled two brownstone town houses at 180–190 East End Avenue in 1932.

39. For a discussion of the 1916 New York Zoning Law and its effects on tall building design, see: Weisman, op. cit., 149–50.

40. For illustrations of McKim, Mead & White's designs modeled on the Palazzo Davanzati, see: *A Monograph of the Works of McKim, Mead & White* (New York: Architectural Book Publishing Co., 1915), pls. 196–97 (St. Gabriel's Branch, New York Public Library, 1906), and pls. 234–35 (Gorham Building, 1906).

41. The Astor interest in the area of Fifth Avenue and 33rd and 34th streets dated from the location of family mansions here in the mid-nineteenth century. These were, in part, replaced by the Waldorf-Astoria Hotel in the 1890s. In the 1910s Vincent Astor began building and remodeling, with Platt's help, office and commercial buildings on the adjacent lots. Among the more interesting of these commercial structures were two contiguous buildings at 18 and 28–30 West 33rd Street. For more information on the involvement of the Astor family with this area of New York, see: Kavalier, *The Astors,* 232, and Frederick Platt, *America's Gilded Age. Its Architecture and Decoration* (New York: A. S. Barnes & Co., 1976), 133–35. The Empire State Building was built on the site of the Waldorf-Astoria during the 1930s.

42. *Monograph of the Works of Charles A. Platt, With An Introduction by Royal Cortissoz* (New York: Architectural Book Publishing Co., 1913), ix.

43. Charles A. Platt, "Country Houses: Italy," Harvard lectures, 3, Platt Office Papers.

44. Hastings's comments appeared in a December 30, 1894 article in the *New York Tribune* discussing Bruce Price's winning design for the American Surety Building.

45. Herbert D. Croly, "The Leader News Building," *Architectural Record* 33 (June 1913), 503.

46. Croly, "Leader News," 504–6.

CHAPTER 6

1. There were fifteen unexecuted projects out of the 109 commissions for these years. In addition to the consultancies discussed in the text, Platt advised Phillips Academy, Exeter, New Hampshire, and the Metropolitan Square Corporation in New York.

2. In addition to those monuments mentioned in the text, Platt designed: The Daughters of the American Revolution Fountain, 1920; Eugene Meyer Mausoleum, 1923–24; Justice Chase Monument, 1923; Palmer Cemetery Gates, 1925; Crowninshield gravestone, 1925; St. Mihiel Monument, 1926; Winchester War Memorial, 1926; Goadby Memorial, 1926; Washington Irving Memorial, 1927; Cornell gravestone, 1927; Russell Monument, 1927; Henry White Memorial Tablet, 1927–28; Fitchburg War Memorial, 1927–29; Greenwich War Memorial, 1927–28; Rainey Memorial

Gates, 1929–33. For further information on these commissions, consult the catalogue of Platt projects. These should be compared to the three commissions received previously for monuments. In addition, most of Platt's institutional structures were intended as memorials to a donor or important individual.

3. Letter, Charles Moore to Charles Platt, October 18, 1919. Commission of Fine Arts, Washington, D.C., Archives. As early as 1913, Platt was involved with Arlington Cemetery when he was asked to advise on a master plan for development.

4. Contract for Professional Services, December 3, 1926, Platt Office Papers, Contracts. The chapel, designed in 1927, was still under construction in 1929 when Platt visited the site.

5. Independently, Platt designed an obelisk for the War Memorial (1927–28) in Greenwich, Connecticut. He collaborated with Daniel Chester French on the Russell Monument (1927), Greenfield, Mass.; Henry White Memorial Tablet (1927–28), National Cathedral, Washington, D.C.; St. Mihiel Monument (1926); and the Washington Irving Memorial (1927), Irvington, N.Y. With Herbert Adams, he designed the World War I Monument (1927), Fitchburg, Mass.; the World War I Monument (1926), Winchester, Mass.; and the McMillan Memorial Fountain (1908–11), Washington, D.C.

6. In Detroit, Platt also collaborated with Stanford White on the landscape and architecture of the Hecker Mausoleum (1898). Freer recommended Platt in 1898 to William G. Mather, eventual builder of "Gwinn" (1908) in Cleveland, and served on the McMillan Memorial Commission that chose Herbert Adams as sculptor and Charles Platt as architect for the McMillan Memorial Fountain (1910) in Washington, D.C. Thus, it was no surprise that Freer commissioned Platt to design a permanent home for his Oriental and American art collections.

7. For biographical information on Freer, see: Leila Mechlin, "Charles Lang Freer" in the *Dictionary of American Biography* (New York: Charles Scribner's Sons, 1937), VII, 14–15; and Agnes E. Meyer, *Charles Lang Freer and His Gallery* (Washington, D.C.: Freer Gallery of Art, 1970), passim. For information on Freer as a collector of American art, see: Nichols Clark, "Charles Lang Freer: Patron of American Art in the Gilded Era," (master's thesis, University of Delaware, 1975).

8. The earliest correspondence between Freer and Platt concerning the gallery was dated January 5, 1913. Freer Papers, Freer Gallery of Art, Washington, D.C.

9. By oral tradition, this sketch is held to be Freer's earliest proposal for the gallery. He also recorded on this sheet, in a different ink, "Blueprint sent Dr. Walcott on April 26." Charles D. Walcott was the Secretary of the Smithsonian Institution, recipient of the Freer bequest; the April 26 blueprint was probably dated 1913, since the earliest floor plans were sent from Platt's office in November of that year. Unfortunately, Freer's original sketch has been lost, but a slide of the drawing is held by the gallery.

10. Fig. 110 shows three early elevation renderings by G. T. Goulstone for the Freer Gallery. The top drawing is the one possibly derived from Freer's five-part plans.

11. Freer made notes on Tudor houses that he liked in books, such as A. H. Malan's *More Famous Homes of Great Britain.* His list included: Layer Marney Hall, Sutton Place, Cowdray, Parmham Manor House, Hengrave Hall, Chavenage Manor House, Athelhampton Hall, Haddon Hall, Yaverland Manor House, Forde Abbey, Compton Wynyates, Montacute House, Barrington Court, Coughton Manor House, Crosby Hall, Lytes Cary, Horham Hall, Borwich Hall, Houghton Tower, and Hampton Court.

12. On one corner of a classically derived plan Freer wrote, "See South Wraxall Manor House Vol. I."

233

13. In a November 23, 1914 letter, Freer mentioned that he was sending Platt a book and photographs of Japanese bridges (Freer Archives). There is no indication, however, that Freer wanted to use a Japanese bridge in the garden court of the gallery.

14. For a description of the McMillan Commission plans for Washington and the role of the Commission of Fine Arts, see: John W. Reps, *Monumental Washington. The Planning and Development of the Capital Center* (Princeton: Princeton University Press, 1967), chaps. 4–7. Platt held a four-year term on the Commission of Fine Arts from September 1, 1916, to September 1, 1920. For information on his activities, see *Minutes of the Commission of Fine Arts,* Commission of Fine Arts, Washington D.C., Archives. One of the commission projects on which Platt had an important effect was in the early planning of Meridian Hill Park. Horace Peaselee was the architect, but Platt offered extensive criticism of the design during the summer months of 1919.

15. Commission of Fine Arts, *Message from the President of the United States transmitting the report of the commission of fine arts for the fiscal year ended June 30, 1914* (Washington, D.C.: U.S. Government Printing Office, 1915), 22.

16. Interview, Schell Lewis with Henry Hope Reed, Jr., January 23, 1958, Platt Office Papers. Lewis stated: "I spent one year laying out perspectives. . . . Did over 100 versions . . . pinned on the office wall and discussed."

17. Letters between Charles Platt and Charles Walcott, January 12, 1914, through December 9, 1915, Smithsonian Institution Archives, Freer Gallery File, detail the consideration of various sites.

18. Freer's health is discussed in letters between Platt and Freer, January 1 through July 14, 1915, Freer Papers. See also Agnes Meyer, *Charles Lang Freer and His Gallery,* 18. Letters from Freer to Mrs. Meyer during this period discussed problems in finding and keeping hotel rooms because of the rumors of his disease. Agnes E. Meyer Papers, Manuscript Division, Library of Congress, Washington, D.C. For a further discussion of Freer's financial situation and Eugene Meyer's role in selling the Parke, Davis stock, see: Merlo J. Pusey, *Eugene Meyer* (New York: Alfred A. Knopf, 1974), 111.

19. Letter, Charles Platt to Charles Walcott, May 23, 1916, Smithsonian Institution Archives, Freer Gallery File.

20. Letter, Charles Freer to Agnes Meyer, July 29, 1917, Agnes Meyer Papers.

21. Just over two months after the construction contract for the Freer Gallery was signed on January 30, 1917, Woodrow Wilson asked Congress to declare war on Germany. The cutting and transporting of stone for the Freer became the major problem, caused by labor shortages and the nationalization of the transportation industries for war. And in September 1918, Herbert Hoover asked Platt to open a branch of the U.S. Food Administration in Rome.

22. Interview, Schell Lewis with Henry Hope Reed, Jr., January 23, 1958: "Freer inspired by Sanmicheli's gate at Verona"; and May 26, 1958: "Platt used Schutz, *Die Renaissance in Italien* . . . for pictures of Verona . . . Freer inspired by the Porta Nuova" (Platt Office Papers). Platt owned both Michele Sanmicheli, *Le fabbriche civili, ecclesiastiche e militari* (Venezia: Giuseppe Antonelli, 1832); and two copies of Alexander Schutz, *Die Renaissance in Italien* (Hamburg: Strumper and Co., 1891), Heft I, abt. B and D; Heft IV, abt. C.

23. Letter, Kenyon Cox to Allyn Cox, June 15, 1917, Kenyon Cox Papers, Avery Library, Columbia University.

24. In 1916, Platt's foreman and engineer did inspection tours of other museums to

study their heating and ventilating systems, including the Frick Gallery, the Brooklyn Museum, and the Museum of the Hispanic Society (Freer Archives).

25.   On December 4, 1917, Freer wrote to Platt, "I have selected a Chinese painting for use in your experimental room, which will give you a fair notion of those to be shown in Washington." On December 14, 1917, Platt responded: "Since my last letter to you I have received the Chinese picture, which I have hung in the Gallery. It is going to help me a good deal about the question of lighting. I have concluded to take no chances on the amount of glass above the diffusing lights in the galleries and get all I can get" (Freer Archives).

26.   For illustrations of these buildings and a discussion of their relationship to other work by the firm, see: Leland Roth, *McKim, Mead & White, Architects* (New York: Harper & Row, 1983), 165–66 and 288–92.

27.   Drawings of the Allen Art Museum were published in "Art Building, Oberlin College, Oberlin, Ohio," *American Architect* 108, no. 2076 (October 6, 1915).

28.   John Canaday, "The Aristocrat of American Museums Has a Birthday," *New York Times,* June 17, 1973, D:23.

29.   Letter, Charles Walcott to Charles Platt, May 14, 1923, Smithsonian Institution Archives.

30.   Letter, Charles Platt to W. H. Holmes, n.d., Smithsonian Institution, Archives of the National Collection of Fine Arts. Platt continued: "if I am a member of the Commission especially chairman of the Committee on *Architecture* it would be quite impossible for my name to be considered for it would be my province to suggest the method of selecting an architect or to name the architect best qualified to do the work."

31.   The research notes and drawings from this tour are preserved in the "museum studies" folder, Charles A. Platt Collection, Avery Library, Columbia University.

32.   The fullest description of Platt's National Gallery project is: Royal Cortissoz, "National Gallery of Art," *American Magazine of Art* 16 (March 1925), 115–20.

33.   Platt's other museum commissions included: Aldrich Gallery, Museum of Art, Rhode Island School of Design, Providence, R.I., 1905; Lyme Art Gallery, Old Lyme, Conn., 1920–21; Wilkes-Barre Art Museum, project, Wilkes-Barre, Penn., 1923; Columbus Gallery of Art, project, Columbus, Ohio, 1927; Lyman Allyn Museum, New London, Conn., 1928–30; Addison Gallery of American Art, Phillips Academy, Andover, Mass., 1929; and Clark Wing, Corcoran Gallery of Art, Washington, D.C., 1925–28.

34.   For further information on the Clark Wing, see: Keith N. Morgan, "Charles Platt's Designs for the Corcoran Gallery Additions," in *The William A. Clark Collection* (Washington: Corcoran Gallery of Art, 1978), 15–23.

35.   In addition to the Washington competition, Platt was also invited to compete for a Roosevelt Memorial in New York City. He was among the New York State architects selected to submit designs for a monument to be located in front of the Museum of Natural History. Letter, Chauncey J. Hamlin to Charles Platt, January 12, 1925, George N. Pindar Collection, Houghton Library, Harvard University. In April, however, he decided to withdraw.

36.   Platt's designs were published in *American Architect* 129 (February 1926), no. 2490. A recent graduate of the Columbia University School of Architecture, William Platt supervised the office entry, adding his knowledge of Beaux-Arts-derived competition procedures.

37.   Pope's winning designs were published in *American Architect* 129 (January 1926), 183ff. The other competitors included: Pond & Pond; Egerton Swartwout; John Mead Howells; McKim, Mead & White; C. Grant LaFarge; Delano & Aldrich; and Albert Randolph Roos.

38.   Interview, William Platt with Henry Hope Reed, Jr., n.d., Platt Office Papers.

39.   Among the prestigious competitions for which Platt was invited to serve as a juror were those for the Nebraska State Capitol and the Harvard Business School.

40.   Letter, Charles Platt to an unidentified trustee, 1902, The Johns Hopkins University, Archives. Letter, Miss Carolyn Smith to the author, February 13, 1975. Bills, 1923–30, Platt Office Papers.

41.   For information on Grosvenor Atterbury and John Russell Pope, respectively, see: "Grosvenor Atterbury," *The Britannica Encyclopedia of American Art* (Chicago: Encyclopaedia Britannica, 1973), 49, and *The Architecture of John Russell Pope* (New York: William Helburn, 1924).

42.   Letter, Rush Rhees to Charles Platt, October 20, 1926, Rush Rhees Papers, University of Rochester, Archives; Edwin S. Gordon, "Construction Work Starting on Oak Hill Site," *Rochester Review* 5 (April–May 1927), 100–101; and Hugh A. Smith, *The University of Rochester: A Story of Its Expansion and Background* (Rochester: University of Rochester Press, 1930), passim.

43.   *Transactions of the Board of Trustees of the University of Illinois, Urbana, Ill.,* 31 (July 6, 1921, to June 13, 1922), 137.

44.   Leon D. Tilton and Thomas E. O'Donnell, *History of the Growth and Development of the Campus of the University of Illinois* (Urbana: University of Illinois Press, 1930), 98–99. See also: Paul Turner, *Campus, An American Planning Tradition* (New York and Cambridge, Mass.: The Architectural History Foundation and MIT Press, 1984).

45.   Ibid., 117–18. Both Platt's twenty-year and ultimate plans for the university were published here.

46.   Ibid., 112.

47.   The Harvard and Johns Hopkins expansions are discussed by G. H. Edgell, *American Architecture of Today* (New York: Charles Scribner's Sons, 1928), 160–68. For further information on the Business School competition, see: Charles W. Killam, "Harvard Graduate School of Business Administration," *Architectural Forum* 47 (October 1927), 305–32. George F. Baker of New York City gave the money and suggested that the architects be chosen by a competition. McKim, Mead & White was the final winner, announced on January 10, 1925.

48.   For illustrations of the World's Columbian Exposition, see: J. W. Buel, *The Magic City* (Philadelphia: Historical Publishing Co., 1894), passim.

49.   University of Illinois, *The Library Building* (Urbana: University of Illinois Press, 1929), not paginated.

50.   McKim, Mead & White established the college library image as the central campus landmark in its designs for Columbia University and New York University, both in the 1890s. See: *A Monograph of the Work of McKim, Mead & White,* rev. ed. (New York: Benjamin Blom, 1973), 30–31. Francesco Passanti, "The Design of Columbia in the 1890s, McKim and His Client," *Journal of the Society of Architectural Historians* 36 (May 1977), 69–84, provides an in-depth analysis of the Low Library and its relationship to the Columbia University plan.

51. For a further discussion of these and other academic libraries of the period, see: Edgell, *American Architecture,* 259–69. For a discussion of the placement of reading rooms in earlier libraries, see: William H. Jordy, "The Beaux-Arts Renaissance: Charles McKim's Boston Public Library," in *American Buildings and Their Architects,* III (Garden City: Doubleday & Co., 1972).

52. Barry Faulkner painted mural maps of the Eastern and Western hemispheres and Celestial and Terrestrial globes with allegorical figure surrounds, as he had for an earlier project for the Cunard Building in New York. For a discussion of Platt's and Faulkner's friendship and collaboration, see: Barry Faulkner, "Charles Adams Platt," typescript, Barry Faulkner Papers, Manuscript Division, Library of Congress, Washington, D.C.

53. Illinois, *Library Building.*

54. It is one thing to have a fine plan, but quite another to put it into effect. To do so, it is necessary to have some continuing force or official with sufficient authority to carry out the plan in the face of changing conditions. The University Trustees were far-sighted enough to realize this and as a result they had created, in 1907, the office of Supervising Architect, and had appointed Professor James M. White to that office (Tilton and O'Donnell, *History,* 113).

55. Platt's role in establishing a campus plan and architectural style that was carried out in his own and other architects' later projects was a frequent case in the early twentieth century. McKim, Mead & White's work at Columbia, Shepley, Rutan & Coolidge's at Harvard, or Day & Klauder's at the University of Delaware were similar situations.

56. The earliest reference to Platt's involvement with Andover is a letter concerning a request by Platt for Olmsted Associates to send topographical plans of the academy. Letter, James C. Sawyer to Charles Platt, September 22, 1921, Archives, Phillips Academy, Andover, Massachusetts.

57. Letter, Guy Lowell to Alfred Ripley, May 28, 1920, Phillips Academy, Archives. Lowell argued in this letter for the placement of new academy buildings away from the increasingly noisy Main Street.

58. Cochran's desire to have Platt replace Lowell as school architect created a rather awkward situation. Platt advised on Lowell's last two buildings, Samuel Phillips Hall and Samuel F. B. Morse Hall, and he designed George Washington Hall (1925) because Cochran was the donor. After Lowell's death in 1927, Platt assumed control of all projects although he was never officially appointed school architect.

59. Claude Moore Fuess, *Independent Schoolmaster* (Boston: Little, Brown & Co., 1952), provides information on the funding, relocation, and architecture of Andover Theological Seminary.

60. Fuess, *Schoolmaster,* 148–49.

61. Fuess, *Schoolmaster,* 150–51.

62. Letter, Thomas Cochran to James C. Sawyer, July 11, 1928, Phillips Academy, Archives. Cochran continued:
    Those people coming to the Academy would go through this beautiful memorial gate into a lovely shady corner where the Chapel and Headmaster's house, the Inn and the Art Gallery were all assembled in juxtaposition to each other, and I can think of no more appealing corner in any educational institution in this country than this would make.

63. The model was begun in 1926 under the direction of Platt and the Olmsted

Associates and was funded by Cochran. Letter, Thomas Cochran to James C. Sawyer, October 15, 1926 Archives, Phillips Academy, Andover, Massachusetts.

64. Letter, Thomas C. Cochran to James C. Sawyer, July 30, 1929, ibid.

65. Platt's office library included: Charles A. Place, *Charles Bulfinch, Architect and Citizen* (Boston: Houghton Mifflin Co., 1925); and Edward W. Root, *Philip Hooker, A Contribution to the Study of the Renaissance in America* (New York: Charles Scribner's Sons, 1929). Folded in Platt's copy of the book on Hooker was a print of a measured drawing by J. L. Dykrusan of the tower of the Second Presbyterian Church in Albany.

66. Letter, James H. Ropes to Thomas Cochran, January 21, 1930, Phillips Academy, Archives. Ropes further commented, "We may find ourselves up against a square issue between a New England meeting-house (like those of Bulfinch) and a London City church, such as Wren designed."

67. Platt also served briefly as a consultant to Phillips Academy, Exeter, New Hampshire, in 1929, and designed a recitation building for Northfield Academy, Northfield, Massachusetts, in 1926–27, a building given by George T. Palmer of Eastover.

List of Buildings, Gardens, and Projects

This catalogue comprises a complete list of Charles A. Platt's known architectural and landscape commissions, including unexecuted designs. As far as possible from available information, the list is arranged chronologically according to the order in which projects were designed. When a series of commissions for one client at a single site were designed and executed at different times, these are grouped with the first project. For example, the designs for William Fahnestock's country house, gardens, and outbuildings, executed in stages between 1909 and 1924 at "Girdle Ridge" in Katonah, New York, are treated as a unit, while his adjacent farm complex, his New York City town house, and his Newport summer house are discussed separately.The entries are organized in a compact and abbreviated format explained below. When a category of information is unavailable or not pertinent, it is excluded.

Name of *Client. Name* and *location* of project. (Even if Platt's work only consisted of a minor alteration or professional consultation, the name of the building or site is provided.) *Condition* (Ex. = extant; al. = altered; dem. = demolished; Ex? has been used for minor projects, such as gravestones or minor alterations, where the location of the commission or its current condition have not been determined). *Description* of project type (e.g., summer house, garden, library alteration, etc.). *Date* (Ds. = designed; ec. = executed; al. = altered). *Cost* followed by the source of information. "Professional services" or "commission" indicates just what Platt was paid, not the total project cost. *References* include manuscript collections with relevant material followed by significant published sources. These references are definitely not intended as a comprehensive listing of publications on the project. *Discussion* of each entry will vary with its importance and the degree to which it is discussed in the text. Information on subsequent changes and current condition will be found here.

ABBREVIATIONS: MANUSCRIPT COLLECTIONS AND LOCATIONS

Platt Office Papers	Geoffrey Platt, Bedford, N.Y.
CAPB	Bills, Platt Office Papers
CAPC	Contracts, Platt Office Papers
Avery	Platt Collection, Avery Library, Columbia University, New York, N.Y.

Archives, AIA	Archives, American Institute of Architects, Washington, D.C.
Archives, C.F.A.	Archives, Commission of Fine Arts, Washington, D.C.
Archives, Illinois	Archives, University of Illinois, Urbana, Ill
Archives, Phillips	Archives, Phillips Academy, Andover, Mass.
Faulkner, L.C.	Barry Faulkner Papers, Manuscript Division, Library of Congress, Washington, D.C.
Freer, Gallery	Charles L. Freer Papers, Freer Gallery, Washington, D.C.
French, Chesterwood	D. C. French Papers, Chesterwood, Stockbridge, Mass.
French, L.C.	D. C. French Papers, Manuscript Division, Library of Congress, Washington, D.C.
McCormick, Wisc.	Harold McCormick Papers, State Historical Society of Wisconsin, Madison, Wisc.
A. Meyer, L. C.	Agnes Meyer Papers, Manuscript Division, Library of Congress, Washington, D.C.
E. Meyer, L.C.	Eugene Meyer Papers, Manuscript Division, Library of Congress, Washington, D.C.
F. L. Olmsted, L.C.	F. L. Olmsted Papers, Manuscript Division, Library of Congress, Washington, D.C.
Olmsted Associates, L.C.	Olmsted Associates Papers, Manuscript Division, Library of Congress, Washington, D.C.
Olmsted, Brookline	F. L. Olmsted and Olmsted Associates Papers, Brookline, Mass.
Saint-Gaudens, Dartmouth	Augustus Saint-Gaudens Papers, Dartmouth College Library, Hanover, N.H.
Shipman, Cornell	Ellen Shipman Papers, Cornell University Library, Ithaca, N.Y.
Smithsonian Archives	Archives, Smithsonian Institution, Washington, D.C.
White, N.Y.H.S.	Stanford White Papers, New-York Historical Society, New York, N.Y.

Periodicals and Secondary Sources

AA	*American Architect and Building News*
AF	*Architectural Forum*
Arch.	*Architecture*
Architect	*Architect*
ARc	*Architectural Record*
ARv	*Architectural Review*
Baker	John Cordis Baker, *American Country Houses and Their Gardens* (Philadelphia, 1906)

BB	*The Brickbuilder*
CAPM	*The Works of Charles A. Platt* (New York: 1913)
CL	*Country Life in America*
Elwood	Philip H. Elwood, *American Landscape Architecture* (New York, 1924)
Ferree	Barr Ferree, *American Estates and Gardens* (New York, 1904)
GM	*Garden Magazine*
H&G	*House and Garden*
Le Moyne	Louis Valcon Le Moyne, *Country Residences in Europe and America* (New York, 1921)
Lowell	Guy Lowell, *American Gardens* (Boston, 1902); not paginated
Shelton	Louise Shelton, *Beautiful Gardens in America* (New York, 1915)

WALKER, Henry Oliver. Residence, Platt Rd., Cornish, N.H. Ex., al. Summer house. Ds. 1889, completed 1890. Frances Duncan, "The Gardens of Cornish," *The Century Magazine* (5/06), 9.

PLATT, Charles A. Residence, Platt Rd., Cornish, N.H. Ex. Summer house, gardens, tennis court, and studio. Ds. 1890, 1892–1912. CAPM 178–79; *AA* (5/12), 198–201; *GM* (1/22), 230–53; *H&G* (4/24), 66–67; Baker, 134–38; Shelton, 27, 29–30. Platt enlarged and altered his summer house on several occasions. The garden assumed its final form after the 1892 trip to Italy. The large living room was added in 1904.

LAZARUS, Miss Annie. "High Court," Cornish, N.H. Ex., al. Summer house, garden, and studio. Ds. 1890, completed 1891, rebuilt 1896, studio 1914. Avery; White, N.Y.H.S.; Freer, Gallery. CAPM 11; *H&G* (1901), 413–15. The house was designed in 1890, when Platt asked Stanford White's advice. The first house, built of stucco over wood, burned and was rebuilt in brick in 1896. The studio, designed by Platt, was added by A. Conger Goodyear.

JENCKS, Francis May. Residence, 1 West Mount Vernon Place, Baltimore, Md. Ex., al. Interior alterations. Ds. ca. 1890. Mrs. Jencks was Platt's sister, Elizabeth. His remodelings included a new mantel in the drawing room, ceilings in the dining room and library, and a circular hanging staircase.

ELLIOT, Dr. John. Residence, 1191 Greendale Ave., Needham, Mass. Ex., al. Country house and garden. Ds. ca. 1895. Avery. The property is now owned by the Y.M.C.A. of Needham which maintains the house on the exterior and has constructed a new gymnasium, attached to the rear of the house.

LAWRENCE, Misses Grace and Elizabeth. Residence, Freeman Rd., Plainfield, N.H. Resort house. Ds. ca. 1896. Avery. Miss Grace Lawrence was a concert pianist, and the parlor and porch were planned for small recitals. The sisters were cousins of Annie C. Hoe, Platt's first wife.

CROLY, Herbert. Residence, Saint-Gaudens Road, Cornish, N.H. Ex. Summer house, garden, and barn. Ds. 1897, al. 1902, garden 1904. Avery. *ARc* (3/04), *H&G* (5/02), 199–204; Lowell. Platt extended the service ell in 1902, converting the original kitchen to a dining room. Minor modifications were made by William Platt in 1937. The gardens have been altered.

PLATT, John C. "Villa Narcault," 68 (formerly 62) Eagle Rock Way, Montclair, N.J.

Ex., al. Formal garden. Ds. ca. 1897. Lowell. John Platt was Charles's older brother. A swimming pool has been constructed in the center of the garden.

SPRAGUE, Charles F. "Faulkner Farm," Allandale Rd., Brookline, Mass. Ex. Garden and grounds. Ds. 1897, ec. 1897–98. Avery. CAPM 18–22; *CL* (4/02), 206ff.; Lowell; Ferree, 131–37; Baker, 108–18; Le Moyne, 427–33. The gardens were added to an 1895–96 clapboard house designed by Little & Browne, which in 1902–3 they encased in brick and to which they added a ballroom. Although the flower beds have been replaced by grass, the basic framework of the garden remains. The pavilion in the formal garden has lost its frescoes, and a large window and pool have been added to the rear.

HECKER, Col. Frank J. "LaSalle Gardens South," Detroit, Mich. Never executed. Residential subdivision with central park. Ds. 1897. Avery; Freer, Gallery. The Thomas Dewing letter to Charles Freer of June 21, 1897 is the fullest description of the plan. Hecker was Charles Freer's business partner.

HECKER, Col. Frank J. Hecker Mausoleum, Detroit, Mich. Ex? Mausoleum. Ds. 1898. White, N.Y.H.S. Platt supplied the grading and planting plan for the Hecker family tomb designed by Stanford White.

UPHAM, Susan. Residence, Lake Road East, Dublin, N.H. Ex., al. Summer house. Ds. ca. 1898. Rebuilt after fire in the early 1920s.

SMOOT, Mrs. Mary Banks. "Blow-Me-Down," Platt Road, Plainfield, N.H. Ex., al. Summer house and garden. Ds. ca. 1899. Avery. The house has been extended to the west, and the former first floor bedroom has been converted to a dining room.

PRATT, H. L. Entrance gates, "Tower Hill," Glen Cove, N.Y. Ex. Ds. 1900. Avery. Platt designed three stone entrance gates for this estate.

WEIR, Julian Alden. Residence, 1 Nod Hill Road, Ridgefield, Conn. Ex. Additions and alterations to summer house. Ds. ca. 1900. Blueprints held by current owner.

CHENEY, Miss Mary. Residence, Hartford Road, Manchester, Conn. Dem. Flower garden. Ds. 1900. Avery.

PAGE, George H. "Heavenly Hill," Chocorua, N.H. Ex. Summer house. Ds. before 1901. Avery.

ANDERSON, Larz. "Weld," 15 Newton St., Brookline, Mass. Al. Garden added to earlier house. Ec. 1901 (inscription). CAPM 112–15; *Arch.* (1909), 56; Ferree, 275–77; Baker, 156–59; Le Moyne, 437–42; Shelton, 38, 45–49. At Mrs. Anderson's death, the property was given to the City of Brookline for use as a park. The Italian garden has been replaced by an ice rink although some of the architectural and sculptural elements remain.

CHENEY, Frank J., Jr. Residence, 20 Hartford Road, Manchester, Conn. Ex., al. Country house, garden, and garage. Ds. 1901, al. 1921. Avery. *ARc* (3/04), 239–42. The house is now used as a social center by a nearby church. A third story was added in 1921.

PAGE, Lilias. Residence, Chocorua, N.H. Ex., al. Summer house. Ds. 1901. Avery. A small shed addition on the rear was not part of the original house. Miss Page built the house as an investment and rented it to the nearby Chocorua Inn for their guests. Lilias's sister, Annie, was a friend of and model for Saint-Gaudens, which probably explains the Platt connection.

HUTCHESON, Rev. Joseph. Study, "North Farm," Hope St., Bristol, R.I. Ex. Study or cottage in the garden of "North Farm." Ds. 1901. Avery. This study was built for Rev. Hutcheson on the Clarks' "North Farm" property before he married Mrs. John Waterman and they built the nearby "Villasera."

MELLUS, Dr. E. Lindon. Residence, Old Common Road, Dublin, N.H. Ex., al. Summer house. Ds. 1901. Avery. The center rear entrance has been removed. Mrs. Mellus was the sister of Francis M. Jencks who paid for this house and who had Platt, his brother-in-law, design his own house on the opposite side of the same hill.

DUNHAM, Dr. Theo. Residence, Manchester Road, Northeast Harbor, Maine. Ex. Summer house. Ds. 1901–2. Avery.

MAXWELL, Francis T. "Maxwell Court," Rockville, Conn. Ex., al. House, garden, gate lodge, and stable. Ds. 1901, ec. 1901–3; swimming pool added 1913. Avery. CAPM 1–10; Baker, 91–98. The house is now occupied by the B.P.O. Elks Lodge of Rockville which has left most rooms in original condition. In addition to other commissions for members of the Maxwell family in Rockville, Platt designed a country house in 1931 at Dedham, Mass., for Francis Maxwell's daughter and son-in-law, Mr. and Mrs. H. Wendell Endicott.

CHURCHILL, Winston. "Harlackenden Hall," Rt. 12a, Cornish, N.H. Partly dem. Country house and garden. Ds. 1901–4. Avery. *ARc* (3/04), 213–17. Part of the service wing and the garden walls remain standing.

CLARK, Randolph M. "Glen Elsinore," Pomfret, Conn. Ex., al. Formal flower garden with loggia and casino. Ds. before 1902. CAPM 49–50; Lowell; Shelton, 90, 95–97. The casino has been partially demolished and the openings onto the garden have been walled shut. The architectural format of the garden is still visible.

SCHOFIELD, Mrs. W. H. "Hilltop," Peterborough, N.H. Ex., al. Gardens. Ds. before 1902, 1914. Avery. Lowell. Platt seemingly designed the flower garden to the rear of this house before 1902 and a small oval garden descending the hill to the south of the house in 1914. The framework of both gardens remains.

YONDOTEGA CLUB. Yondotega Club, Jefferson Ave., Detroit, Mich. Dem. Garden. Ds. 1902. Avery; Freer, Gallery. *ARc* (3/04), 237–38. Charles Freer sought Platt's assistance in designing first a verandah, and then a garden. Albert Kahn served as the executant architect. The walled fountain was Freer's personal gift to the club.

CABOT, Dr. Arthur Tracy. "Cherry Hill," 2468 Washington Street, Canton, Mass. Ex. Country house and garden. Ds. 1902. Avery. CAPM 150–52; *ARc* (3/04), 218–21.

CLARK, Howard L. "North Farm," Hope Street, Bristol, R.I. Country house dem.; gardens and study ex. Ds. 1902. Avery. *ARc* (3/04), 242–44. The property has been developed for condominium living, but the gardens and study have been preserved for the residents' use.

RICHMOND BEACH PARK ASSOCIATION. Richmond Beach Park, Hylan Ave., Huguenot, Staten Island, N.Y. Dem. Two bathing pavilions, administration building, service building, superintendant's house, gardener's cottage, and lavatories. Ds. 1902, two schemes proposed. Avery. *ARc* (3/04), 230–34. The property is now occupied by St. Joseph's-by-the-Sea High School, and all the original buildings have been demolished. The scheme was supported by Charles G. Schwab, steel magnate, and included a large dining facility, as well as bath houses.

OSGOOD, Anna Parkman (later Mrs. Frederic S. Culver). "Blendon Hall," Selden Rd., Hadlyme, Conn. Ex., al. Country house and garden. Ds. 1902. Avery. CAPM 129–32; *ARc* (10/06), 336–40. It is not known whether Platt designed the Italian-inspired garden descending the hill behind the house. In about 1930, Bill Douglass designed a library addition and relocated the service wing flanking the entrance court. A winter cottage, swimming pool, tennis court, and garages have subsequently been added to the property.

MAXWELL, Harriet K., et al. George Maxwell Memorial Library, Union St., Rockville, Conn. Ex. Public Library. Ds. 1902, ec. 1902–3, opened 1904. $150,000 lot, building and furnishings. Avery. The library building is well maintained, and a sympathetic addition has been constructed at the left front corner.

JENCKS, Francis M. Beech Hill Farm, New Harrisville Rd., Dublin, N.H. Ex., al. Summer house and garden. Ds. 1902–3; garden ds. 1906. Avery. The house is now used as an alcoholics' rehabilitation center and has been radically altered. Dormitories have been constructed near the house and a swimming pool attached to the rear.

ADAMS, Herbert. "The Hermitage," Meriden Stage Road, Plainfield, N.H. Ex. Summer house and studio. Ds. 1903. Avery. *ARc* (3/04), 202. The plans included a walled courtyard between the house and studio to contain a formal garden and for display of sculpture. Recent owners have added a one-story wing to the west end of the house and have made major changes to the entrance facade and interior arrangement.

CHURCHILL, Winston. Freeman house, Freeman Road, Plainfield, N.H. Ex. Alterations and additions to earlier house. Al. 1903; additions 1914. Avery. The changes consisted primarily of loggias and porches.

RAND, William H. Residence, 179 Forest St., Rye, N.Y. Ex. House, garden, stable, and squash court. Ds. 1903; squash court 1907. Avery; blueprints held by owners. CAPM 175. Recent owners have altered the interior of the service area.

RING, Clark Lombard. Residence, 1126 North Michigan Ave., Saginaw, Mich. Ex., al. House, garden, two garden structures, and garage. Ds. 1903–4, 1904 over door; garage 1926. $501.36 commission for garage. CAPB. Avery; blueprints held by owner; Freer, Gallery. CAPM 133–36. Mr. Ring was a lumber baron, whose daughter married William G. Mather of "Gwinn." The building now serves as the Saginaw Art Museum. A modern wing connects the house and garage, and the house has been altered slightly on the interior.

HUTCHESON, Rev. Joseph. "Villasera," Main St., Warren, R.I. Dem. 1973. Country house, gardens, and stable. Ds. 1903–6. Avery. CAPM 42–48; Shelton, 80, 87; *ARc* (20/21), 294–336. A children's cottage was planned but never executed.

CHENEY, Clifford. Residence, 40 Forest Street, Manchester, Conn. Ex. Country house. Ds. 1904. Avery. CAPM 170–71; *Arch.* (8/12), LXXIV. Platt later added a loggia with sleeping porch on the west end of the house.

LEE, Frederick S. Residence, 125 E. 65th St., New York, N.Y. Ds. 1904, ec. 1905. Avery. CAPM 116–19; *ARc* (11/06), 427–36; *BB* (9/07), 90. The house is presently owned by China Institute in America, Inc., which has made minor changes on the interior.

LLOYD, Robert MacAlister. "Tapis Vert," Syosset, N.Y. Ex., al. Country house and garden. Ds. 1904. Avery. A third floor was added by Platt or in his style; no drawings for this enlargement are in the Platt Collection at Avery Library.

SLADE, Augusta and Emily. "Dingleton House," Dingleton Hill, Cornish, N.H. Ex. Summer house and gardens. Ds. 1904–5. Avery. CAPM 155–62; *AA* (5/12), no. 1898; *ARc* (10/07), 288–89.

SLADE, Marshall P. "Woodston," Mt. Kisco, N.Y. Dem. Country house, gardens, swimming pool, and bath house. Ds. 1904–8; pool and bath house 1909. $74,813.05, Miscellaneous Architectural Services, Platt Office Papers. Avery. CAPM 84–89; *ARc* (10/07), 261–72. Marshall was the brother of Emily and Augusta Slade of "Dingleton House."

CHAPMAN, John Jay. "Sylvania," Barrytown, N.Y. Ex. Country house, garden, grounds, and stable. Ds. 1904–9. $60,000 estimate for house, stable, and grounds, letter, Platt to Mrs. Chapman, 11/10/04, Avery. John Jay Chapman Papers, Houghton Library, Harvard University. CAPM 15–17; *ARc* (9/08), 107–217. Mrs. Chapman was a sister of Mrs. C. Temple Emmet, another Platt client.

HOWARD, Henry. Residence, 36 Amory St., Brookline, Mass. Ex., al. Detached town house and garden. Ds. 1905. Avery. CAPM 176–77; *AA* (4/08), 145. The basement garage, unique in Platt's work, has been filled, the kitchen has been moved from the basement to the first floor, the garden is gone, and the rear porch has been enclosed with glass.

CHENEY, J. Davenport. Residence, 151 Hartford Road, Manchester, Conn. Ex. Country house. Ds. 1905. Avery. CAPM 172–74.

RADEKE, Mrs. Gustav. Museum of Art, Rhode Island School of Design, 224 Benefit St., Providence, R.I. Ex., al. Ds. 1905; opened October 1906. Gallery and stairwell. Avery. *Rhode Island School of Design Year-Book* (1905), 10. The gallery was constructed to connect the Pendleton House (1904) to the addition given in 1897 by Mrs. Radeke's father. Another donor to the project was Howard L. Clark, for whom Platt designed "North Farm" at Bristol, R.I. In the 1950s, the gallery was remodeled by the insertion of 18th-century English paneling as a backdrop for the Lucy Truman Aldrich Collection of European porcelain figurines.

POOLER, Louis J. Residence, Tuxedo Park, N.Y. Ex? Additions and alterations to a country house. Ds. 1905. Avery. CAPM 75–76; *Arch.* (2/12), XII–XV, XXII–XXIV. Platt removed the western section of this late-19th-century house and added to the north a library and service area with two floors of bedrooms above.

EMMET, C. Temple. "The Mallows," Saint James, N.Y. Ex., al. Country house, garden, and squash building. Ds. 1905; 1906 over door. Avery; blueprints held by owner. The squash building has been remodeled to serve as an apartment. The window in the west pediment of the house has been enlarged and minor alterations have been made on the interior.

CHENEY, J. Platt. Residence, East Center Street, Manchester, Conn. Dem. Additions and alterations to 18th-century house. Ds. 1905 alterations, 1906 additions. Avery.

SAINT-GAUDENS, Augustus. "The Pilgrim," Philadelphia, Pa. Ex. Alterations to pedestal of statue. Ds. 1905. Saint-Gaudens, Dartmouth.

HAPGOOD, Norman. Residence, 107 East 73rd St., New York, N.Y. Ex. A previously remodeled town house redecorated by Platt. Ds. ca. 1905. *ARc* (1/05), 8–11.

CULVER, Frederick S. Studio Building, 131–134 East 66th St., New York, N.Y. Ex., al. Apartment building with studio rooms. Ds. 1905–6. Avery. CAPM 140–43; *ARc* (7/08), 1–18; *ARv* (1909), 19–22. Platt designed or altered the interiors of various apartments, including those for Howard C. Hart, Percy Kent, Theodore F. Luling, F. S. Culver, Gordon Grant, H. O. Taylor, John M. Woolsey, Otis Skinner, C. F. Schallcross, "Mrs. Thaw," and himself. Certainly, interiors of apartments have subsequently been altered, but only window air conditioners mar the intended exterior appearance.

PALMER, George T. "Eastover," New London, Conn. Dem. ca. 1933. Country house, gardens, and garage. Ds. 1906; garage 1920–22. Avery. CAPM 51–60; *ARc* (4/09), 249–58; *CL* (1/16). At the request of the client, Platt modeled this house on "Westover" (1730), the Virginia mansion.

NICHOLS, George L. "Alderbrook," Katonah, N.Y. Ex., al. Country house and garden.

Ds. 1906, 1909–11. Platt office drawings. *ARc* (4/11), 310–17. There have been minor interior alterations.

ASTOR Estate Office. Residence, 844 Fifth Ave., New York, N.Y. Dem. Ds. ca. 1906. CAPM 166–67; *ARc* (6/07), 469–72. Platt remodeled a four-story brownstone town house, using a rusticated limestone facade with basement entrance nearly identical to the Astor property at 7 East 65th Street.

MAXWELL, William. "Kellogg Lawn," Union St., Rockville, Conn. Ex., al. House, garden, squash court, tennis court, stable. Ds. 1906–8; stable 1907. Avery; blueprints held by owner. CAPM 120–28; *ARv* (12/09), XII. "Kellogg Lawn" was built on the site of William Maxwell's mother's home, from which the name was taken. He shared the house with his sister, Miss J. Alice Maxwell. In 1942, the property was purchased and adapted for use by the Rockville General Hospital, the present occupant. All additions have been to the rear, leaving the entrance facade as originally designed. The gardens and squash building have been demolished. Contents of the house were sold at auction by Parke Bernet, Sale No. 387, 1942.

LEE, Frederick S. Residence, River Road, Woodstock, Vt. Ex. Country house, garden, garage, and stable. Ds. 1906–7, addition to house 1913. Avery; blueprints held by owner. The house is still owned by descendants, and its original character is carefully maintained.

SMITH, W. Hinckle. "Timberline," Bryn Mawr, Pa. Dem. 1976. Country house, gardens, pavilion, stable, coachman's and gardener's cottages. Ds. 1907. $169,929.35 CAPC. Avery; Olmsted Associates, L.C. CAPM 95–111; *ARc* (10/12), 162, 280–86; Elwood, 132–34; Shelton, 188, 199. The property is held by the W. Hinckle Smith Foundation, but the site is in the path of a planned highway, and the house has been demolished. The stable and cottages remain in decaying condition. The Olmsted Associates assisted in the site planning here.

ROOSEVELT, Mrs. James S. Residence, 47–49 East 65th St., New York, N.Y. Ex., al. Double town house. Ds. 1907, completed 1908. $132,129.88 CAPC. Avery; blueprints held by Franklin D. Roosevelt Library, National Archives and Records Service, Hyde Park, N.Y. CAPM 163–65; Eleanor Roosevelt, *This Is My Story,* 152. The property now serves as the Sara Delano Roosevelt Memorial House. The walls between the dining rooms and drawing rooms of the two houses have been removed to provide larger meeting spaces.

EDWARDS, Allen F. Residence, 776 Seminole Ave., Detroit, Mich. Ex. Detached town house. Ds. 1907. Drawings for this house were in the Platt Collection when Henry Hope Reed, Jr., inspected it in 1958 but have since disappeared. No. 776 Seminole Avenue is so close to Platt's Henry Howard house of 1905 in Brookline that it must have been designed by Platt or someone who knew his work well. Edwards is listed as living at Nos. 212 and 1111 Seminole Avenue before his move to Lothrop Road, but street renumbering may be confusing the question.

OPPENHEIM, Dr. Nathan. Residence, near Ferrisburg, Vermont. Ex. Summer house. Ds. 1907, ec. 1909.

SCHUTZ, Robert M. Residence, 1075 Prospect Ave., Hartford, Conn. Ex., al. Country house, garden, gardener's cottage, and garage. Ds. 1907–8. Avery; blueprints held by owner. CAPM 168–69. The first set of plans for the house were rejected by the client as too large, but the drawings have been preserved by his son, the present owner. The garden has been reduced in size and redesigned. Mr. Schutz was a trustee of Trinity College, Hartford, as was William G. Mather of "Gwinn" in Cleveland.

MATHER, William G. "Gwinn," 12407 Lake Shore Boulevard, Cleveland, Ohio. Ex.

Country house, gardens, tea house, coachman's cottage, gardener's cottage, greenhouses, garage, and stable. Ds. 1907–8, various alterations and additions 1911–20. Avery; William G. Mather Papers, privately owned, Cleveland, Ohio; Freer, Gallery. CAPM 23–41; *ARc* (11/09), 313–20; *CL* (9/12), 28–30; Shelton, 227–79; Howe, 133–35. The house and gardens are owned by a descendant and have been carefully restored with the assistance of Platt's successor firm, Platt, Wyckoff & Coles.

CATLIN, Daniel K. Residence, off Lake Road North, Dublin, N.H. Ex. Summer house. Ec. 1908.

ALGER, Russell A., Jr. "The Moorings," 32 Lake Shore Drive, Grosse Pointe Farms, Mich. Ex. Country house, gardens, and garage. Ds. 1908–10; ec. 1910; al. 1928. $16,526 fountain and forecourt alterations, 1928. CAPC; Avery; Shipman, Cornell; Freer, Gallery. *CL* (9/12), 28–30; *ARc* (12/13), 480–86; Howe, 34–41. After Mr. Alger's death in 1934, "The Moorings" was given to the Detroit Institute of Fine Arts and is now the Grosse Pointe War Memorial. Ellen Shipman designed the formal garden to the right of the entrance court in 1917–19, remodeled it in 1931, and redesigned it as an English knot garden in 1934. A large auditorium has recently been constructed on the southeast corner of the property, and the lawns flanking the entrance drive have been converted to parking lots. After leaving "The Moorings," Mrs. Alger moved to a house on Provencal Road, Grosse Pointe, designed by William & Geoffrey Platt, with gardens by Ellen Shipman.

BALCOM, H. Tracy. Residence, 1193 Delaware Avenue, Buffalo, N.Y. Ex., al. Detached town house, garden, and garage. Ds. 1908–10. Avery. *Arch.* (11/12), XCIII–XCIX. The property is now used as a day nursery, and various interior alterations have been made.

McMILLAN MEMORIAL COMMISSION. Senator James McMillan Memorial Fountain, McMillan Park, Washington, D.C. Ex., al. Architectural and landscape setting for fountain and statue by Herbert Adams. Ds. 1908–11, ec. 1913. $15,000 appropriated for foundation, Olmsted Associates, L.C.; Freer, Gallery; Olmsted Associates, L.C., *Washington Post*, 4/9/57. The fountain stood in McMillan Park until the reservoir was enlarged in 1941 and is currently in storage.

McCORMICK, Harold F. "Villa Turicum," Sheridan Rd., Lake Forest, Ill. Dem. 1965. Country house, gardens, pavilion, water staircase and fountains, bridge, garage, and service buildings. Ds. house stage I 1908, stage II 1910–11, stage III (unexecuted) 1917–18; gardens and service buildings 1912–13. Avery; blueprints held by property owner; McCormick, Wis. CAPM 61–74; *CL* (9/12), 28–30; Shelton, 266–69; Le Moyne, 533–42. After initially commissioning Frank Lloyd Wright in 1907, the McCormicks gave the project to Platt in 1908. For the next twenty years, Platt was intermittently involved with additions, alterations, or unexecuted projects. Mrs. McCormick died in debt in 1932, and the property was in litigation for many years. The house was finally demolished in 1965, the land being divided for residential development. The garden pavilion and parts of the water staircase remain, though in vandalized condition.

MERRILL, Richard D. Residence, Harvard Ave., Seattle, Wash. Ex. House, garden, and garage with pergola. Ds. 1909; garage additions 1922; new fountain 1929. Avery. CAPM 90–94; Shelton, 324–29. There is also an unlabeled blueprint for a house and garden at the Country Club, Seattle, located in the Merrill folder, Platt Collection, Avery Library.

McCREA, J. A. Residence, Woodmere, N.Y. Dem. Country house. Ds. 1909. Avery.

LOWELL, Josephine Shaw. James Russell Lowell Memorial Fountain, Bryant Park,

New York, N.Y. Ex. Fountain. Originally intended for Corlears Hook Park, the Lowell Fountain was erected in the park behind the New York Public Library.

DYER, George R. Residence, 16 Brookville Road, Brookville, N.Y. Ex. Country house. Ds. 1909–10. Avery. *ARv* (8/12), LXX–LXXI.

PRATT, John T. "Manor House," Dosoris Lane, Glen Cove, N. Y. Ex., al. Country house, gardens, pavilion, grounds, playhouse, garage, stable, laundry building, camp, and farm house alterations. Ds. 1909–11; garage, stable, laundry building, playhouse, camp, and farm house 1913–15. $271,890.28 CAPC. Avery. CAPM 77–83; *ARc* (10/19), 296–97; *BB* (1912), 1–13; Shelton, 129, 153–55. The property is now occupied by a conference center which has expanded the water side of the house and built a freestanding dormitory. A swimming pool was placed in the center of the formal garden.

FAHNESTOCK, William F. "Girdle Ridge," Katonah, N.Y. Dem. Ds. 1909–24; house and garden ec. 1910–11; outbuildings ec. and al. 1914–24. Avery; Olmsted, Brookline; Olmsted Associates, L.C.; Shipman, Cornell. CAPM 144–49; Ellwood, 189. Platt requested the collaboration of Olmsted Associates for the planting plan in 1911. They were dismissed by the client in 1912.

ASTOR Estate Office. Putnam Building, 1497 Broadway, New York, N.Y. Dem. Decoration of Tap Room and Café. Ds. 1910. Avery.

McCORMICK, Harold F. Residence, 1000 Lake Shore Drive, Chicago, Ill. Dem. Int. al. Ds. 1910, 1917, 1924, 1928–30. Avery; McCormick, Wis. The 1920s alterations are recorded only by bills, CAPB. In 1958, H. H. Reed, Jr., recorded drawings for the 1922 alterations which have since disappeared from the Platt Papers.

CHAPIN, Willis O. Residence, 1205 Delaware Avenue, Buffalo, N.Y. Detached town house. Ds. 1911. Avery. The property is used by the Delaware Nursing Home. It has constructed a large wing to the rear and made internal and external alterations to the house.

ASTOR Estate Office. Residence, 7 East 65th Street, New York, N.Y. Dem. Town house alterations. Ds. 1911. Avery. CAPM 137–39. An earlier house was altered by bringing the facade forward and placing the entrance at the basement level.

THE LEADER-NEWS COMPANY. Leader Building, Superior Ave. and 6th St., Cleveland, Ohio. Ex. Office building. Ds. 1911, ec. 1911–12. Avery; blueprints held by owner. CAPM 180–82; *Arch.* (9/12), LXXXII-LXXXVIII; *ARc* (6/13), 501–17. Minor alterations include removal of the bronze elevator grilles and modernization of some storefronts.

BAKER, George F. Monument, Kensico Cemetery, Valhalla, N.Y. Ex. Monument and planting plan. Ds. 1911. Olmsted Associates, L.C. Platt designed the monument and made recommendations for the planting scheme carried out by the Olmsted Brothers. In 1924, Platt designed entrance gates for the lot.

ASTOR Estate Office. Bawo & Dotter Building, 28–30 West 33rd Street, New York, N.Y. Ex. Commercial building. Ds. 1911. Avery. This twelve-story building is loosely derived from the Palazzo Davanzati, Florence, to which photograph album 38 in the Platt Library, Century Club, is devoted.

PRUYN, R. D. "Apple Orchard," 300 Millwood Rd., Mt. Kisco, N.Y. Ex. Country house and stable. Ds. 1911–12. Avery.

ASTOR Estate Office. Mercantile Building, 24 West 34th Street, New York, N.Y. Dem. Commercial building. Des. 1911–12. Avery. This building was demolished to make way for the Empire State Building.

WELD, Francis M. "Easterly," 16 West View Drive, Lloyd Harbor, Huntington, N.Y. Ex., al. Country house, garden, grounds, and stable. Ds. 1911–14; stable 1915. Avery. *AA* (7/15), no. 2063; *ARc* (10/21), 201–25. The property has been subdivided for residential development, and the stable has been converted to a dwelling. A swimming pool and pavilion have been constructed in the formal garden, and the service wing has been extended.

GOODRICH, David M. Residence, West Orchard Rd., Mt. Kisco, N.Y. Ex., al. Additions and alterations to country house and garden. Ds. garden 1912; house 1920. Avery. The plans at Avery Library show alterations and additions to include a theater wing and a ballroom. Although these specific plans were never executed, the house was altered in the early 20th century, and the present elevations and details resemble certain Platt drawings, suggesting that he was the architect for the work. The David M. Goodrich Theater was later built in the area, but Platt was not the architect.

ASTOR Estate Office. Commercial building, 18 West 33rd Street, New York, N.Y. Ex., al. Ds. 1912. Avery. The ground floor windows have been altered. It is surprising that this property was not incorporated in the adjacent Bawo & Dotter Building, also owned by the Astor Estate Office and designed by Platt in the previous year.

PARMALEE, James. "The Causeways" (later "Tregaron"), 2946 Macomb St. (formerly entered from 3029 Klingle Rd.), Washington, D.C. Ex., al. Country house, garden, grounds, stable, superintendent's house, and greenhouse. Ds. 1912–14. $326,216.29 CAPC. Avery; Shipman, Cornell. *BB* (1915), pl. 67; *ARc* (8/14), 80–97. The property is now occupied by the Washington International School, but there are proposals to divide the estate for residential development. A cottage imported from Russia by subsequent owners was erected partially across the formal garden.

BROKAW, Clifford V. "The Elms," Dosoris Lane, Glen Cove, N.Y. Dem. 1946. Country house, grounds, and garden house. Ds. 1912–14. Avery. *ARc* (10/16), 383–85; *BB* (6/16), 85–90.

GRISWOLD, Frank T., Jr. Residence, Newton Rd., Radnor, Pa. Ex. Country house, garden, and garden house. Ds. 1912; garden and garden house 1921. Avery. Platt also designed additions to the service wing in 1928 and to the gardens in 1930.

PULITZER, Ralph. Residence, Manhasset, N.Y. Partially dem. Garden, swimming pool, and bath house. Ds. 1913. Avery. *AF* (8/18), 53; *Architectural League of New York Annual* (1917), not paginated; *Architect* (5/27), 167–70.

STEPHENS, Mrs. Henry. Residence, 241 Lake Shore Drive, Grosse Pointe Farms, Mich. Ex. Country house and garden. Ds. 1913. Avery. Ferree, 228.

MEEKER, Arthur. Residence, 303 Barry St. (formerly 3030 Lake Shore Drive), Chicago, Ill. Ex., al. Detached town house, garden, and stable. Ds. 1913. Avery; rendering by Schell Lewis, Print Department, Cooper-Hewitt Museum, New York, N.Y. Arthur Meeker, *To Chicago with Love* (New York, 1955), 68–69. The house is now used as a convent. The Catholic Church has constructed a new entrance wing between the house and stable and a dormitory addition extending into the garden behind the house.

BRADLEY, J. Cameron. "Wolf Pen Farm," Sears Road, Southboro, Mass. Ex., al. Country house, garden, grounds, and barn. Ds. 1913. Avery; blueprints held by owner. The property is now owned by the Southboro School for Girls. The house has been altered for classroom and dormitory use, the garden is now a lawn, and new dormitory buildings have been erected on a hill overlooking the entrance court.

CLARK, Herbert L. Residence, Radnor, Pa. Ex., al. Country house, gardens, laundry, stable, garage, and two cottages. Ds. 1913–16. Avery; Olmsted Associates, L.C. The

Clarks began to work with the Olmsted Brothers on the planting in 1911 and brought Platt in as architect in 1912. The property has been converted to a country club with a major addition on the rear of the house.

FREER, Charles Lang. Freer Gallery of Art, the Mall, Washington, D.C. Ex. Art museum. Ds. 1913, ec. 1918–21, opened 1923. $1,166,416.39 CAPB. Avery; blueprints held by owner. Freer, Gallery; Smithsonian Archives; A. Meyer, L.C.; Archives of the Commission of Fine Arts. *Arch.* (11/20), 332–34, *Arch.* (9/23), 293–97; *AA* (12/19), 748–50; Agnes Meyer, *Charles Lang Freer and His Gallery.* The sculpture intended to decorate the interior and exterior of the building was never commissioned.

FAHNESTOCK, William F. "Little Farm," Katonah, N.Y. Dem. Cottage, dairy farm (barn, hog pen, pig pen, ice house, etc.), pheasant run, laundry, garage. Ds. 1913-23; ec. farm 1915, pheasant run 1921, garage 1923, dairy al. 1923–24. $35,931.05 dairy alterations, 1924, CAPB. Avery. "Little Farm" was located adjacent to "Girdle Ridge."

LEDYARD, L. C., Jr. Residence, Route 25a, Syosset, N.Y. Ex., al. Country house, garden, tea house, garage, and stable. Ds. 1914, tea house 1917. $60,000 house, $100,000 with land and outbuildings (client's daughter). Avery. The house resembles Platt's contemporary design for J. Cameron Bradley, Southboro, Mass. It now serves as the Greek Orthodox Church in America Chancery. The drawing room has been remodeled as a chapel, and a shrine has been constructed in the garden. The outbuildings remain unaltered.

PLATER, Richard C. "Boxwood," 810 Jackson Boulevard, Nashville, Tenn. Ex., al. Country house and garden. Ds. 1914. The house has been partially encased in brick, fronted by a monumental tetrastyle portico, and altered by a subsequent owner through the addition of imported interior woodwork.

ASTOR Estate Office. Astor Court, 2424 Broadway, New York, N.Y. Ex. Apartment building. Ds. 1914–15; ec. 1915. Avery. *Arch.* (1916), 134–36; *AA* (11/16), 331–35.

PAUL, A. J. Drexel. "Box Hill," Radnor, Pa. Ex., al. Country house, gardens, garage, and farm buildings. Ds. 1914–15. Avery; Shipman, Cornell. *CL* (10/37), 62–68. Platt designed the gardens here, but Ellen Shipman supplied the planting plan. The house was partially destroyed by fire in 1947; the service wing survives.

ASTOR Estate Office. Astor House Building, Broadway and Vesey Street, New York, N.Y. Dem. Alterations of the Astor House Hotel for use as office building. Ds. 1915. Avery.

PRATT, John T. Residence, 6–9 E. 61st., New York, N.Y. Dem. Town house. Ds. 1915. $177,858.67 CAPC. Avery. *Arch.* (6/17), XCV.

HAMMOND, John Henry. Residence, Mt. Kisco, N.Y. Ex. Country house, garden, and children's cottage. Ds. 1915. Avery.

CAMPBELL, J. A. Residence, 3434 Logan Lane, Youngstown, Ohio. Ex., al. Country house and garage. Ds. 1915–16. $81,240.57 CAPC. Avery; Olmsted Associates, L.C. Olmsted Brothers handled the general site development for this and the adjacent Garlick property, where Platt also built the house. The breakfast room and loggia on the garden side of the Campbell house have been removed, and the formal garden has been returned to grass.

MEYER, Eugene. "Seven Springs Farm," Oregon Rd., Mt. Kisco, N.Y. Ex. Country house, garden, orangerie, grounds, and laundry building. Ds. 1915–17; completed 1919. Avery; A. Meyer, L.C.; E. Meyer, L.C., *Architect* (10/27), 27–30; *AF* (1920), 123–30. Platt was recommended to the Meyers by their mutual friend, Charles L. Freer. The property was bequeathed to Yale University in 1970 by Mrs. Meyer, for use as a conference center. It is the largest of Platt's country houses still maintained basically in its original condition, including the Meyers' furnishings.

STARR, Isaac T. "Laverock," Willow Grove Ave., Chestnut Hill, Pa. Dem. Remodeling of country house, gardens, pavilion, greenhouse, stable, garage, and cottage. Ds. 1915–18. Avery; Shipman, Cornell. Platt extensively remodeled a 19th-century country house in an irregular manner. The gardens were designed by Ellen Shipman.

GARLICK, Richard. Residence, 1025 Ravine Drive, Youngstown, Ohio. Ex., al. Country house, garden, and garage. Ds. 1916. Avery; Olmsted Associates, L.C. The loggia on the garden end has been removed, and the garden has returned to grass.

COTTIER, Alonza D. "Heathcote" (now "Southlawn"), Birchall Drive, Scarsdale, N.Y. Ex. Country house and garage. Ds. 1916. Avery.

ASTOR Estate Office. Commercial building, 295–305 Sixth Avenue, New York, N.Y. Floor plan and structural alterations. Ds. 1916. Platt remodeled for the Astor Office the 1895 building designed by Kimball Thompson for B. Altman and Company.

COOPER, J. Fenimore. "Fynmere," Estlie Avenue, Cooperstown, N.Y. Ex., al. Alterations and living room addition. Ds. 1916. Avery; Shipman, Cornell. The house was designed by Frank Whiting and completed in 1911. In 1916–17, Platt handled interior alterations and a large living room addition, and supervised Ellen Shipman's designs for the gardens and the tool shed and study building. The living room was subdivided after the residence was presented to the Presbyterian Church in 1952 for use as a ministers' retirement home.

ASTOR Estate Office. "Ferncliff," Rhinebeck, N.Y. Garden dem.; farm buildings ex. Formal garden with pool and grape arbor; farm buildings, including three barns, a dairy, and a cottage. Ds. garden 1916; farm buildings 1916–17. Avery. The property is currently held by the Catholic Church. The garden was removed before 1942. The farm buildings were designed by Harrie T. Lindeberg, but the working drawings were prepared in Platt's office. Although still standing, the farm buildings are deserted and decaying.

HARE, Meredith. "Pidgeon Hill," Huntington, N.Y. Ex. Country house, studio, playhouse, two cottages, and garage-stable. Ds. 1916–17. Avery. *ARc* (9/20), 178–91.

STEPHENS, Mrs. Henry. Residence, Santa Barbara, Calif. Unexecuted project. Country house and garden. Ds. 1916–18. Avery. The drawings in the Platt Collection, Avery Library, are variously labeled Santa Barbara, Montecito, and Pasadena. A June 1919 bill for decorating samples mentions "for Montecito," but it is addressed to Santa Barbara.

FREER, Charles Lang. Residence (now called "Aston Magna"), Berkshire Heights, Great Barrington, Mass. Ex., al. Summer house. Ds. 1917. Avery; blueprints held by owner; Freer, L.C.; A. Meyer, L.C.; E. Meyer, L.C.; Arthur Spaulding, *Rise to Follow* (New York, 1943), 296–99. Subsequent owners have made minor alterations. The property now serves as a retreat for musicians.

WELLESLEY COLLEGE. Alumnae Hall competition, Wellesley College, Wellesley, Mass. Never executed. Two proposals for Alumnae Hall with 1,500-seat auditorium and clubrooms. Ds. 1917. Avery. Alumnae Hall was eventually designed by Cram & Ferguson and dedicated in December 1923.

WILLIAMS, Clark. "Hawthorne Beach," Byram Point, Greenwich, Conn. Dem. Remodeling of beach house. Ds. 1917. $400 preliminary plan for a house in 1923 CAPB. Platt Office Papers; Shipman, Cornell. Clark Williams, *The Story of a Grateful Citizen* (New York, 1934), 234. There are two undated photographs of the Williams garden in the Ellen Shipman Papers. The Platers of Nashville were relatives of Mrs. Williams and

251

probably introduced her to Platt.

SPEED, William S. "Kanawha," 515 Altagate Rd. (formerly 2828 Lexington Rd.), Louisville, Ky. Ex., al. Country house and gardens. Ds. 1917–21, east porch added 1929. $175,247.14 CAPC. Avery. The interiors were redesigned after a fire. Mrs. Berry V. Stoll, the clients' daughter, thinks the gardens were designed by Ellen Shipman (letter to author, 10/12/76). The property has been subdivided for residential development. An earlier stable still stands near the house.

HANNA BUILDING COMPANY. Hanna Building, Euclid Ave. and East 14th St., Cleveland, Ohio. Ex. Office building. Ds. 1919. Avery; blueprints held by owner. *ARc* (1/22), 12–31; *ARc* (3/22), 237–40. An indication of the care taken in designing this building are the bills for more than twenty plaster models of sections and details.

HANNA BUILDING COMPANY. Hanna Building Annex, East 14th St., Cleveland, Ohio. Ex. Office building and theater. Ds. 1919. Avery; blueprints held by owner. The plans for the annex are dated only one month later than those of the adjacent Hanna Building. The David Garlick Theater is now called the Cleveland Playhouse.

PRUYN, Miss Nell K. Residence, Glens Falls, N.Y. Ex? Additions to studio. Ds. 1919. Platt designed an addition of a kitchen, stairwell, and maids' rooms for a studio planned by Bigelow & Wadsworth in 1912 (letters to the author from Hilda Cameron, Crandall Library, Glens Falls; and from Mrs. Lyman A. Beeman, a relative of Miss Pruyn). In 1958, Henry Hope Reed, Jr., recorded drawings for this commission that have since disappeared from the Platt Collection.

COMMISSION OF FINE ARTS. Gravestone, Arlington Cemetery, Washington, D.C. Ex. Gravestone model for World War I dead. Ds. 1919. Archives, C.F.A. Platt designed this stone while serving on the Commission of Fine Arts. In 1913, he had been named as consultant for a master plan of Arlington Cemetery development.

SHIPMAN, Ellen. Residence, 421 East 61st St., New York, N.Y. Ex. Town house alterations. Ds. 1919. Henry Hope Reed, Jr., recorded drawings in 1958 that have since disappeared from the Platt Collection.

THE JOHNS HOPKINS UNIVERSITY. Homewood Campus development, the Johns Hopkins University, Baltimore, Md. Ex., al. Professional consultant, 1919–1933, CAPB & C. As early as 1902, Platt wrote to Johns Hopkins, offering to assist in planning the new campus. In 1912, he was appointed to the Homewood Advisory Board and continued as a consultant until his death in 1933. With John Russell Pope and Grosvenor Atterbury he advised on: the Chemical Laboratory (1923); dormitories, University Hall, the Gilman Terraces and other landscaping (1924); the Medical Center and YMCA Building (1927); Welch Library, Hunterian Laboratory, and the Homewood restoration (1928); the Physical Laboratory and the Institute of Law (1929); and dormitories and the Physiology Building (1930).

ROGERS, W. A. Residence, Rumsey Rd., Buffalo, N.Y. Unexecuted project. Ds. 1920. Avery. A drawing in the Platt Collection, Avery Library, is labeled "Rumsey Road elevation," but Mr. Rogers was living at 196 Soldiers Place in the 1920s. There is no house presently standing on Rumsey Road or at 196 Soldiers Place that resembles this design or Platt's work.

SCOTT, Mrs. L. Grame. Residence, 155 East 70th St., New York, N.Y. Ex., al. Town house alterations. Ds. 1920. $63,090.10 CAPC. Avery. The rusticated facade designed by Platt has been replaced by stucco.

DAUGHTERS OF THE AMERICAN REVOLUTION, Orford Parish Chapter. Drinking fountain, East Center Street (now located at the Public Works Garage, 236

Olcott St.), Manchester, Conn. Ex., al. Memorial fountain. Ds. 1920. Avery. After being hit and damaged by an automobile, the fountain has been moved several times.

ASTOR Estate Office. Knickerbocker Hotel, Broadway and 42nd Street, New York, N.Y. Dem. Alterations. Ds. 1920. Avery. Platt altered floor plans and elevations in the hotel, including the grill, lunch room, barbershop, and Pani's restaurant.

NICHOLS, George L. Residence, 108 E. 37th St., New York, N.Y. Ex., al. Town house. Ds. 1920. $186,921 CAPC. In 1958 Henry Hope Reed, Jr., recorded drawings that are no longer in the Platt Collection. The house has been converted to apartments, but it remains unaltered on the exterior.

PARKER, Lawton. Lyme Art Gallery, Old Lyme, Conn. Ex., al. Art gallery. Ds. & ec. 1920–21. $16,170.26 CAPC. Avery; blueprints held by owner. Minute Book, Lyme Art Association, 12/4/19–6/19/20; *AA* (9/21), 184–87; *Arch.* (11/20), 335. Platt offered his services gratis to the members of this summer art colony in the design of a gallery. A wing has been added to the rear and its basement recently renovated for studio space.

INGRAM, Erskine B. Residence, Grove St., Eau Claire, Wisc. Ex., al. House, garage, barn, gardener's cottage, garden pavilion, formal garden. Ds. 1921. $188,582.25 CAPB. Avery; blueprints held by owner. Immanuel Lutheran College has owned the property since 1963. Between 1959 and 1962, the house was used as a retirement home by the Minnesota Foundation which remodeled the gardener's cottage as a dormitory and constructed an ambulatory between that structure and the main house. Platt supplied furnishings and art work, including two of his own paintings for the dining room and four photographs of Italian gardens.

PALMER, George T. Palmer Library, Connecticut College, New London, Conn. Ex. College Library. Ds. 1921–22. $124,038.64 CAPB. Avery. Lateral wings were constructed by Shreve, Lamp & Harmon in 1941, following designs suggested by Platt in 1929. The building was replaced by a new library in 1976.

AMERICAN INSTITUTE OF ARCHITECTS. Headquarters proposals, American Institute of Architects, The Octagon, 1800 New York Ave., Washington, D.C. Never executed. Ds. 1921–31. Archives, AIA. *Proceedings of . . . AIA* (1926), 38–44; *Journal of the AIA* (6/12), 175–77; *The Octagon,* 16–26. Platt and D. Everett Waid collaborated on a series of proposed designs for a headquarters building and convention center, to be located behind the Octagon. A building roughly based on Platt's early schemes was designed by Eggers & Higgins and constructed in 1940–41. The present building for the AIA was designed in 1974 by the Architects Collaborative.

UNIVERSITY OF ILLINOIS. Campus development, the University of Illinois, Urbana, Ill. Ex., al. General plan, landscaping, and building placement. 1921–33. Avery; blueprints held by owner. David Kinley Papers, Archives, University of Illinois; CAPC. Working with James M. White as supervising architect, Platt established a master plan for the university and designed or consulted on twelve buildings discussed below. In 1928, Ferrucio Vitale was brought in as landscape consultant, but Platt's ideas continued as the basis for all development. Some attempts were made to follow Platt's building style and, more importantly, his proposals for building locations in post-1933 construction.

UNIVERSITY OF ILLINOIS. Mumford Hall, the University of Illinois, Urbana, Ill. Ex. Agriculture classroom building. Ds. 1922. $400,311 CAPB. Avery. This building set the style model for all of Platt's work at the university.

GERRY OFFICES. Residence, Lake Delaware. Professional services. Ds. 1922. $1,245.03 professional services CAPB.

FAHNESTOCK, William F. Residence, 457 Madison Avenue, New York, N.Y. Ex., al. Remodeling of interior of town house. Ds. 1922–24, ec. 1923–24. $544,622.04 CAPB. Avery. Platt thoroughly remodeled the north section of McKim, Mead & White's Villard Houses, 1882–85. Fahnestock inherited No. 457 from his father, Harris C. Fahnestock. The interiors were further altered by subsequent owners. Platt also purchased furnishings for the house.

PHILLIPS ACADEMY. Landscaping, Phillips Academy, Andover, Mass. Ex. Grading, planting, walls, gates, steps, and lighting. Ds. 1922–30. Avery; Archives, Phillips; Olmsted Associates, L.C. Although the landscaping was executed in relation to each building, it all followed a master plan, worked out by Platt with Olmsted Associates. Of course, subsequent buildings have been constructed, but the general character of Phillips Academy still reflects Platt's conception.

WILKES-BARRE ART MUSEUM. Wilkes-Barre Art Museum proposals, River Common, Wilkes-Barre, Pa. Never executed. Art museum. Ds. 1923. $5,095.34 professional services CAPB. Avery. Only floor plans have survived. "Professional services" included preparation of a promotional pamphlet.

GARRETT, E. T. Residence, Seattle, Wash. Ex? Examination of house sites 1923. $100 CAPB. Platt also received a commission from Mr. Garrett on an order from H. Galland & Co. in 1923.

HOLT, Mrs. Henry. Hariette Taber gravestone, Dublin, N.H. Ex. Ds. 1923. $170.67 CAPB & C.

INDIANA WAR MEMORIAL. Project for a monument. Ex? Professional services. Ds. 1923. $2,000 CAPB.

STARR, Edward. Residence, Willow Grove Ave., Chestnut Hill, Pa. Dem. Country house. Ds. 1923. $67,618,04. CAPB & C. Avery. The house was paid for by Isaac Starr.

GLENS FALLS PRESBYTERIAN CHURCH. Church, Glens Falls, N.Y. Ex. Professional services. Ds. 1923. $2,057.08 professional services CAPB.

UNIVERSITY OF ILLINOIS. Dairy Manufacturing Building, the University of Illinois, Urbana, Ill. Ex? Improvements to dairy barn. $1,102.90 professional services CAPB & C. Ds. 1923. Avery. Platt was James White's associate architect for this building, with most of the drawings evidently produced in Illinois. A proposal of connecting a dairy barn to a three-story classroom building by an arcade was never executed.

PHILLIPS ACADEMY. Phelps House, Phillips Academy, Andover, Mass. Ex. Alterations and enlargement of headmaster's house. Ds. 1923, completed 1924. Avery. Archives, Phillips.

AMERICAN BAR ASSOCIATION. Chase Monument. Ex? Project for monument to Chief Justice Chase. Ds. ca. 1923. $260 project CAPB.

EATON, Estate of Sir John C. Residence, Toronto, Canada. Professional services. Ds. 1923. $500 professional services CAPB. The bill was sent to 480 Davenport Road, Toronto, which may have been the location of the work.

MERRILL, Richard D. Preliminary plan for development of property at The Highlands, Seattle, Wash. Ds. 1923. $750 CAPB.

UNIVERSITY OF ILLINOIS. McKinley Hospital, the University of Illinois, Urbana, Ill. Ex., al. Teaching hospital. Ds. 1923–24; cornerstone 1924. $4,100 professional services CAPB & C. Avery; blueprints held by owner. Platt and White were associate architects, with major elevation, plan and section drawings, as well as the usual details, coming from the New York office. Platt also designed future expansion, one wing of which was constructed.

UNIVERSITY OF ILLINOIS. Kinley Hall, the University of Illinois, Urbana, Ill. Ex. Classroom building for Commerce Department. Ds. 1923–24. $11,810.35 professional services CAPB. Avery; blueprints held by owner. According to the contract, Platt served as associate architect to James M. White for this commission, but the drawings, especially for details, were produced in the Platt office.

MEYER, Eugene. Meyer mausoleum, Kensico Cemetery, Valhalla, N.Y. Ex. Mausoleum. Ds. 1923–24. $23,509 CAPC. Avery. E. Meyer, L.C.

TOMKINS, Mrs. Ray. Residence, East Rd., Drive C, Strathmont Park, Elmira, N.Y. Ex. Country house, garden, tennis court, swimming pool and pavilion, garage, greenhouses, cottage, and shed. Ds. 1923–25. $260,159 CAPC. Avery.

STIMSON, Thomas D. Residence, Olympic Drive, The Highlands, Seattle, Wash. Ex. Country house, garden, casino, swimming pool, and garage. Ds. 1923; garden 1927. $150,319.31 CAPC. Avery. In 1929 Platt executed four landscape panels for the dining room. The house was variously remodeled and enlarged in minor details by the Stimsons.

ASTOR Estate Office. Nicholas Biddle Memorial Room, Harvard Club, 27 West 44th Street, New York, N.Y. Ex. Meeting room. Ds. 1924. Avery. *Architect* (1925), 109–11. Nicholas Biddle directed the Astor Estate Office and was the brother of Ellen Biddle Shipman, Platt's garden collaborator.

SMITHSONIAN INSTITUTION. National Gallery of Art, the Mall, Washington, D.C. Unexecuted project. Art museum. Ds. 1924. $10,000 preliminary plans CAPB. Smithsonian Archives; Archives, C.F.A. *Evening Star* (Washington), 3/2/24. Platt's design was never executed because the necessary appropriation was not secured from Congress. The present building (1939) was designed after Platt's death by John Russell Pope.

REED, Lansing F. Residence, 38 Snake Hill Road, Lloyd Harbor, N.Y. Ex. Country house, gardens, garage, barn, and gardener's cottage. Ds. 1924–25, ec. 1926–27. Blueprints held by current owner. Flower gardens adjacent to the house designed by Ellen Shipman; blueprints of garden plans held by current owner.

UNIVERSITY OF ILLINOIS. Huff Gymnasium, the University of Illinois, Urbana, Ill. Ex. Men's gymnasium. Ds. 1924–25, addition 1926. $10,170 professional services 1923–26 CAPB & C. Avery; blueprints held by owner. *AA* (10/27), 541–44. Platt served as associate architect for White's designs.

UNIVERSITY OF ILLINOIS. Evans Hall, the University of Illinois, Urbana, Ill. Ex. Women's dormitory. Ds. 1924–25. $7,000 professional services CAPB & C. Avery; blueprints held by owner. Platt served as associate architect to White, and the New York office produced drawings for ornamental details and suggested modifications.

McCONNELL, J. W. Residence, Montreal, Canada. Ex? Interior alterations. Ds. 1924–25. $559.92 professional services CAPB. Avery. The Platt Collection, Avery Library, contains designs for a drawing room, living room, dining room, library, stairhall, vestibule, and corridor.

PRATT, Frederick B. "Poplar Hill," Dosoris Lane, Glen Cove, N.Y. Ex., al. Country house and gardens. Ds. 1924–26. $449,452 CAPB. Avery. Although Platt was commissioned to design iron gates for this estate as early as 1914, the final plans and construction were in 1925–26. The house was used as a retirement-convalescent home until a modern facility was constructed behind the building. It currently serves as the Chancery of the Russian Orthodox Church in America. There have been interior alterations, and the garden is totally overgrown.

UNIVERSITY OF ILLINOIS. Armory, the University of Illinois, Urbana, Ill. Ex. Armory addition. Ds. 1924–26. $2,500 commission CAPB & C. Avery; blueprints held by owner. Platt designed a brick, two-story shell to encase and improve an airplane hanger for use as an armory.

UNIVERSITY OF ILLINOIS. Library, the University of Illinois, Urbana, Ill. Ex. Library with two additions. Ds. 1924, additions 1926, 1927–29. $1,750,000 The University of Illinois, *The Library Building,* 2 and passim. Avery; blueprints held by owner; Faulkner, L.C.; Archives, Illinois. *Architect* (11/27), 181–83; *Architect* (6/29), 253–56. This building was the second Platt alone designed for the campus, using White as the supervising architect. Although Platt designed and constructed two additions, the rear of the building was always left ready for future expansion. Barry Faulkner was commissioned to paint four maps in the stairwells.

PAUL, Gilman d'Arcy. "The Woodlands," Blythewood Rd., Roland Park, Baltimore, Md. Ex. Country house, gardens, and garage. Ds. 1924, entrance gates 1927, wall fountain 1931. $99,026.21 CAPB. Avery. There have been some changes made in the garden, but the house has been carefully maintained.

THE ARCHITECT OF THE CAPITOL. Coolidge Auditorium, G-118, Library of Congress, Washington, D.C. Ds. 1925. $92,867.35 *Annual Report of the Architect of the Capitol . . .* (1926), 29. Avery; Office of the Architect of the Capitol; Archives of the Library of Congress; Archives, Office of the Architect of the Capitol. The auditorium was the gift of Elizabeth Sprague Coolidge (1864–1953). Because of legislative policy, David Lynn, Architect of the Capitol, was technically the architect and Charles Platt the consultant architect for the Coolidge Auditorium, but Platt designed the building and his office produced the working drawings.

PHILLIPS ACADEMY. George Washington Hall, Phillips Academy, Andover, Mass. Ex. Administration building and auditorium. Ds. 1925. Avery; blueprints held by owner. Archives, Phillips. Phillips *Bulletin* (10/25), 30–32 and (10/26), 28.

ASTOR Estate Office. Saint Regis Hotel, Fifth Avenue and 55th Street, New York, N.Y. Ex. Alterations to first floor and mezzanine, and new entrance and shopfronts. Ds. 1925. Avery. In 1933–34, Platt's successor firm did further alterations to the hotel, including the design of the King Cole Room with earlier murals by Maxfield Parrish.

ASTOR Estate Office. Apartment house, 840 Fifth Avenue, New York, N.Y. Dem. Apartment house. Ds. 1925. $16,078.27 Miscellaneous Architectural Services, Platt Office Papers.

PALMER, George T. Gates, Cedar Grove Cemetery, New London, Conn. Ex? Ds. 1925. $8,912 CAPC.

CROWNINSHIELD, Frank. Project for a gravestone. Ex? Ds. 1925. $140.05 professional services CAPB. Mr. Crowninshield lived at 19 West 44th Street, New York, N.Y., but there is no mention of the person for whom the stone was intended.

ROOSEVELT, Theodore, New York State Memorial Association. Competition drawings, Theodore Roosevelt Memorial, Central Park West, New York, N.Y. Unfinished designs. Ds. 1925. George N. Pindar Collection, Houghton Library, Harvard University. In January 1925, Platt was selected as one of ten architects to compete for the Roosevelt Memorial in front of the Natural History Museum, New York City. In April, however, he decided not to submit a design.

ROOSEVELT, Theodore, Memorial Association. Competition drawings, Theodore Roosevelt Memorial, Washington, D.C. Unexecuted designs. Ds. 1925. $2,000 CAPB. *AA* (2/26), pl. 2490. The competition was won by John Russell Pope, but the monument was never erected.

ASTOR Estate Office. Fifth Avenue Astor Building, 330 Fifth Avenue, New York, N.Y. Ex. Office building. Ds. 1925–26, minor alterations 1929, 1932. Avery. This building is adjacent to Astor properties on West 33rd Street.

RUMSEY, C. C. Residence project, Port Washington, N.Y. Never executed. Ds. 1925–26. $514.96 preliminary sketch CAPB. Olmsted Associates, L.C. H.H. Henderson, Platt's engineer, mentioned the commission in a 12/28/25 letter to the Olmsted Brothers, but only preliminary sketches were prepared.

MORGAN, Henry S. Residence, 34 East 36th St., New York, N.Y. Dem. Town house. Ds. 1925–26. $271,381.83 CAPB. Avery. Located across the street from the Morgan Library, this house was designed for a son of J. P. Morgan.

CORCORAN GALLERY OF ART. Clark Wing, Corcoran Gallery of Art, 17th Street at New York Avenue, Washington, D.C. Ex. Gallery and office additions. Ds. 1926. $816,025.81 CAPB & C. Avery; blueprints held by owner. Archives, Corcoran Gallery of Art. As early as 1919, Platt had redecorated the galleries of Ernest Flagg's 1897 building and had served as a consultant on painting acquisitions. The Clark Wing comprised space for display of the W. A. Clark Collection and additional galleries for the permanent collection.

McGRAW, Mrs. Arthur. Residence, 340 Lakeland Ave., Grosse Pointe, Mich. Ex. House and garden. Ds. 1926. $135,632.44 CAPB. Avery.

FRENCH, Daniel Chester. St. Mihiel Monument project. Ex? Ds. 1926. French, L. C.; French, Chesterwood. Undated blueprints for a marble tablet also are located in the French Papers, Chesterwood.

ASTOR Estate Office. Hurley Shoe Store, 215 Broadway, New York, N.Y. Dem. Interior alterations. Ds. 1926. $4,457 Miscellaneous Architectural Services, Platt Office Papers. Avery. Platt altered this store within the Astor House Building, which he had remodeled in 1915.

BRONXVILLE, Village of. Village Hall project, Bronxville, N.Y. Never executed. Competition drawings. Ds. 1926. $300 competition fee CAPB.

ADAMS, Herbert. War Memorial, Winchester, Mass. Ex. Public monument. Ds. 1926. $600 professional services CAPB. Platt designed the pedestal and landscape treatment.

STRONG, William Everard. Goadby Memorial project. Ex? Monument. Ds. 1926. $1,000 commission CAPB.

MERRILL, Richard D. Residence, Bainbridge Island, Wash. Ex? Country house. Ds. 1926. $211.55 professional services CAPB. Avery.

NICHOLS, George L. Residence project, Cooper's Bluff, N.Y. $2,340.17 professional services CAPB 3/5/26.

PALMER, George T. Recitation Building, Northfield Academy, Northfield, Mass. Ex. Classroom and science building. Ds. 1926, ded. 10/25/27. Avery; blueprints held by owner. Platt Office Papers; Archives, Northfield Academy. Mr. Palmer was a cousin of Northfield's principal, Miss Evelyn S. Hall. The money for this building was provided by the sale of Mr. Palmer's American furniture collection to Mrs. Russell Sage.

FAHNESTOCK, William F. "Oaklawn" (now "Bois Doré"), Narragansett Ave., Newport, R.I. Ex. House, grounds, two gate lodges, and alterations to stables. Ds. 1926–27, ec. 1927–28, stables al. 1928. $434,895 house and $10,297 stables CAPB. Avery; blueprints held by owner. Platt replaced an earlier house by James Smith. The "Sullivan Cottage," a shingled stable with apartment which Platt remodeled, was presumably by Smith too. The interior of the house was redecorated slightly by a recent owner, who also added a formal garden to the west of the house.

UNIVERSITY OF ILLINOIS. Architecture Building, the University of Illinois, Urbana, Ill. Ex. Classroom building and library for "Architecture and Kindred Subjects." Ds. 1926–27. $432,040 CAPB & C. Avery; blueprints held by owner.

DARTMOUTH COLLEGE. Professional Services, Dartmouth College, Hanover, N.H. Architectural consultant, 1926–31. $5,123.96 commissions CAPB. As early as 1915, Platt was involved with Dartmouth when he presented for exhibition a collection of blueprints of his country houses. Although he advised on designs for the library in 1926, Platt was not formally retained as a consultant until 1928. He was involved with plans for Carpenter Hall, Sanborne House, and the Tuck School. In 1928, Dartmouth conferred on Platt the honorary degree of Doctor of Letters.

THE UNIVERSITY OF ROCHESTER. River (or Oak Hill) Campus, The University of Rochester, Rochester, N.Y. Ex. Consultant architect, 1926–33. $10,706.04 commissions CAPB. Olmsted Associates, L.C.; Rush Rhees Papers, Archives, University of Rochester. *Rochester (Alumni) Review,* (April/May 1927), 100–101. Platt served as consultant to the executant architects, Gordon & Kaelber of Rochester. Frederick Law Olmsted, Jr., was the consultant for landscape planning. Unlike the relationship with the University of Illinois, the Platt office did not design buildings for Rochester. Platt's involvement lasted from the 10/4/26 invitation through his death.

ASTOR Estate Office. "Nourmahal." Dem. Interiors for motor yacht. Ds. 1927. $630.52 commission, Miscellaneous Architectural Services, Platt Office Papers. Avery. Platt designed the living room, dining room, and library for Astor's yacht.

BLACK, Mrs. H.V.D. Washington Irving Memorial, Irvington-on-Hudson, N.Y. Ex. Superstructure and site planning for bust and two relief sculptures by Daniel Chester French. Ds. 1926–27; ded. 6/27/27. $18,860 CAPC. Avery; blueprints at Chesterwood, Stockbridge, Mass. French, L.C., Container #22. French requested Platt's assistance in February 1925. The monument was delayed on several occasions because of problems with fundraising and attempts to incorporate an adjacent brook in the landscape.

CORNELL, Allen D. Project for a headstone. Ex? Headstone. Ds. 1927. $60 professional services CAPB. Mr. Cornell lived at 1528 Cherry Street, Philadelphia, Pa., but there is no mention of the person for whom the stone was intended.

FRENCH, Daniel Chester. Russell Monument, Greenfield, Mass. Ex? Public monument. Ds. 1927. $200 CAPB. French, L.C. Work included adding an inscription and designing the landscape treatment for a monument by French.

RUMSEY, Trustees of, School of Art. The Evelyn Rumsey Carey School of Art, Buffalo, N.Y. Never executed. Project. Ds. 1927. $4,000 commission CAPB. Henry Hope Reed, Jr., recorded drawings in 1958 that have since disappeared from the Platt Collection.

COLUMBUS GALLERY OF ART. Columbus Gallery of Art, Columbus, Ohio. Never executed. Art museum. Ds. 1927. $640,000 estimate CAPB. Avery. Platt signed a contract for the design of this building in January 1927, but the project died the following year.

CHAMBER OF COMMERCE, Greenwich, Conn. War Memorial, Post Office Plaza, Greenwich, Conn. Ex. Granite obelisk. Ds. 1927; ded. 1928. $32,000 estimate, CAPC.

FRENCH, Daniel Chester. Henry White Memorial Tablet, National Cathedral, Washington, D.C. Ex. Memorial plaque. Ds. 1927–28. French, L.C.; French, Chesterwood. The tablet vaguely resembles an earlier one for Mrs. White, on which Henry Bacon collaborated with French.

ASTOR Estate Office. Astor Apartments, 528–540 East 86th Street, New York, N.Y. Ex. Apartment building. Ds. 1927–28. Avery. This building differs only in detail from 520 East 86th Street, also by Platt.

CHENEY, Philip. Residence, 50 Forest St., Manchester, Conn. Country house and garden. Ds. 1927–29. $157,684.71 CAPB. Avery; blueprints held by owners. Platt totally rebuilt this residence on the site of a house reputed, incorrectly, to have been built by H. H. Richardson, but the influence of the late-19th-century dwelling can be seen in the unusually planned living room.

EDWARDS, Allen F. Residence, 99 Lothrop Road, Grosse Pointe Farms, Mich. Ex. House, garden, and garage. Ds. 1927–29. $195,460.30 CAPB. Avery. Ellen Shipman designed the landscape treatment for the house.

ADAMS, Herbert. War Memorial, Fitchburg, Mass. Ex. Public Monument. Ds. 1927–29. $500 professional services CAPB. Platt designed the pedestal and landscape treatment.

AMERICAN BATTLE MONUMENTS COMMISSION. Chapel, Military Cemetery, Suresnes, France. Ex., al. Ds. 1927–29, completed 1929. $95,000 CAPB. The Platt Office Papers contain the contract, dated December 3, 1926, and allotting $80,000 for the budget. Platt visited the site in the summer of 1929 while work was in progress. William & Geoffrey Platt added lateral wings to the chapel.

PHILLIPS ACADEMY. Paul Revere Hall, Phillips Academy, Andover, Mass. Ex. Dormitory. Ds. 1928. Avery; blueprints held by owner. Archives, Phillips. Phillips *Bulletin* (10/28), 19 and (10/29), 16.

ASTOR Estate Office. Apartment building, 640 Park Avenue, New York, N.Y. Ex. Alterations to exterior, lobby, and ground floor offices. Ds. 1928. Avery. The building was originally designed by J.E.R. Carpenter in an Italian Early Renaissance style. Platt moved the entrance one bay to the east, replacing a large pointed arch by a flat-pedimented doorway.

PHILLIPS ACADEMY. Commons, Phillips Academy, Andover, Mass. Ex., al. Dining hall. Ds. 1928. Avery; blueprints held by owner. Archives, Phillips. Phillips *Bulletin* (4/28), 19 and (10/29), 14. In 1929, Barry Faulkner painted monochromatic brown murals of the Andover landscape in the masters' dining room. The first floor hall and the stairwells have been redecorated, and there are plans to construct a new dining facility at the rear of this building, leaving the future of Platt's structure in question.

ASTOR Estate Office. Astor Apartments, 520 East 86th Street, New York, N.Y. Ex. Apartment building. Ds. 1928. Avery. This building is adjacent to and similar to 528–540 East 86th Street, also owned by the Astor Estate Office and designed by Platt in 1927–28.

SWITZER, John M. Project for a residence. Ex? Study for placement of a house. Ds. 1928. $100 commission CAPB. Avery.

PHILLIPS Academy. Oliver Wendell Holmes Library, Phillips Academy, Andover, Mass. Ex., al. Library and gallery. Ds. 1928–29. Avery; blueprints held by owner. Archives, Phillips. *AF* (6/32), 567; Phillips *Bulletin* (4/28), 17. A skylighted gallery on the second floor was originally intended as the school art museum, a function that was assumed in 1929 by the Addison Gallery. The Architects Collaborative constructed an addition at the rear of this building and more book space is again needed.

ALLYN, Harriet U., Trust. Lyman Allyn Museum, New London, Conn. Ex., al. Art museum. Ds. 1928–30; ec. 1928–30. $874,677.26. CAPB. Avery; blueprints and specifications held by owner. The museum has been enlarged with a major wing to the rear and the raising of the roof for conversion of the attic to storage area. The property is adjacent to Connecticut College, where Platt built a library and administration building during the 1920s. The donor of the library, George T. Palmer, was also a trustee of the museum.

PHILLIPS Academy. Addison Gallery of American Art, Phillips Academy, Andover, Mass. Ex. Art museum. Ds. 1929, ec. 1929–30; opened 5/16/31. Avery; blueprints held by owner. Archives, Phillips. Thomas Cochran provided the money to build the museum and named it in honor of his friend, Keturah Addison Cobb. Platt also served as professional advisor to Cochran in purchasing the paintings for the collection. The Architects Collaborative, Cambridge, Mass., added a wing at the rear.

ASTOR Estate Office. Apartment building, 903 Park Avenue, New York, N.Y. Dem. New terrazzo and marble floor in entrance. Ds. 1929. Avery.

GARRETT, E. H. Residence, The Highlands, Seattle, Wash. Ex? Professional services. Ds. 1929. $1,400 professional services CAPB.

UNIVERSITY OF ILLINOIS. General planting plan, the University of Illinois, Urbana, Ill. Ex., al. General landscape treatment, foundation planting, and architectural elements. Ds. 1929. Blueprints held by owner. These plans were developed by Ferrucio Vitale in collaboration with Platt and James M. White.

McCONNELL, J. W. Residence, Dorval, Ontario, Canada. Ex? Study for a garden. Ds. 12/2/29. Avery.

METROPOLITAN SQUARE CORPORATION. Opera House Development, Columbia Leasehold, New York, N.Y. Professional services. Ds. 1929. $2,500 professional services CAPB. This project eventually developed in the scheme for Rockefeller Center.

SMITH, Jeremiah, Jr. Phillips Academy, Exeter, N.H. Advice; 1929. $500 CAPB.

McCORMICK, Edith Rockefeller. Residence, Chicago. Never executed. Town house and museum project. Ds. ca. 1929. Elevation drawing owned by Platt family.

CONNECTICUT COLLEGE. Fanning Hall, Connecticut College, New London, Conn. Ex. Administration and classroom building. Ds. 1929–30. Avery. *Bulletin of Connecticut College, New London, Conn.* (1958), 24.

UNIVERSITY OF ILLINOIS. Freer Gymnasium, the University of Illinois, Urbana, Ill. Ex. Women's gymnasium. Ds. 1929–30. $11,000 professional services CAPB & C. Avery; blueprints held by owner. That the contract called Platt the Associate Architect and the drawings refer to White as Supervising Architect shows the confusion in assigning responsibility for this university building.

DEERFIELD ACADEMY. Campus development, Deerfield Academy, Deerfield, Mass. 1929–33. Archives, Deerfield Academy. Through Frank D. Cheney and Thomas Cochran, Platt became involved with Deerfield in 1929, replacing Perry, Shaw & Hepburn as academy architect. Platt's successor firm continued to oversee campus development through the 1950s. In addition to the buildings discussed below, Platt made recommendations for the academy's general plan and provided designs for a dining hall, infirmary, and dormitory, not constructed during his life.

ROGERS, Grace Rainey. Paul J. Rainey Memorial Gateway, Bronx Zoological Park,

New York, N.Y. Ex. Gate houses to accompany gates by Paul Manship. Ds. 1929–33, ded. 6/14/34. $6,221.02 commission CAPB. Avery. Although the commission is credited to the Platt office, the gate houses were designed by William Platt.

DEERFIELD ACADEMY. Academy Building, Deerfield Academy, Deerfield, Mass. Ex. Administration and classroom building. Ds. 1930. Avery; blueprints held by owner. Archives, Deerfield Academy. *Am. Mag. of Art* (6/34), 383–88. The Academy Building replaced a Queen Anne Revival structure by Peabody & Stearns and set the tone for later campus buildings.

DEERFIELD ACADEMY. Gymnasium, Deerfield Academy, Deerfield, Mass. Ex., al. Gymnasium, swimming pool, locker rooms, and offices. Ds. 1930. Avery; blueprints held by owner. Archives, Deerfield Academy. An indoor ice rink was constructed behind and attached to the gymnasium in the 1960s.

PHILLIPS ACADEMY. Infirmary project, Phillips Academy, Andover, Mass. Never executed. Ds. 1930–31. Avery.

PHILLIPS ACADEMY. Cochran Memorial Chapel, Phillips Academy, Andover, Mass. Ex. Memorial chapel. Ds. 1930–31. Avery; blueprints held by owner. Archives, Phillips. Phillips *Bulletin* (4/31), 8.

ASTOR Estate Office. Astor Apartments, 120 East End Avenue, New York, N.Y. Ex. Apartment building. Ds. 1930–31. Avery.

UNIVERSITY OF ILLINOIS. President's House, the University of Illinois, Florida Ave., Urbana, Ill. House, garden, and garage. Ds. 1930. $3,000 professional services CAPB & C. Avery; blueprints held by owner. Platt was White's associate architect, but most of the extant drawings were produced in New York. The design resembles Platt's Philip Cheney residence, and he even planned the furniture arrangement for the president.

CRANDALL LIBRARY. Crandall Library, Glens Falls, N.Y. Ex., al. Public library. Ec. 1931. Blueprints held by owner. Herbert Putnam Papers, Archives of the Library of Congress. Platt ran into opposition with the building committee over the question of a stack wing, which he opposed, and appealed to his friend, Herbert Putnam, Librarian of Congress, for support. In 1970, William & Geoffrey Platt were the architects for a stack addition.

ENDICOTT, H. Wendell. Residence, 80 Haven St., Dedham, Mass. Ex. Country house and grounds. Ds. 1931–34. $250,000, Massachusetts Institute of Technology, "History of Endicott House." Avery; Olmsted Associates, L.C. The Endicotts employed the Olmsted Associates as site planners and Platt as architect. Because of the Depression, construction was suspended during 1932 and much of 1933, and the house was completed after Platt's death by his sons. The residence is now used by MIT as a conference center.

ASTOR Estate Office. Residence, 180–190 East End Avenue, New York, N.Y. Dem. Avery. Platt designed alterations for two brownstone town houses since replaced by a large apartment building.

DEERFIELD ACADEMY. Science Building, Deerfield Academy, Deerfield, Mass. Ex. Classroom and laboratory building. Ds. 1932. $90,000 estimate, letter, Platt to Frank Boyden, 3/10/32, Archives, Deerfield Academy. Avery; blueprints held by owner.

PHIPPS, L. C. Residence, Denver, Colo. Ex. Interior of library and dining room. Ds. 1933. Avery. After Charles's death, William & Geoffrey Platt completed the Phipps house with Fisher & Fisher as supervising architects.

HOLT, Mrs. Henry. Henry Holt Tablet. Ds. 1933–34. $332 professional services CAPC.

UNDATED COMMISSIONS AND PROJECTS

PRUYN, Misses Mary and Nellie. Residence, Easthampton, N.Y. Ex? Summer house and garden. Shipman, Cornell. Ellen Shipman designed the garden for this unlocated Platt house.

ASTOR Estate Office. Residence, Newport, R.I. Ex? Alterations project. In 1958 Henry Hope Reed, Jr., recorded two preliminary plans that are no longer in the Platt Collection at Avery Library. The dates 1921 and 1924 were penciled on the folder containing these plans.

DEERFIELD ACADEMY. Dormitory project, Deerfield Academy, Deerfield, Mass. Never executed. Project. Watercolor rendering by Schell Lewis, Avery.

Index

Figure numbers are given in italics following page numbers.

263

Sources of the Illustrations

Unless otherwise noted, all drawings, paintings, etchings, gardens, and buildings illustrated were the work of Charles A. Platt. He also took the photographs illustrated in Figs. 4, 17, 28, and 55.

Richard W. Cheek took all the modern photographs of Platt buildings and a major portion of the copy photographs including the frontispiece and Figs. 5, 6, 8, 13, 14, 16, 23, 24, 27, 29, 30, 37, 39, 40, 41, 42, 44, 45, 49, 50, 52, 53, 54, 63, 72, 73, 79, 83, 84, 90, 93, 94, 95, 99, 102, 110, 114, 115, 117, 118, 121, 122, 123, 124, 125, 129, 130, 131, 134, 135, and 136.

Michael Vest took copy photographs of Figs. 38, 96, 101, 112, 116, and 119.

The Avery Architectural Library, Columbia University, provided the drawings from the Charles A. Platt Collection as illustrations for Figs. 16, 30, 73, 93, 96, 101, 110, 112, 114, 116, and 118.

Monograph of the Works of Charles A. Platt (New York, 1913) was the source for Figs. 10, 19, 25, 32, 43, 47, 48, 51, 57, 58, 65, 67, 70, 76, 81, 86, 88, 89, 91, 92, and 105.

All other drawings, photographs, paintings, and sculpture are contained in the Platt Office Papers or are owned by the Platt family with the following exceptions:

Fig. 2.   The St. Botolph's Club, Boston, Mass.

Fig. 9.   The Stanford White Papers, New-York Historical Society, New York, N.Y.

Fig. 12. *A Monograph of the Works of McKim, Mead & White, 1879–1915* (New York, 1915), I, pl. 38.

Fig. 18. Charles A. Platt, *Italian Gardens* (New York, 1894), frontispiece.

Fig. 20. Society for the Preservation of New England Antiquities, Boston, Mass.

Fig. 21. The Metropolitan Museum of Art, New York, N.Y.

Fig. 22. Courtesy of The Museum of Fine Arts, Boston, Mass.

Fig. 23. Courtesy of Mrs. Lawrence Taylor, Plainfield, N. H.

Fig. 26. The Frances Loeb Library, Graduate School of Design, Harvard University, Cambridge, Mass.

Fig. 29. *Architectural Record* 29 (January 1910), 19.

Fig. 31. The Library of Congress, Washington, D.C.

Fig. 33. Society for the Preservation of New England Antiquities, Boston, Mass.

Fig. 34. Guy Lowell, *American Gardens* (Boston, 1902), not paginated.

Fig. 35. Copyright The Frick Collection, New York, N.Y. Ezra Stoller photograph.

Fig. 36. *Architectural Review* (London) 31 (January 1912), 15.

Fig. 37. American Architect, *American Churches* (New York, 1915), I, pl. 97.

Fig. 38. *Architectural Record* 14 (October 1903), 297.

Fig. 59. Frank Cousins and Phil M. Riley, *The Colonial Architecture of Philadelphia* (Boston, 1920), not paginated. Book in Platt Office Library.

Fig. 60. The Society for the Preservation of Long Island Antiquities, Setauket, N.Y.

Fig. 74. Copyright © The Frank Lloyd Wright Foundation, 1942, revised 1970, Taliesin, Scottsdale, Ariz.

Fig. 78. *Architectural Record* 31 (March 1912), 223.

Fig. 86. *Architectural Record* 15 (March 1904), 232.

Fig. 107. The Commission of Fine Arts, Washington, D.C.

Figs. 108, 109. The Freer Gallery of Art, Washington, D.C.

Figs. 111, 137. Platt Office Papers, Kenneth Clark photographs, 1923.

Fig. 119. *American Architect* 129 (February 1926), pl. 2490.